Come take a narrated tour of the life Calabria, Jr. This fascinating, humorous, and insightful book is a series of short stories that help the reader see life as Calabria has lived it.

A top salesman and manager for IBM and other corporate giants, Calabria and his wife started their own business that has generated hundreds of millions of dollars in revenue.

Calabria shares his laws of business and life through a non-stop barrage of mind-bending anecdotes. He makes his points while sharing 100+ Memorable Moments of his life, and he encourages his readers to work on their own list.

Does success lead to greed? Calabria is clearly successful, but he freely shares his secrets of success. At the same time, he reveals a purposeful desire to give back to others and the educational institutions that help better our society.

The pages will turn almost effortlessly as you laugh your way to the next insight. In this book, everyone is welcomed into the life and times of Joseph Calabria, Jr. And each of us will come out a little better because of it.

REVIEWS

*We couldn't fit all the reviews in on the back cover, so here
are a few more reactions to this masterful book:*

"Hilarious and insightful. Shakespeare would be jealous!"
—DENNIS QUINN, AUTHOR, AND EDITOR-AT-LARGE

"This book put me in the hospital. I split a gut while reading it!"
—ANONYMOUS (HIPAA REGULATIONS PREVENT THE
RELEASE OF THIS PATIENT'S INFORMATION)

"I laughed, I cried, I held my breath in suspense, this book
is destined to become a Pink Panther movie."
—SCOTT WALKER, SOCIAL ACTIVIST AND AUTHOR
OF *DON'T SQUAT WITH YOUR SPURS ON*

"When you read Joe's book, it is best to wear sun-
glasses. His humor and stories are brilliant!"
—DAVID V. GUTIERREZ, CPA, J.D.

"I want to be like Joe when I grow up. Plus,
this book is good for killing flies."
—NEIGHBOR KID

"I learn something new every time I read it! Must be
chewed, swallowed, digested, and read again."
—JOE CALABRIA, AUTHOR

"If I have said it once, I have said it a hundred times. It is the best book my
son has ever written. Now, can we please go to dinner like you promised?"
—MRS. JOSEPH CALABRIA, SR.

HELLO

How Are You?

Joseph M. Calabria, Jr.

ISBN: 978-1-945028-18-2 (hardcover)
ISBN: 978-1-945028-19-9 (paperback)

Book design by Adam Robinson for Good Book Developers.
Cover photo from Unsplash by Juan Gomez

For questions, comments, or bulk purchases, contact the author directly by emailing: Joe@HelloHowAreYou.US

I dedicate this book to Providence College—Dominicans, athletes, students, faculty, administration, staff, and alumni, all those fondly and proudly known as the "Friars."

I thank my parents, my wife, my children, my grandchildren, my friends, and my co-workers. Without you, I wouldn't have the experiences to write this book, or have any readers to enjoy it! I am indebted to Dennis Quinn and Tom Sparough for their guidance and counsel.

CONTENTS

205 SECTION 3

What Makes Me Tick

SECTION 1

HELLO

CHAPTER ONE

Hello, How Are You?

F ROM MY EARLY YOUTH, I CONSIDERED MYSELF A SALESMAN. SO, it was no surprise that my first job out of college in 1965 was in sales working for IBM. I was given a sales quota to achieve. All year I strove to make my quota, and when I finally made it, I got my invitation, that long-awaited, pined-for invitation to the Annual Sales Recognition Convention. That year we went to Miami, to the Fontainebleau, a luxurious, 1,504-room masterpiece.

At the appointed time, I made my way among the hundreds of other guests in the lobby and came face to face with our VP of Sales.

He asked, "Hello, how are you?" He shook my hand and beamed vigorously. With that quick introduction, he moved past me to the next group of people. He greeted everyone the same way, "Hello, how are you?"

It struck me as inauthentic. He was feeding everyone the same line. It wasn't just the words of his greeting. It was about how he said it. There seemed to be an underlying entitlement in his voice and posture, as though he'd paid for each and every one of us to be there out of his pocket, which we all knew he hadn't.

I participated in all the activities of the convention. It was a good time with lots of fun, drinks, and camaraderie.

But that interchange with the VP of sales stuck with me throughout the gathering. Here I am, 50 years later, writing about it. Things happen in all of our lives that stick with us.

But, will we learn from those things that stand out in our memory?

I knew back then that I didn't want to be like that arrogant VP. I wanted to be authentic. I wanted to treat each person for who they were. I wanted to extend my hand and have it mean something.

I have always known I wasn't perfect. My college grade point average will forever remind me of this fact, but I have learned a thing or two in my 70 plus years of life.

This book is my attempt to share some of the important things I have learned. I would like to look you in the eyes and say, "Hello, how are you?" And then linger with you, find out your stories, share some of mine. Have some fun, and drinks, and camaraderie.

To that point, much of this book is about fun, and occasionally I have stretched the truth, but only one inch here, and, OK, two inches there. And, yes, I have added a little spice. But I was once told that the general rule of storytelling is as follows:

All stories are true, and some of them actually happened! Don't worry; most of my stories actually did happen.

With this approach, I have written my book as a series of short stories. These stories illustrate and inform what I call Calabria's Laws. These are 12 lessons stated as laws that have helped shape my life and business. In some ways, each of us is a hero, amazing, remarkable, and exceptional. Our stories need to be told.

And so my stories begin.

"Hello, how are you?"

CHAPTER TWO

A Friar's Story of Life, Laws, Luck, and Love

WHEN I WAS YOUNG, I HAD A DREAM TO BE SUCCESSFUL. IN that dream, I wanted to own my own business and achieve financial independence. My dream came true.

Even my seventh-grade teacher, Sister Mary Louise, had told my parents I was going to shoot for the stars. She advised my parents not to break that dream, because the worst case would be a lasso around the moon.

My parents helped me to reach my dreams.

My life changed one day while watching basketball on TV. That moment, I was thinking about an alternative to admission to the Coast Guard Academy, which looked like my destiny. I picked up a book with short descriptions of colleges and happened to open the book to the page detailing Providence College. This was a Saturday afternoon in March of my junior year in high school. By coincidence, I had the National Invitational Tournament (NIT) basketball championship game on, and there was Providence College in the playoffs. Providence's big man, Jim Hadnot, was electrifying the screen with his amazing dunks. He averaged more than 19 points per game in the 1960-61 season. I took it as a sign! Maybe Providence College was the place for me. It was a small school, not overly expensive, and with a caring teaching staff willing to work with anyone wanting to get a solid education. Anxious to learn more about the Friars, I soon found that here was a school full of first and second-generation immigrant kids from working class families eager to learn about the philosophy of life, basic truths, and the search for the universal laws.

That was a description of me, so with my parents approval, I applied to Providence College. I had a smile from ear to ear the day I got my acceptance letter.

From 1961-65 I attended Providence College, which is in Providence, RI. I was a Providence College Friar, and I loved every minute of it. It helped to form me into who I am today. I guess once the Friar-lore is in us, it goes deep and stays there, affecting everything we do through life. While a student at Providence, I put together a list of my goals in life, i.e. first to marry the perfect loving wife; second to start and own our own business; and the third to.... well, you get the point.

As the years have passed, I developed at least 100 of these goals, most of which I have achieved. I call them "Memorable Moments." Throughout this book I will make reference to many of these moments. It is part of what makes me tick. As you'll soon read, my ticker has needed lots of work along the way. But having goals and achieving them is huge. It is the Friar way.

I guess we all should believe in Divine Providence, that idea that something greater than myself is at work in my life. I think it was Divine Providence that brought me to Providence College.

My wife and I have been dedicated fans and donors of Friar basketball. We believe that the men's basketball program is an important part of the Friar community. Of course, it is more than basketball that fills me with gratitude. I am thankful for the impact that the Dominicans, the religious order that founded and runs the college, has had on my life, and the life of my family. My gratitude is why I dedicated this book to my Friars. They have helped me to strive for the absolute best.

That desire to strive for the absolute best starts with imagination. Divine Providence leads this. That is how the best ideas first come to us. We need to imagine what is possible. From there, we collaborate to shape the vision and develop the plan. When I am in the game, we could call it CA-LAB-O-RA-TION. Later in the book, I'll tell you about how that spelling was first developed. It is a combination of my name and the word "collaboration." That process is really important to me. Few things in life get done without it. From there, we add in perseverance. This is how we achieve and overachieve our goals. We use imagination with collaboration and perseverance.

As proof that I have strived for the absolute best, I include my wife's picture on the next page. Take one look, and now you know that this Friar REALLY overachieved! This is especially true if you look at my picture, and then hers. She's so sweet her name is Sugar, and that's the truth. As of this writing, she hasn't read my book. However, she does know I intend to brag about her looks. Recently, with the book almost done, she entered my office, and I asked her if she wanted to see where I had decided to include her picture. To my surprise, she coyly eyed me and commented, "That little space! It's hardy big enough to hold a wallet-sized picture. Don't you think I deserve a whole page?" God, I love that woman.

Truth be told, I am a non-liberal, traditional, right-wing, unwavering individual. I have more than 50 years of business experience that I am sharing in these pages. As Confucius said, "Words are the voice of the heart." I am sharing my heart with you. This book's mission is to preserve complete information for those people interested in learning more about my views, methods, and laws of success. Admittedly, that will probably be mostly my family and friends. At least, I hope they will be interested! Also writing a book is one of my lifelong goals. You, the reader, are now an important part of this achievement. In fact, you can be part of the movie, but all in good time.

My experience in the work world is probably similar to yours, full of interesting characters, and realizations, that have coalesced into my laws of life and business. I remember these people through a diverse, interwoven series of vignettes. These stories bring to light for me the functional departments of the work world, alongside the nuttiness of people and business, and, shhh, come closer, because they might be listening—GOVERNMENT. If you know me, you know that I don't actually care if they are listening. I am telling the truth. These varied stories fit together in my puzzle of life. We each have a puzzle of life. My puzzle has had me baffled, mystified, stumped, foiled, and sometimes hoodwinked, yet I have tried to make sense of this riddle that runs through my life. My objective is to present to you a concise, easy-to-read, and humorous set of stories.

The woman of my dreams

Before going further, I want to share a bit more about my desire to write a book. It has not been easy for me. I am not a natural writer. It has taken a lot of inspiration, and perspiration, to finally get it done. Most people never finish their book, which I guess actually does make me an overachiever. I share this challenge of writing the book to illuminate why we do certain things, specifically things that no one says we have to do, and some people tell us we can't do.

Several years ago one of my best friends, Dennis, sent me an email announcing his book publication. He then suggested I buy it on Amazon for $7.95 before the price increases. My response to him was a heartfelt "thank you," but no $7.95 was coming out of my pocket for his book. My wife got wind of this and quickly reminded me that I vowed to myself more than 50 years ago that I would write a book.

My wife said, "Here you are 50 years later, and your college friend prevails with his book publication. When are you going to join the club?" Her remark and Dennis' book lit a fire under me. The flames forced me to get out of my immobile, unresponsive state and to start my book.

I sent Dennis a second email saying, "Haven't saved enough to buy your book, but let's trade for my future book."

Dennis replied, "Joe, you have a deal!"

Truth be told, I saved my quarters, dimes, and pennies and eventually had enough to purchase Dennis' book. I became one of his customers.

A few months passed. I then wrote back and asked, "How are the sales?"

Dennis emailed, "Better than we initially expected. We published during the December holidays, three and a half months ago, and now we are pushing a thousand copies sold."

"Hmmm," I thought to myself. I know Dennis too well. When he says, "pushing a thousand" that probably means he had only sold a hundred, and still had 900 more to "push." But hey, that was more than I had done. So now I was getting psyched.

I emailed back saying, "Expect a draft sometime this year for comments."

Dennis encouraged, "I'm looking forward to it. I know you'll enjoy writing it. The act of writing the book was a lot of fun for me, more than I expected. Honestly, the characters just took over the keyboard in ways I had not expected. On average it took me about 6-8 hours to write, rewrite, and edit a single page. You may not need to do that, but be ready for it, if you do. The hardest part of finishing the book was getting a good editor without paying a lot of money. But looking back, a really good editor would have been worth the money. Good luck, but most of all, HAVE FUN DOING IT!"

"Hmm," I thought. This time I think he was telling the truth. My next thought was, "If Dennis can do it, and have fun, why not me?" That was the day I said, "Joe, go for it!"

What will it take for you, my reader, to put your long-held plans in motion?

Even when you resolve to start on a project, not everyone believes you can do it. Sometimes those closest to you doubt your ability the most. After all, they think they know what you are capable of doing. It can be confusing, because one minute they encourage you, and the next minute, they try to hold you back.

Shortly after my pledge to "go for it," I was in my office with a couple of pencils (all with erasers). My wife spied me and questioned what I was doing. I replied, "I am writing my book."

After she had picked up her jaw off the floor, she said, as if she was an investigative reporter, "Come on, Joe, you can't really write a book!"

"Why not? I have a razor-sharp wit," I answered.

She shook her head slowly, and silently. Then verbally added, "Joe, I love you, but you can't spell items on the grocery list. You couldn't write a note to our kids' teachers. But now, you are really going to write a book?"

As she left the room, still shaking her head in disbelief, and rhythmically swaying her hips to distract me from the important work at hand, she looked back over her right shoulder and chuckled, "Some of your friends would be surprised to find out that you have even read a book, much less can write one."

I tossed out the famous George Reeves comment, "Knock the 'T' off that 'can't.'"

The following morning, she acquiesced halfheartedly in agreeing with me that I might amuse myself in trying to write a book. She did mention that she didn't believe my book had the slightest chance of becoming a major motion picture. Somehow it seemed to me, of course, it would be a major motion picture. Once again she stuck a pin in my bubble saying that some natives living in the remote jungles of Brazil have better betting odds in securing a major motion picture contract.

Her agreement in supporting me in my book-writing endeavor came with certain frugal economic conditions. It had to be a low-budget project. For instance, when I got thirsty, she said, I was only to use tap water from the refrigerator with a two-ice-cube maximum. I wasn't to go to the grocery store and stock my office with purchased bottled "tap" water. I used my razor-sharp, internal wit to justify these demands from my lovely wife. Effortlessly the old African proverb came to mind, "A razor may be sharper than an ax, but it cannot cut wood." I agreed to my wife's ground rules and continued on my goal to start and FINISH writing my book.

In reality, this book has no real ending, because my life and lessons learned are not finished yet. You will have to hold your breath, along with me, as I find out what crazy things life still has in store for me. I hope I have the chance to fill in the remaining blank chapters in a second book, which I plan to title, "Illegitimi Non Carborundum," or for you non-Latin scholars out there (which I guess is most of us): "Don't Let the Bastards Get You Down!"

For all the Friars trying to overachieve, always remember, "For the things we have to learn before we can do them, we learn by doing them." —Aristotle.

CHAPTER THREE

Success

I HAVE ALREADY STATED THAT I REACHED MY GOAL OF BEING A success in life. Of course, there are many ways to measure success. For instance, I graduated college with a grade point average just barely above the minimum. That didn't make me the valedictorian, but I see myself at the top of the class. I am not trying to brag, but I am proud of the things that I have achieved.

Remember, my intention is to help you learn from my success. Just as if we were sitting together talking, I would like to learn from your success.

I have 12 laws that have helped guide my success. Before I share them with you, let me give you a thumbnail sketch of some of the highlights of my success. Then the next 12 chapters will explain my laws. After that, I'll describe some of what makes me tick, and I'll also include a complete list of my 100+ Bucketload of Memorable Moments, some of which I am still working toward. You will find them at the back of my book.

As I explain my laws, I am going to bounce around a lot, so this little summary will give you the big picture of my career right from the start.

A Brief Summary of My Success

- I started saving for college when I was just a kid cutting lawns and delivering papers, and I actually used that money to pay for my first year of college.

- While in college, one summer I sold cookware and became the top salesman in the nation and paid for an entire year of my college tuition.

- Also while in college, I started my own pick up and delivery service for laundry. This business also helped pay my expenses and tuition costs.

- As an upper classman, I created an algorithm that predicted horseracing results. I won enough money to pay off my remaining college tuition expenses.

- I was elected to student government and eventually became the treasurer of our student government.

- I was listed in Who's Who Among Students, the national college student recognition program.

- Even though my parents hadn't been to college, and my grandparents hadn't graduated from high school, I graduated from Providence College with a 1.73 GPA. Please note, I could have graduated with a 1.66 GPA, but I exceeded minimum standards!

- I was hired before I graduated by IBM as a salesman. I surpassed my yearly quotas for six straight years, accepted a series of promotions, and climbed to the position of multi-branch manager. I remained there for about two years, surpassing my office quotas both years.

- I was selected to join the Bachelor's Ball planning committee in Reading, PA, which helped set my life-long path of supporting worthy charities.

- The woman of my dreams came into my life, and I married her. We have now celebrated more than 50 years of marriage together!

- The blessings of two children entered my life. Not sure how that happened, but I know there are six grandchildren now.

- My career expanded as I accepted positions with the international firm Olivetti, and then Exxon. I gained invaluable experience in sales, marketing, and financial forecasting.

- I accepted my first top-level position with a start-up computer firm in Boulder, CO. Unfortunately, I also received a lesson in corporate bankruptcy.

- While transitioning to my next job, I mortgaged our house and planned and orchestrated a multi-million-dollar business deal.

- With my wife, I started and grew our business CPI into a 260 million dollar per year business with more than 60 employees.

- My wife and I became major donors to numerous institutions, and I joined the Board of Trustees of Providence College, my alma mater.

- I wrote this book about my guiding laws and the things that have motivated me throughout my life. I may not have graduated at the top of my class, but I have been rising ever since. For all I know, with the writing of this masterpiece, I may be in a class all of my own!

- Reaching the fine age of 77 years old, I am still hard at work. The reason is simple: to support causes I believe in.

- We started a foundation for the purpose of offering scholarships to needy students. This non-profit corporation meets the 501(c)(3) requirements of the IRS code.

Conclusion

Here is a little tip on celebrating success. Write out one of your goals on a piece of paper. Place that goal in your desk drawer or bedroom bureau. Work hard and continue to believe you will succeed. One day, open that drawer and experience the excitement of realizing you have achieved your goal. Moments of success like this are one of the satisfying thrills in life! I have been filling my bucket with them and have no intention of stopping. This is good, old-fashioned horse sense that will get you across the finish line in the winning position.

SECTION 2

CALABRIA'S
12 LAWS

Calabria's Laws

1. Nothing was ever accomplished …
   … By a reasonable man.

2. Without procedure …
   … There is chaos.

3. Primary considerations …
   … Usually conflict.

4. When in doubt …
   … Hesitate.

5. Everything is negotiable …
   … Except failure.

6. Sacrifice today …
   … For tomorrow's reward.

7. When you're fast and efficient …
   … You don't go unnoticed.

8. Excellence is …
   … Our ultimate goal.

9. Time is my most precious commodity …
   … Don't waste it.

10. When a reasonable offer to buy is refused …
    … Lower it.

11. Soar as rapidly as possible …
    … To achieve a longer glide pattern.

12. Service measured not by gold …
    … But by the Golden Rule.

CHAPTER FOUR

Calabria's Law Number 1

Nothing was ever accomplished...
...By a reasonable man

L IFE IS FUNNY. IT DOESN'T GO ACCORDING TO PLAN. YOU CAN'T reason your way through it. To be successful, you have to be unreasonable, go the extra mile, try one more thing, and keep working when others give up.

Let me tell you about my graduation from college, Memorable Moment #15. If you have ambitions, use your educational experience as a springboard to get on your train of life. My grandfather was an Italian immigrant who couldn't speak English and worked as a laborer in a brick factory. However, he was smart enough to insist his children learn to speak fluent English and earn a high school education. My father embraced America and refused to speak Italian in our home. He insisted I go to college. It didn't matter to him what I studied. It mattered only that it was a meaningful degree and that I complete all necessary course work. My only regret of my college years is that the course work didn't include a class in learning the Italian language. That is one of my Memorable Moments I am still working toward!

For me, college was four years of questions and laughter between childhood and the real world. It produced these three big results. None of them are what your typical, reasonable person would call success. In this chapter, though, we are talking about being unreasonable.

1. Enough credit hours surpassing a 1.66 GPA on a 4.0 scale. No sweat. My 1.73 GPA was enough with room to spare. It didn't

torpedo my dreams of 100 things I wanted to accomplish in life. I recently reviewed my college transcript and was surprised to find most of my semesters had 20 credit hours in them. In case you haven't been to college, let me put this in terms you will understand. "That's a lot!" An average load is 15 credit hours, so 20 is a heavy load. In spite of this heavy study load, I started a laundry business on campus to help pay my expenses, and I built and used a complicated algorithm to frequently pick the winning horses in races at the local track. The laundry business and the winning algorithm helped pay my college tuition. My higher than expected GPA helped me finish as number 532 out of 597 graduates. But hey, I both graduated and I and I graduated debt free! That is my Memorable Moment #15.

2. I didn't just pay off my college debt before graduation. I made my parents proud. I was going to school for everyone in my family who didn't get that opportunity. Along the way, I also helped my roommate. My horse track results gave me the opportunity to change ten dollars from my financially strapped roommate into 67 dollars. He used that money for his class ring. If you're curious about how I won at the track, it's no secret. It's science, and I am going to describe it in detail later in the book. Remember, I am a college graduate, so I know stuff.

3. Get a job. Anyone who has ever been to college knows this isn't a sure thing. Christmas of my senior year my mother had set me up with an interview at IBM. She had seen a help-wanted ad in the newspaper and made a phone call to get an appointment for me. After that interview, I received an offer from IBM, but after graduation I was still considering becoming a professional gambler. My mother grabbed me by my ear and whispered in that ear, "Apple Pie, Motherhood, American Flag, AND IBM!"

The president of Providence College recently told me I owed the college rent for using the dorm parlor as a business storefront. This was after I told him my story of starting a cleaning service for shirts and slacks in the dorm. The old college rules of the 1960s forced us to wear a shirt and tie for all classes, but this offered me the opportunity to provide a delivery laundry service for shirts and slacks. I felt responsible for helping my fellow students to have personal neatness and cleanliness (for a small token of appreciation, of course). I offered pick-up on Tuesdays and delivery on Thursdays or vice versa. After hearing my story, the president asked how I got so many customers so quickly. Remember, this was before computers, hash tags, or any social media. I told the president that I hung a tampon over the door with a little sign that said, "We clean everything." My business exploded because I discovered the keys to advertising, "corporate identification" and "product familiarization." It may not have been reasonable, but hey, it was effective.

And the president wasn't being reasonable when he asked for rent from my business of 50 years ago. But, that request worked, as well. Any and all proceeds from this book and movie will go directly back to the Friar family. Year-to-date presales have already yielded enough for two, premium, Venti cups of Starbucks. That will supply the president the funds to give a couple of honor students a much-needed coffee break!

Order of the Arrow— Memorable Moment #37

When I was a kid, I learned lots of lessons, just like we all did. I want to tell you a story about one of those early lessons. I was involved in the Boy Scouts of America and moved up through the ranks. There is an honor society in scouting called the Order of the Arrow, and I was invited into the special trials that a scout has to perform to be admitted into the society.

I knew many scouts had survived these trials, but they didn't seem reasonable to me. If you haven't guessed it, I am a guy who likes to talk, but the first rule was that you had to be silent for 24 hours! Then you only got a small portion of food to survive on, and you had to spend the night by yourself in the woods.

So there I was with my two pieces of bread, my canteen of water, my sleeping bag, and a block of wood that I was supposed to carve into an arrow with my pocketknife. It was a daunting task, definitely unreasonable in my eyes. In retrospect, it was great. For the first time in my life, it taught me that I could do something that seemed impossible to me.

The hardest part for me was sleeping alone under the stars in a sleeping bag in the woods. I was especially scared of snakes. After finally getting myself to sleep, I woke up in the middle of the night. I heard a swishing noise, something slithering near me. It was right next to the sleeping bag I was lying in. Whatever it was, it was moving through the leaves on the ground within striking distance of me. My sleeping bag was thin. Where was my safe shelter? I was vulnerable as I lay on the ground. An overwhelming feeling filled me that I was about to be bitten.

At that moment, I thought I smelled cucumber. That was the scent of the copperhead, one of the most deadly of the poison snakes. They emit a musk that smells like cucumber. I could smell it and hear the snake moving next to me. Then I noticed that the sound was coming from more than one spot. There were two of them!

I pulled my sleeping bag up over my head and tried to lie as still as possible. I told myself that I was safe, that I was OK, that I was going to make it through the night. I talked myself back into a kind of a drowsy state, yet slightly wakeful. I just couldn't get back to sleep.

In the morning, I got out of bed exhausted, but very carefully. I did not want to step on a snake. I thought I could still smell the cucumber. Fortunately, I never did see a snake during that ordeal. I had made it through the night and hiked to the destination point carrying my arrow I had carved out of wood. It wasn't easy by any stretch of the imagination, but I passed the inspection and was inducted into the Order of the Arrow.

As I look back on this story, I think I realized what William Wordsworth meant when he said, "Nature never did betray the heart that loved her." I had experienced a unique outdoor adventure, even if I didn't sleep in a safari tent with an air mattress.

All of us have stories from when we were younger of things that we got through, even though they were very difficult, perhaps unreasonably so. We should always pay attention to those stories. They set the stage to overcome even greater things in our later lives.

District Sales Manager Joins Me for the Day

I am going to hop around a bit on some of the highlights of my life, and I want to jump to a couple of sales stories that show part of what I think is important about not being reasonable, and how it can pay off.

A couple of years into my sales career with IBM, the district manager showed up one day at our branch office and announced he was going to accompany me on my sales calls that day. I didn't have a plan for what I was going to do that day, but I knew I wanted to impress him.

The structure at IBM was that I was a salesman who reported to a sales manager, who reported to a branch manager, who reported to a district manager. Did you get that? My boss' boss' boss had shown up at our office unannounced and was now in my car, and I didn't have a plan for what I was doing that day. It was intimidating to say the least, and I was thankful I had put on antiperspirant, because I was sweating behind the wheel.

He asked me, "What are we going to sell today?"

I told him, "We are going to sell everything today—office supplies, a graphics machine, a dictation machine, a typewriter, and a copier."

It was a mighty ambitious agenda, and frankly, I had never sold that many things in a day. But he smiled at me, and said, "Well, I know you're a hot shot salesman who doesn't even stop to eat lunch, except for a hot dog in the car, but today we are stopping for lunch. I am a district manager, and we take the time for lunch."

That morning every call we made, I got a sale. Sometimes everything clicks into place and this was one of those days. Later in the book, I'll explain my sales secrets. We had lunch and got back to work. At the end of the day, I had done it. I had sold at least one of everything we offered!

The district manager said something that I will never forget. "It was the most incredible sales day I have ever seen."

The whole day was unreasonable. A reasonable employee would have set a modest sales goal so that he could have looked good in front of his top boss. I set an unreasonable goal. That day everything came together. Great things can come from being unreasonable.

Not in My Vocabulary

After I had the outstanding sales day with our manager, one of my fellow salesmen, Bill, who was down on himself and in a real slump, asked to spend the day watching me perform what he called my "sales magic." I agreed. I had been on a tear, and perhaps I did have just what he needed!

We started calling on potential clients early, but didn't have any luck. All day long we got nothing but rejection. As the day came to a close with no tangible results, we headed back to the office. I felt like I had a neurotic condition much like soldiers in a combat zone. The lack of sales on this day while trying to help my fellow salesman produced anxiety, hysteria, and utter exhaustion. However, I refused to accept the consequences of failure and its impact on Bill.

Before we got back to the office, I saw a small business in a building just past the exit we were approaching and decided to pull over and give it one more try. I really wanted to motivate Bill. He needed to learn that he wasn't an empty bottle, but rather a candle waiting to be relit. When we entered the prospective customer's office, I was determined to salvage the day with a sale. A few minutes later, in spite of all my efforts, we left empty handed. I had failed Bill.

Bill, however, was keenly appreciative, and as we got into my car he said, "Joe, that was an awesome call. What I saw you do was powerful enough to change my attitude. Thank you. This is really going to help."

I asked Bill what he thought happened in the call. He in turn asked me a question. "Joe, how many times did they say 'no' in that call?"

"I don't think they ever said 'no,'" I told Bill.

Bill said, "I counted 29 times. And after each one, you came back with a well-reasoned response why they should buy our product. Joe, when someone tells me 'no,' I immediately leave and look for another client. I'm going to change that."

"That's great," I said. "My philosophy is if at first you don't succeed, pretend nothing is wrong and continue forward. 'No' is not part of my vocabulary."

I know this isn't reasonable, yet that day Bill became determined to change negative responses into sales. He committed to a solid game plan, and he executed it brilliantly in the weeks and months that followed. He realized he couldn't take it personally when someone closes the door. Rather, in a relationship business like this, he had to stay motivated and remember how good victories feel.

Legendary college basketball coach Jim Valvano may have said it best in his famous speech at the 1993 Excellence in Sports Performance Yearly Award. He gave the speech only months before he died of cancer. His message was clear and to the point, "Never give up. Don't ever give up,"

The Lottery Winners

Conventional wisdom says, "Lottery: A tax on people who are bad at math." In other words, it's not reasonable to expect to win big in the lottery.

I remember walking down Penn Street in my hometown of Reading, PA, after graduation in 1965 thinking I wanted to achieve financial independence. For me, that meant a great income and no financial problems. Yes, you're right. Everyone wants financial independence. So, OK, I'm not an amazing, original thinker, but hey, it's still a good thought. However, the important question in wanting financial independence is: "Do you have a plan to achieve it, or do you wait for luck, like winning the lottery?"

I like the first question, because I am a reasonable guy. But, I like the second question, too, unreasonable as it is.

In the 1960s, many states were introducing their version of the lottery, which in many cases featured a million-dollar payout spread over 20 years. Looking across Penn Street and observing people strolling, I remember thinking that if I did achieve financial independence, I didn't want people I knew thinking I was just a lucky son of a gun who had won the lottery. Rather, I wanted to convince myself, and I wanted others to know, that I had made my money as a result of personal drive and hard work. I wasn't going to spend the money to buy a lottery ticket, because if I did win, I'd never be able to prove that I was worthwhile without my lucky win. And plus I knew the odds were mathematically totally unrealistic to think I had a chance to pick the right grain of sand while looking at a whole beach!

Ironically enough, given my views on playing the lottery, I have personally known three actual lottery winners. How about you? Do you know anybody who has hit it big with the lottery? If the odds are so terrible, how come so many of us know someone who has won?

I didn't begrudge any of the people I knew for their lucky paydays. The first was my cousin Consette, who lived across the dirt alley from my house in Reading. When we were kids, it seemed like she was always in her backyard working in her garden. On my side of that dirt alley, I remember using the hose on my mom's garden in our backyard during those long, hot summer evenings. When I would see my cousin weeding her garden, it didn't take much contemplation to direct the spray from my hose over our garden, across the alley, and high enough to glide the water over the garden hedge, and drench my cousin. I did it often and thought it funny every time.

Years later, after receiving a promotion at IBM, I moved out of town. Several years after that, I heard my cousin Consette was a million-dollar lottery winner. I called to congratulate her.

"Consette, it's Giusseppe," I started my call.

"Too late," she barked and slammed down the phone.

The story doesn't end there. Recently, I was visiting my mother a few months before her 99th birthday. Cousin Consette called. My mother handed me the phone. I told Consette that she was going to be in my book, and I wanted her to make a cameo appearance in my movie. She would be able to tell her version of the dangers of late-day gardening and the constant threat of sudden showers without a cloud in the sky.

She asked, "How much will I get?"

"Well, that will depend on book sales and how well the movie does, but I assure you a check will be coming. What's your address?"

"Look it up!" She slammed the phone down on my sensitive ear. I was trying to listen to my cousin carefully. I guess time doesn't heal all wounds. Maybe she needs a cold shower? Anybody got a hose?

I met my second lottery winner after moving to Colorado in 1983. I remember meeting him on a golf practice range. He won more than

$2,000,000. He told me he quit his job and improved to a two-handicap golfer, sent his wife to work, and was living an "unexciting, uninteresting, and mostly dull life." A bit after this, he decided to go back to work and took a part-time consultant contract. A year later, he was back to full-time work with 60 plus hours a week of responsibility and no time off for golf.

Someone once said, "Don't start a diet that has an expiration date. Focus on a lifestyle that lasts forever."

The third lottery winner was a friend named Maureen. My wife and I attended a wedding in 2006. I remember walking a few blocks from the church on a cold, snowy Saturday night to get to the reception. Maureen joined us, but came in complaining that an uncivil, disrespectful, and impolite lout had skipped in front of her at the convenience store to buy a lottery ticket. She had been anxious to get to the reception. As I listened to her, I truly began to feel that karma was in the air that snowy night. I wondered if Maureen would be the lottery winner, and so it was!

What are the odds? You don't want to do the math. There is no reasonable way to expect to win.

```
        Check winning numbers at
        www.coloradolottery.com
         The lottery has returned
          more than $3.0 billion

Term: 03379200                    013669
Ret: 033792
0893-016881666-127864

                         20171027 13:19

POWER            $2.00-1 DRAWS
                     10/28/2017
BALL®

                          PowerPlay No


A  03  09  13  27  33  PB  03

         Expect the Unexpected

          Estimated Jackpots
Powerball:            $40,000,000
Mega Millions:        $30,000,000
Lotto:                 $1,300,000
Lucky For Life:  $1,000 a Day for Life!

            0893-016881666-127864
```

After success in my business career, and being witness to these three lottery winners, I know I can now purchase the mega millions or power ball lottery ticket, with no guilt, no shame. I realize, of course, that the odds of winning the lottery are one in umpteen hundred million, proving the total randomness of winning. This is unlike the scientific basis of my horseracing algorithm mentioned earlier in this chapter, and which will be explained later in this book, and which I used successfully while wearing a very stylish hat.

If you want me to apply the same skills to the lottery, so far my limited, fickle research for a lottery-wining algorithm led me to this conclusion. The winning combination of numbers must contain the number "3" in it. You can take that to the bank.

For me it's worth the $2 to settle back in a comfortable rocking chair (preferably with a motor) and fantasize on what to do with all the winnings. This is pure enjoyment for me. I get more out of it than a $10 movie ticket. I have extravagant notions, elaborate dreams of what I would do if I won the money. Why I might fund the building of a basketball arena at the campus of Providence College, or perhaps an aquatic center. I indulge in these gratifying daydreams until the actual winning numbers are announced. Then the fun is over, at least until the next ticket is bought. And I will buy that next ticket, as unreasonable as that might seem.

If I ever won big, I think the first thing I would do is wait for my water-soaked cousin to call me on the phone. Of course, for that to happen, I would have to send her my phone number. I would love to hang up on her just once. Then, I'd probably need to take a cold shower. Anybody got a hose?

Honestly, though, in a more charitable vein, I would set up a trust to spread my good luck to others. I don't need the money, but others do. Every time I buy a ticket, it's in the hopes that I will hit it big so that I can give it all away, every last penny to those who need it most.

One of my unreasonable goals of my life is to have Memorable Moment #34—to win the lottery. Please remember the German proverb, "There is no one luckier than he who thinks himself so."

I am pretty sure I am going to hit it big! After all, I was schooled by the **DO**m**I**ni**CAN**s. They have that "I Can Do" attitude! They remind me that it "Can" happen. And they inspire me to get off my lazy "Can" and buy a ticket. You might want to "Do" the same.

Engagement

Eight months after leaving college in 1965, and fully engaged in my first job, I found myself in a two-day business show in Lackawanna County, PA. The branch manager of the local Office Products Division at IBM was also in attendance. Dinner options included chicken nuggets, tomato basil soup, fries, and a menu of sandwiches. The locals considered these options a food marriage. It was all they would get when eating out in their sprawling metropolis, since there wasn't another available restaurant in town.

During dinner, Bob, the manager of this local IBM branch office, suggested I transfer and take a selling position in his office. He talked about the advantages of eliminating all the software program training I was scheduled to attend. Since starting at IBM, I had spent almost 70% of my time in school. I was scheduled for seemingly countless trainings for two more years. My life so far, and for the foreseeable future, was centered on data processing. I saw Bob's offer as an immediate opportunity for some golden nuggets, instead of only being able to afford chicken nuggets, and finally get the chance to use my skills as a natural salesman.

My then-girlfriend, who would eventually become the Chick in Charge (CIC) of my life, was apprehensive about the switch. It meant that my salary would switch to commission, which was not the surest of incomes, unlike my current data processing division job. I assured her the move would help facilitate getting her an engagement ring. Hmmm, that seemed to change her mind.

Accepting this offer meant I wasn't taking the reasonable course with my career. After all, those classes I was scheduled to attend were there for a reason. It was a well thought out plan that helped reasonable people to climb the corporate ladder. But, I didn't go that route. I accepted that offer to unreasonably skip class and take a salary dependent on my sales success.

Off I went to White Plains, NY, for a two-week sales school for orientation on my new job. The Yonkers Race Track was a short distance from my hotel. I'm sure you already see where this is going. Although I had never before used my algorithm on harness-racing horses, I tried without much success on Wednesday of the first week. On Wednesday of the second week, most of the first weeks' horses were slated to race again. It seemed appropriate to revisit this 67-year-old, historic half-mile, standard-harness racing track.

The results were exactly what I had been working toward my whole life. I won big. My girlfriend accepted my proposal and my racetrack winnings paid for her diamond ring. It wasn't the reasonable way to get a fiancée, but Sugar, the Chick in Charge of my life, loved her ring. Once again, I thanked the racing gods who were very kind to me. Just kidding, it was the science of my algorithm that allowed me to win. My number one achievement in life was to marry the woman of my dreams. I am happy to report Memorable Moment #1 became a reality!

Breakfast at Jerry's

It is not enough to follow any one of my laws of success. They work in unison. This next story will illustrate that fact by the time we get to the end. My wife, Sugar, and I had a favorite little diner run by a guy named Jerry. He was certainly unreasonable, and that was part of the fun of why we kept going back. Jerry had returned from Vietnam and opened his "greasy spoon." It was a small, cheap restaurant specializing in fried foods. Jerry would advertise his restaurant as "the little place you would not want to ever pass."

He reminded me of one of my ancestors, 5' tall, great coordination of hand and mouth motion, and always ready for a quick conversation about all the oppressively heavy or onerous happenings in the world. My wife and I often stopped by his restaurant, not because we enjoyed his coffee or the greasy smell, but because we loved to listen to his semi-philosophical discussions with his patrons. It was an avenue of humor for me. Jerry knew better than to try to get me to talk about anything too deep. He was all emotion, but I took things a bit more seriously. As Tacitus said, "Think, therefore, as you advance to battle, at once of your ancestors and of your posterity."

One day a business acquaintance of mine, John, arrived at Jerry's diner and was questioning the cost for a cup of coffee. Jerry got indignant and told him to pay what he thought it was worth. John reached into his pocket and flipped a quarter to Jerry. From that day forward he would order a coffee and leave a quarter. When Jerry would object, John answered that was the contracted price.

Neither of them was being reasonable, but in a way it was marketing genius. Jerry created a little drama show that patrons could come and observe, or even take part in the banter. It really was fun. My wife and I loved to watch it all unfold, and sometimes I'd get involved.

Jerry had small packs of jelly/jam on each table. You could find grape, strawberry, and black raspberry. He was always unhappy when he saw too much free jam being used, and often expressed his dissatisfaction verbally if he saw you spreading black raspberry on your toast. One day Jerry told me that it was more expensive for him to buy the black raspberry jam. It was a big mistake telling me that! Now I was part of the act. From then on, I put the punctuation mark on our table by gathering as many black raspberry packs as I could find from other tables and slathering the stuff on my toast and rolls, always making sure Jerry saw me doing it. Not nice, but fun! There is a Scottish proverb that says, "A good tale never tires in the telling." Messing with Jerry never got old.

On any given day, the check was not very expensive. Even so, I always paid by credit card. One day Jerry asked me to pay my bills with cash. I responded that I didn't think this was suitable, or proper, since the IRS already had a difficult task trying to distinguish total revenue for taxing purposes. I told him, "The credit card payments will assist the IRS and ensure that Jerry's Restaurant was not under taxed." As you will read in future chapters, I am not a fan of the IRS, but this was all in fun! It was the reason we kept coming back, and we weren't alone.

The unreasonableness of the whole scene made it successful.

Jerry's Restaurant had a few sleek, well-dressed patrons as regulars who really got under his skin, even more than I did. Take Peter for example. He would order the pancake breakfast special. This was advertised as "two pancakes, each containing only 64 calories." Peter always ordered the special, but with only one pancake, not two, and only wanted to pay half price since he was only getting 32 calories!

Jerry had a sense for how all this commotion was good for business.

Unfortunately, he lacked some other sense. For one, he was mean to his wife, and ended up getting a divorce. Problems like that drain the fun from the establishment, and that started the road to the restaurant's demise.

A coffee shop opened up across the street. I told Jerry, "You should offer cappuccino at 50¢ and drive them out of business."

"They are no competition to me. They don't sell food, and I don't sell cappuccino, and I never will," Jerry said.

Well, the new coffee shop was fast and efficient, and they didn't go unnoticed. That's one of my upcoming laws that Jerry didn't get. The coffee shop started selling food and Jerry went out of business. We can't always be unreasonable, or we will suffer the consequences.

My First Track Meet

When I was a kid, just like clockwork my Uncle Nicholas would make the family rounds on Thursday every week, always willing to sit at our dinner table, experiencing the flavor of a forkful of this and a spoonful of everything my Italian mother had in our refrigerator. When I was in the seventh grade, Uncle Nick used to come around a lot. At that time, he was in his fifties and out of shape. One visit led to an exchange of who was a faster runner, him or me. After a five-minute exaggeration by my uncle on his past sports performances on the track, Uncle Nick suggested we race around the block. The bet? The loser would push the winner in a wheel barrel down Main Street. Of course, I reminded him I was "All Neighborhoods Champ." My advice to him was to seriously reconsider his bet. It would be the reasonable thing to do.

We lived on a hill, and we were about two houses away from the top of that hill. It was a steep grade and Uncle Nick started the race by letting me go down the hill first. The race route went down the hill, turned right for a block, turned right again back up a hill, and then back to our house, approximately four blocks in total distance. I flew down the hill, across the next block, and back up the opposite hill, dashing the last 50 yards past the two houses next to ours, only to find my uncle enjoying a beer and claiming to have passed me on the third leg of the race. What really happened was Uncle Nick waited for my start, never moved past the front yard, and had a good laugh waiting for me to complete the race. I was exhausted.

I told him he had cheated and wouldn't get the prize of the wheel barrel ride down Main Street. He told me that the real prize was watching me huff and puff around the block!

Years later, I ran for the Providence College Friars cross-country team. I never found it any easier to finish the races. Now I run on my treadmill in my man cave, watching sports on TV with the air set at 70° Fahrenheit. Like golf, I find workouts on my treadmill best defined as an endless series of tragedies obscured by the occasional miracle of the finish.

But hey, I also learned a good lesson from Uncle Nick that day. If I was giving a speech, I might say it this way, "In life's many races, some of the competitors may try to cheat. Keep an eye on your path and an eye on them." Uncle Nick's unintended little lesson has served me well over the years. When it comes to achieving success, sometimes you have to be unreasonable. In fact, I think it is a requirement, but that doesn't mean you get to be dishonest.

Go ahead and be unreasonable. Keep trying when others quit. But make sure you do it with integrity. None of my laws of success are enough by themself. They work with each other. There is more to success than being unreasonable, even if it is one of my favorite parts. So let's move on to the next of Calabria's Laws.

CHAPTER FIVE

Calabria's Law Number 2

Without procedure…
……… *There is chaos*

L ET'S FACE IT. CHAOS ISN'T GOOD FOR US. WHEN WE ARE IN chaos, and we have all been there, it is hard to get anything done. It slows everything down. It's confusing, frustrating, and unproductive. It is bad for our heart, our head, and our bottom line.

Your office shouldn't look like a bad hair day.

Procedures don't have to be set in stone, but they do need to be set in place. We need guidelines and systems so that we are able to do our best work. We, and the people we work with, need to know what to expect. Otherwise, not just our outward appearance is amiss, but inwardly our guts are in a mess. When that happens, it is pretty tough to benefit from our gut instincts.

Putting the right procedures into place starts with knowing who you are, what you want, and how you want to get there. Communication is key.

How to Attend a Meeting

Let me share a brief story that illustrates why procedures are imperative. Without them, there's chaos. I remember attending a strategic meeting in Boulder, CO, where over seventy employees from around the country representing engineering, finance, marketing, production, management, manufacturing, new product research, and forecasting, spent three days hashing out a strategy for a poor-performing product.

When I returned to our division headquarters in New Jersey, I learned that the top-level corporate management ash-canned the product three days before the meeting ended. That's a breakdown in communication and a lack of proper procedure. What a waste of time, effort, and money! Most importantly, it was a blow to morale. I guess that's when I first realized the ultimate career strategy would either be going to as many meetings as possible, or owning my own business. Which strategy do you think I chose?

Along the way I learned from all kinds of people. I have tried to put into practice much of what I have learned. I will share a few of those influences with you.

McCullough's Advice

I seized one of my best opportunities of a lifetime, when I heard David McCullough's 2013 keynote speech at the dedication of the Providence College Raune Center for the Humanities. At the time of his keynote address, this American author and historian had already been honored with two Pulitzer Prizes, two National Book Awards, and had received the Presidential Medal of Freedom. The part of McCullough's advice that really spoke to me that day could be summed up like this:

"Know how to express yourself on paper and on your feet.

You will be way ahead of almost all your contemporaries."

That little tidbit of wisdom is huge. If you want to start your own business, success will ultimately depend on how well you express yourself in writing and on your feet. We need to be clear with what we write and what we say. To be able to do this on our "feet" means that we must know it well enough to express it in new ways, whatever the situation, as questions come to us in real time.

McCullough certainly would encourage everyone to write his or her own book. It wouldn't matter the topic, or whether it was printed in hard cover or created on a website. It only matters that our message is preserved and clear. This helps us, and all of those who would like to follow in our footsteps.

Anderson's Law

If you want to start a business like I did, or if you just want to be successful in your life, you have to know what you are trying to achieve, and what you think it will take to get there. That is what procedures are all about.

When we moved to Colorado in 1983, ValleyLab, a company founded in 1967, had a plant one mile from our new home. Its products included an electro-surgical scalpel, an intravenous infusion pump, and other medical products. I learned an important lesson from Robert Anderson, one of the co-founders of the company. This came after Pfizer, Inc. acquired ValleyLab, a very big moment for this start-up company. Anderson, who was CEO at the time, shared his recipe for success:

> "Take a pinch of new technology;
> Add an understanding of your market place;
> Mix with massive quantities of technology and focus;
> and stir for several years."

Rickey's Law

I'll keep this one short. As the old baseball man Branch Rickey once claimed:

> "Luck is the residue of design."

The Lore of Being Italian

One of my favorite heroes of all time is Lawrence Peter Berra. You may know him as Yogi, a nickname given to him by a friend who likened his cross-legged sitting to a Yogi. This Italian baseball legend is still famous for his fractured English, and sometimes nonsensical quotes, or as I like to think of them, philosophy of "making this day necessary." When you grow up in an Italian family like I did, it was exciting to see a famous Italian baseball player and coach. I'll refer to Yogi and his philosophies again in this book, but for now, here is one of his most famous quotes:

"It ain't over,
'Till it's over."

This is exactly what I was talking about in my first law about "nothing was every accomplished by a reasonable man." Yogi knew from experience that you can be down five runs in the 9th inning, and have two outs, and still win the game. It may not be reasonable, but it is possible. What makes it possible is the right procedures, the right spirit, and the proper practice.

Business and sales are the same way. Everything can change at the last moment. Be ready for the unexpected. New developments should not be the onset of chaos, but the opportunities of an agile system.

Ronald Reagan's Law

Here is another short one. It gives us the big picture. There is a lot to admire about our 40th president of the United States of America. Here is one of the lasting zingers he shared:
"Socialism only works in two places:
Heaven where they don't need it,
And hell where they already have it."

Commission For All

At my company, I don't want everyone to earn the same amount. I want everyone to be on some sort of commission basis. I want people to profit from their hard work. I look for ways that we can quantify the good work that people are doing, and then reward them for it. This is an on-going effort, and we have many procedures in place to make it effective. Someone who finds a cost-cutting measure should get a share of the savings. Someone who sells more should get more. Someone who helps the sales staff to be more efficient so that they can sell more also deserves to make more.

My ideal company has everyone on commission. My ideal country does, as well.

Hap's Law

I worked under Hap at IBM. He was the VP of Operations at the time. He was a very formal man, often sporting a Harvard-type bowtie, and he had his own set of rules. I named one of them Hap's Law. It was summed up in this way: always avoid verbally asking questions when they could be asked in writing. I believe the reason that particular rule stuck out to me was because of our daily interactions at work. Hap would send me a memo, approximately one paragraph, with three sentences. Each sentence would have at least two hundred and seventy-six words, and I'm probably underestimating!

While his memos were extensive in content, because he was trying to give precise instructions on what to do, or what he wanted, I could never seem to get the point. This meant I would have to respond to his memo with a memo. After about the fifth memo of the day, Hap would get fed up with me and agree to have a meeting to explain his request, or talk about the issue at hand. Hap's Law:

"Never ask a question verbally that you can put in writing."

Note: I didn't like this law. I never use it in my business. I think it is a lot faster, and usually more clear, to talk to people rather than to write to them. But of course, I do agree there are times that it is important to document details in writing! My point here is that successful people put procedures into place. Mine are different than Hap's.

Law of Attraction

The Law of Attraction is one of the many universal laws. This one has been important to me. I have tried to keep it in mind to help me be successful. I focus on what I want. That clarity is really important. A universal law can be compared to swimming in a strong river. If you try to swim against the current, you will go nowhere. However, if you swim with the current, you can end up traveling a great distance. Universal laws are always in motion and cannot be stopped, because they are fundamental for life. The Law of Attraction acts like a magnet between people, places, and things.

Every thought that we make is energy. The Law of Attraction takes the energy from our thoughts, both positive and negative, and uses it to help create our reality. This change doesn't always happen automatically, for if it did, we would have everything we could ever want and still feel unsatisfied.

Esther Hicks, writer and motivational speaker, has a wonderful quote about the Law of Attraction: "This incomplete place that you stand is the best place that you could be. You are right on track, right on schedule. Everything is unfolding perfectly. All is really well. Have fun."

Another great Law of Attraction quote comes from author and lawyer William Walker Atkinson: "The best way to overcome undesirable or negative thoughts and feelings is to cultivate the positive ones."

Bacon's Law

Everything tastes better with bacon!

Actually, I am talking about Francis Bacon, the English philosopher, statesman, scientist, jurist, orator, and author. He penned his greatest works in Latin. Those of us who don't read Latin may also have a hard time plowing through the old English translation, but it's well worth the effort. Bacon's Law:

> Reading maketh a full man;
> Conference a ready man;
> And writing an exact man.

Sweeney's Law

I considered Steven "Nap" Napolillo, who works in the Providence College Athletic Department, to be our adopted son. He is smart and wise and hardworking. Nap always says that John Sweeney, Providence

College's Senior Vice President for Business and Finance, "…is the most important Friar hire of all times."

I, and especially my ego, agree with him. I love that John coined one of my favorite laws, as well as one of my favorite words, when he said, "CA-LAB-O-RA-TION helps Providence College succeed."

John combined my name, CALABRIA, with one of my most important procedures, which is COLLABORATING with Providence College leaders. That is how together we achieve the college's goals.

However, sometimes I fear that John thinks that CALABORATION is like letting loose a high-speed, high-power, high-impact, yet unguided missile. I admit, occasionally I can be hard to control. But, hey, our CALABORATION usually ended up right on target.

Since CA-LAB-O-RA-TION qualifies as "coining a phrase," it became my Memorable Moment #44.

Legalese

I want to toss this sentiment into the mix. We need lawyers for some things. But, life and business would be simpler without legalese. I agree with the businessman Philip Lazarus who said, "A consent decree, as I see it, is a legal agreement when the fellow who doesn't admit doing it, agrees not to do it again."

Corporate Jargon (Lingo)

Business is forever putting me back into the classroom to learn about corporate jargon. There is a close connection in time, space, and logic in the development of your personal corporate jargon.

I firmly believe that without corporate jargon there would be pandemonium. For calmness and efficiency to prevail, investors and consultants use this gobbledygook to mesmerize business associates around the world. Yet it's true that in a corporation, everyone needs to speak the same language. Different corporations have different problems, concerns, and measurements. I once worked for a European company and had difficulty in understanding what was going on. Then I read the operations manual and from then on knew how to speak their language.

Even when I got the jargon down, it was still a challenge to understand my boss. She was Italian and loved to dress in a provocative way. I tried my best to pay attention to her words. This was also tough because of her pronunciation of English words. For instance, she would say, "maaa-chine" and "commm-puter."

It is a lot of fun to realize that many American corporations tend to be more technical in their jargon, using impressive phrases such as "econometrics algorithm." Europeans might use a simpler word, such as "haggle," for the same idea. Both "econometrics algorithm" and "haggle" get at negotiating a price.

Another favorite American jargon technique is the formulation and use of acronyms. One acronym, which is included in all my company's strategic planning meetings, is "SWOT Analysis." This is taught in Masters of Business Administration courses across the country, even around the world. These initials stand for Strengths, Weaknesses, Opportunities, and Threats. These categories help us better understand our current position in the market and determine what areas we need to improve, expand, or abandon. Since we compete in the information technology industry, we use computer jargon for creating images in the minds of our associates and customers. Some computer jargon examples we use to communicate are: Browser, Cookie, CPU, Data Base, Download, Firewall, Mouse, Plug and Play, Spam, Virus, Alpha Geek, and Empty Suit.

In 1985, I started buying and selling surplus products. This eventually led me, and my company, to become a key player in the acquisition of computer components, circuits, and memory. One of my favorite jargon words is "Chip Review and Process." That spells CRAP. That is the jargon we use when measuring our inventory of surplus chips.

Here's a suggestion. Have some fun at your business, and at the same time make sure everyone can speak your common language. This is a fun way of keeping procedures in place. Play the "Lingo Game." Create two columns. Have contestants connect column A with the correct definition in column B. Many different versions are possible, but it will always be a hoot. Make sure your employees can score 100%. Here is a sample game:

LingoDefinition

A- CRAP   ___where the cat sleeps

B- Laptop   ___plastic utensils you get at Big Rooster

C- Web   ___what eats the grain in the shed

D- Mouse   ___chip review and process

E- Software   ___flies worst nightmare

Here's a little advice from Warren Buffet about getting in the game:
"The first rule is not to lose.
The second rule is not to forget the first rule."

Rules of Corporate Jargon Game

There will be two teams competing against one another. Each team will consist of 1-4 team members. Each team will create a list of different types of corporate lingo and a list of definitions in random order. Teams will exchange lists and match the opposing team's lingo with the correct definition. Each team will be timed. For each wrong answer the team will have a minute added to their time. The team with the lowest time at the end will win. Make sure the players have emptied the punch bowl before starting the game.

Please note, if you're playing Lingo after hours in Colorado or Washington State, or any of the other states that make marijuana legal, take it easy on the pregame brownies. You might be traded to another team, or cut and not sanctioned to play by the commissioner.

Lingo at Home

This corporate jargon game that I call the "Lingo Game" can be played at your next home party. In fact, that is where I first thought of the idea some 20 years ago. My wife and I had a dinner party. Late in the evening, we split the couples into two groups, all the husbands on one team, and all the "women" on the other team. The wives wanted to rename the husband team and suggested we be called "The Beer Bellies," or "The Tarzan Club," or "The Stubbles." After those suggestions, we men just decided to call the wives, "The Women." That was all that needed to be said.

Well, the game got started with a coin toss and The Women won that and proceeded to create a list of words and definitions that no man could answer, at least no man at our table. The Women chided us, "What's the matter? Cat got your tongue?" We did get a couple of answers correct, though.

We battled it out and The Women kept coming out on top. Evidently they read a lot of books. I hope they are reading this one, and remember how the game finished. We had at the house a series of Walt Disney Limited Edition prints from various movies. The husbands listed in the left column the original artwork, and in the right column the copyright year. All The Women had to do was match the two up correctly, but they couldn't do it. The Husbands won! Sorry ladies. Better luck next time.

Anyway, the game is fun to play, and actually can help people in your office or your home have a common understanding of jargon and other technical information. Putting everyone on the same page is a valuable procedure for any group. Here are a few of the Walt Disney movie print names and copyright years from those original limited edition serigraph artwork pieces. See if you can match them up.

LingoDefinition	
A- Pinocchio	___©1942
B- Winnie the Pooh	___©1940
C- Bambi	___©1941
D- Alice in Wonderland	___©1977
E- Dumbo	___©1951

And the answers are: A- 1940, B- 1977, C- 1942, D- 1951, E- 1941.

My Company Holidays

Clear procedures around holidays are an absolute necessity for any business trying to keep its employees happy. Holidays are important to everyone, so always publish them in your employee handbook. The holidays which include a day off are most important, but don't stop there! Make some holidays up that you can celebrate in your lunchroom or around the office. Here's a few examples:

Important Paid Holidays—With Time Off

– New Year's Day   – Thanksgiving

– Memorial Day   – Day after Thanksgiving

– Independence Day   – Christmas

– Labor Day   – One Floating Holiday*

*Could be used for MLK Day, President's Day, or any other day you consider important.

Important Non-Paid Holidays—Without Time Off

- January 4th is Trivia Day. A prize if any employee can name the non-paid holidays for the coming year.

- February 16th is Do a Grouch a Favor Day. Employees restricted from naming another employee a grouch.

- March 27th is National "Joe" Day and we always close five minutes early. It's important to recognize the owner.

- April 1st is April Fools Day. Play a prank or two, but don't be mean about it.

- April 30th is Honesty Day. Only the employees who partook in April Fools are allowed to participate. Confess who did what.

- May is Older American Month. We hold a raffle on the last Friday of the month for a bottle of Geritol.

- June 7th is the National Donut Day. An event started in the 1930s as a Salvation Army fundraiser (back when donut was spelled "doughnut"). If this holiday falls during the normal workweek, never give time off, but always allow for donut time during coffee breaks. Employee donations are always welcome and proceeds go to the Salvation Army.

- July 29th is National Lasagna Day. Have a special catered lunch with accordion music.

- August 21st is Senior Citizen Day. Buy lunch for those over 50, and have them tell the staff one story of when they were young and reckless.

- September 28th is Ask a Stupid Question Day. Have a meeting and the boss will answer all your thoughtful questions.

- October 2nd is Name Your Car Day. Staff draws pictures of their dream cars and puts names on them and displays them on their desks.

- November 15th is Clean the Refrigerator Day. During one-minute shifts, everyone helps clean because Thanksgiving leftovers are coming!

- December 15th is Corporate Jargon Day. Each employee is given a two-hour lunch break to play the game and the company provides lunch.

Other Fun Rules for Lucky Employees

- Whenever Christmas falls on a Sunday, always close the office early on Christmas Eve (at least by 4:45 p.m. on Saturday).

- Leap years are illegal, except when the extra day occurs on the weekend. No extra pay for the extra day unless employees can jump over a desk in a single bound.

Dumb, Dumber, and Dumbest

I have been joking around here, but let's look at something serious. Fraud is a huge problem in our country and around the world. It takes many different forms. Most of us picture the elderly person taken in by an unscrupulous Internet ploy, investment agent, or door-to-door con artist.

The reality is that a modern businessperson must be constantly on the watch for sophisticated scams. I experienced my first case of fraud in 1996 and my latest one is probably in an email request right now. My company has fallen victim more than once. That says something, right? We know it happens. We train our people to watch out for it. We have procedures in place, but occasionally we still fall victim. Every week, if not every day, someone tries a custom-made scam on our business.

How does it happen? Our salespeople are eager to get sales, and sometimes because of the excitement of closing a deal, they forget the procedures in place to safeguard the authenticity of each sale.

Here is one that got us, at least, at first.

One of our salesmen received a request for a quote on a series of computers. He submitted it and got approval for a $30,000 sale. That's a good day's work! There was an email confirmation, and he talked with the new alleged purchaser. The company named in this order was one of our customers, but the "ship to" address wasn't verified as a company warehouse location.

Furthermore, this is the kind of order that should immediately be suspect, because it sounds too good to be true. There was no prior contact with the purchaser. The call came out of nowhere, and the order didn't require competitive bidding.

Our procedure at this point in the order process is what we call the "buddy system." This means a "buddy," which is another salesperson, must look over the details of the order and sign off on it to confirm it. That happened, but in a sloppy way, and the sale was approved. This order was listed as being purchased by one of our established customers. Unfortunately, that company was not actually placing the order. It was someone else pretending to be that company.

Before the payment had processed, our salesmen got a second offer from the same company, going to the same address. This order was for $100,000, which is a very, very good day's work. By this time, the administrator had noticed that there was not confirmation of a payment date for the first order. She asked the salesmen about it, and they both called the purchaser, the imposter, and he assured them everything was OK. He'd take care of it. At that point, management should have been alerted to this situation, but it wasn't. Our VP of sales wasn't aware of these transactions. Perhaps he was sleeping on the job. The sales rep was eager to process the order. Everything seemed to be legitimate, and we sent the shipment out. When you do the volume of sales that we do, this is not an unusual order.

But when a third order for $170,000 came in before anything had been paid, various people in our company got suspicious. A different "buddy" did the check, and looked up the address and found out it wasn't going to the company, but to a U-Haul dealer in Texas located near the company. They stopped the order. I got involved.

I told my people, "Let's send out the third order, but only half of it, and instead of sending out the product, let's fill the boxes with bricks." I had a plan in mind.

After a little research, I contacted a reliable, private investigator in Texas and put him on the case. He was able to hang out at the U-Haul site and when the order was delivered he saw the office manager was having trouble moving the boxes filled with bricks to the rented storage area. He offered to help, and the employee accepted. Now he knew exactly where the boxes were being stored.

It wasn't long before a woman picked up the boxes and had them moved to a nearby house. The PI followed her to the house. Now the PI had all the information needed, and we got the police involved. We shipped the second half of the third order to catch criminals in the act with the police detective there. It worked!

But was it really fair to catch this con artist who makes a dirty living targeting companies with schemes designed to steal their products? Oh sweet justice, yes!

When the detective arrived at the house where the stolen goods were stored, another woman entered the scene and stormed up to him. She explained to the detective on site that she wanted $10,000 back, because she had just bought computers that turned out to be a bunch of bricks!

It didn't go well for her. She was trying to get the police to refund her money for buying stolen goods. She must have missed that lesson in school, but that is not what the police do.

OK, we were dumb to fall victim to their scheme.

The thieves were even dumber to try the same trick twice.

But, the dumbest was when the woman who complained to the detective that the "hot" merchandise she was trying to purchase turned out to be bricks. I can imagine her pleading her case. "Officer, you don't understand! My clients won't pay me for the bricks. They only want computers!"

Protecting yourself and your company from fraud is a gigantic headache. In the case I just described to you, we are still trying to get our money and product back. It's not easy. With a little imagination, it is easy to envision the havoc that would ensue if we didn't have strong procedures in place. No doubt we would be out of business. Not everybody out there is nice. Be ready or fall victim.

Recognizing Fraud

Fraud is such a problem that we need never-ending education for employees. It never ends, because those who perpetrate the crime are often smart, and they adapt their tactics continually. Regardless of whether or not you are in business, you need to protect yourself and your information. I am going to list here some of the procedures we use with my company. Perhaps they will help you to develop or refine your own safeguards. Fraud attempts happen every day. For us, they have all had the same basic approach:

1. Needed immediate shipments.

2. First contact was direct to a sales representative.

3. "Ship to" and "Bill to" was either to different addresses, or to temporary office rental.

4. Email address changed within one week.

5. Phony bank references were out of state.

6. Pretended to be a department manager of a named institution.

The sophisticated ones have a secretary answering the phone and putting you on hold for a few minutes until the knowledgeable and experienced crook takes over. When you spot them in the act, let them know. Remind them that what they are doing is criminal activity and you are forwarding their information to local authorities.

Rules to Avoid Fraud

1. Don't ship if "bill to" address and "ship to" are different. Especially if ordered by credit card.

2. Confirm order by looking up the company headquarters and calling through the company switchboard to speak to the direct contact. Confirm order with the company procurement department.

3. Ask for copies of driver's license and check if it has been reported lost or stolen.

4. On every first order asking for credit, call the bank and ask if someone there knows or handles the referenced account on a personal basis, how long the account has been opened, and average account balances. Be sure the first order is pre-paid cash, not credit, before the order is shipped.

5. Senior management is responsible to follow up if a crook is apprehended; go to court and insist on no bail.

I followed one criminal taken into custody by the police, only to watch a judge release him on bail. It doesn't take special powers of intuition to know these criminals are a flight risk. My crook never returned. We did catch his associate and had her tried and convicted. Eventually her parents paid off the debt to get her released from prison.

With or Without an HR Director

Throughout my career, I've had many unusual encounters dealing with directors of human resources. It's hard to imagine having a chug-a-lug in a grog shop with any of the ones I knew.

The Cemetery

In 1979, while living in Connecticut, I and four of my company colleagues had to drive more than 70 minutes to get to work. Since we all lived within 5 miles of each other, we decided to carpool to and from work. We carpooled from exit #41 off the Merritt Parkway in Connecticut to IBM in Franklin Lakes, New Jersey. This was a procedure that made the trip easier for everyone.

For me, the benefit was getting home earlier than when I drove by myself, since there wasn't any leeway for working past 5:15 p.m. We had a drop-dead departure time of 5:15 p.m. One of the four of us bought a van and he became "Captain Bob." He equipped it with a CB radio, captain seats, an extra fuel tank, a TV, and many other amenities. We all quickly learned CB lingo. "10-4 good buddy. Is Smokey up ahead?" Translation: "I understand friend. Are there police up ahead?" We got to listen to the darker side of truck driving as we heard announcements such as: "Looking for a skirt for rent."

One day there were only two of us in the van, myself as driver, and the formal, stiff, proper, rigid, precise, methodical, dignified, director of human resources, whose name was Ed. Driving with Ed was a procedural responsibility that I didn't enjoy. He never smiled, made conversation, or opened his eyes all the way. Our route through Connecticut took us over the Tappen Zee Bridge and across some back roads in northern New Jersey. The winds that day were almost at hurricane levels and pushed the van sideways across the lanes of the bridge. I did my best to keep the van straight, but it was tough going. By the time we finished crossing the 2.5 mile-bridge, Ed was pale and his knuckles were white. Somehow that cheered me up.

OK, I should probably say at this point, I did not like Ed. A stick in the mud was more exciting than he was. I tried to be nice to the guy, but it didn't work.

It is my opinion that you have to have some fun along the way. At least I did. Ed needed to learn that lesson. On that day with the winds howling, a devilish idea came to me. I suddenly figured out how I could really bust Ed's chops, and maybe I could shock the guy into relaxing and have a laugh or two.

Halfway through the back roads, I slammed on the brakes creating a screeching sound and a burning rubber smell, causing the cars around me to also come to a screeching halt. With the van stopped, I rolled down my window, pointed to the top of the hill, and announced to Ed, "There under the apple tree is the perfect plot to get buried."

Since Ed was not yet over his scare from the bridge, I admit I was a little afraid the added trauma from the honking horns and screeching tires might cause him to have a stroke. After a brief pause with some heavy breathing, Ed shouted, "WHAT ARE YOU TALKING ABOUT?"

With the van still stopped, and other cars passing us now, I told him this was his chance to carve his niche in tombstone folklore. Beginning today, he could design his gravestone featuring all his business cards from the first one as a trainee to his last as an HR icon, all engraved on the north side of his stone. I added that if he had the contents of the cards etched on his tombstone in gold, his stone would really stand apart from all its neighbors. On the south side, he could engrave each and every score of his past evaluations. He loved to do evaluations.

"What do you think Ed? Would you like to get out and look at the perfect place for your grave?"

Ed slowly shook his head no. I must admit at that moment, I silently thought that "flatulus antiguates" (AKA an old fart) was a better engraving option.

I started driving again, but I added that if he does leave this world, we remaining carpoolers would roll down our window every day on our way to work so he could listen in and stay up-to-date on the latest business gossip.

I finished this little performance by reminding Ed what Yogi Berra's wife Carmen asked, "Yogi, you are from St. Louis, we live in New Jersey, and you played ball in New York. If you go before I do, where would you like me to have you buried?" Yogi answered, "Surprise me!"

All this fuss didn't help Ed to enjoy life any better. It also didn't draw us closer together. He never understood that just because we were striving to achieve the American Dream, we could still have fun along the way. That was the last time Ed and I ever rode alone together to work.

Dinner With the Bell

My story of Ed continues with a dinner party. Let's take another view of how procedures matter, but can be overdone. The procedures are in place to serve the workers, to safeguard and protect them. The procedures should be designed to keep people fast and efficient. They should help people to get along better, not to be on edge, not to be rule bound. Of course, no one should know all this wisdom about procedures better than the VP of human resources, Mr. Ed, at least one would think.

Our carpool gang was invited to dinner at the home of that top executive, and we were to bring our wives. He expected we would be dressed in semi-formal attire. We sat four on each side at that meticulously set dining table, with Ed, the executive, at the head of the table, and his wife as the hostess at the foot.

Just as a side note, my peasant Italian mind was always puzzled after that night, "Was there a rule for determining which end of the dinner table was the head and which the foot?" But, I digress.

The whole evening was quite stiff. The conversation was stilted. After the main course was finished, Ed rang this elegant little glass bell at the "head" of the table. His wife rose from her seat at the "foot" of the table and rushed to clear the dishes. They clearly had a procedure in place! After the dishes were removed, Ed again rang the bell, and his wife hurried to his side. He requested she take coffee orders to be served with dessert.

I squirmed in my seat. And if I looked uncomfortable, you should have seen my wife. No one anticipated dinner would be like this. This was the head of personnel. Wasn't he supposed to be a real people's person?

Coffee and dessert were served. When the meal was over, he rang his bell once again. As his wife approached his side, he took from his suit coat an evaluation sheet and publicly went through his critique of the evening, rating her service.

We couldn't wait to get out of his house. I should mention that at the end of the night, there was no bell notifying us that it was time to leave, but we left anyway. Finally, my wife and I were back in our car. It was a quiet ride home that night. Somehow, it appeared I was partially responsible for what had happened. After all, I was a man, too. Without saying a word, my wife's eyes conveyed to me in no uncertain terms, "Don't ever try that, buster!"

Later that night after we went to sleep, I woke up and went to the bathroom. Half dazed from sleep, I thought I could still hear the bell ringing. I discovered I had a bell strung on a string around my neck.

When I came back to bed, my wife Sugar whispered in the dark to me, "The bell is because I love you so much and always want to know where you are."

For your amusement I have attached a similar evaluation sheet from that infamous dinner. If you are interested in climbing the corporate ladder, you might want to give it a try. You'll have to get your own bell. My wife keeps ours locked in a drawer. Remember, whatever procedures we put in place at home and at the office, we must accept the responsibility for the negativity they create. Be smart. Lose the bell!

Somebody suggested to me that perhaps I shouldn't put this story in my book, because of repercussions from that esteemed VP. I don't think he is around any more, and if he is, I am pretty sure he doesn't want to draw attention to this story! Plus, as every good salesperson knows, a little controversy would certainly be good for book sales.

Host Evaluation Sheet (Check All That Apply)

Attire
[ ] You should have changed
[ ] Better than a Goodwill outfit
[ ] Ok to be seen in public

Manors
[ ] Uncouth
[ ] Not completely annoying
[ ] Acceptable for a date

Conversation
[ ] Talked way too much
[ ] Mostly boring
[ ] Impressed with your quiet

Quality of meal
[ ] Dog wouldn't even eat it
[ ] Full, but not satisfied
[ ] Meal is a do-over, Yum!

Promptness
[ ] Way too slow
[ ] Almost fast enough
[ ] You finally served it on time

Followed direction
[ ] Get hearing checked
[ ] You drool when bell rings
[ ] You are getting the hang of it

The CPI Financial Model

I always wanted to come up with a sound financial model for business, and I did. This is Memorable Moment #11. It's all about putting the proper procedures in place. Without them, there is not only chaos, but also bankruptcy.

Throughout my book, I am sharing some of the nitty-gritty details of my business to help you think about the nitty-gritty details of your life and career. What is at stake? What matters most? What are common pitfalls? What procedures can you put in place to achieve your goals?

When I researched why small businesses fail, I found one of the main causes was a credit policy that was too liberal, which led to bad debt. In other words, company A ships product to company B, but B doesn't have the resources to pay back A. Because of that, there is no way for A to pay its bills. This isn't fiction. It is a common occurrence. I saw that I didn't want to fall victim to this bankruptcy pattern.

Many believe Dun & Bradstreet's fairy-tale reports for credit approval will solve this issue. I am going to lay that claim to waste later in this book, but all in good time my friend. The answer is straightforward. Use bank references, bank account averages (cash only), and the number of years in business to determine creditworthiness. It is also important to put a plan in place to manage cash flow; your credit line, i.e. borrowing money, should be the last tool used to increase company growth.

Here are three procedures that have helped us to stay financially secure as we slowly built our revenues to over $260,000,000 per year.

1. Separate operating funds from taxes and payroll. This necessitates two separate checking accounts. Split daily deposits to each of their appropriate accounts. For our business, one account is restricted for timely disbursement of sales tax, payroll taxes, and commissions paid. The second account is the operating account for fixed expenses and cost of goods that we sell. This may seem obvious to you, but trust me. It's not the norm. My banker was so thrilled when I reported my plan to

him over a coffee break, that with a laugh, his coffee ran out his nose.

2. Maintain a healthy cash reserve. Give your accountant the actual revenue and the bottom line taxes due. When you are all paid up this comes out to zero. All the accountant has to complete is credits and debits to reach the desired results. The net result is a healthy cash reserve. The temptation is to spend this, or take it as income. When you do that, you leave yourself at the mercy of the banker who shoots coffee out his nose.

3. Create a budget and the procedures to stick with it. If you need help, don't hire an out-of-work US Senator as a consultant, unless, of course, you're looking for a clear path to deficit spending. Bankruptcy is just around the corner, right near the coffee shop with your favorite banker. When dealing with a consultant, be careful and ask one simple question: "Are you acquainted with the bottom line basics of owning a business?" The bottom line is profit. The quickest way to bring money down from the top line, which is your gross income, is to slash expenses in your budget. Do that and profit falls right into your hands, or at least, your reserves.

OK, enough about procedures. We have a lot to cover and it's time to move on to the next of my Calabria's Laws. Let's finish this chapter with a bit of wisdom from the former Prime Minister of the United Kingdom, Winston Churchill. He said, "I contend that for a nation to try to tax itself into prosperity is like a man standing in a bucket and trying to lift himself up by the handle."

CHAPTER SIX

Calabria's Law Number 3

Primary Considerations…
…Usually conflict

W HEN THINGS ARE EXTREMELY IMPORTANT, THEY BECOME PRI-
mary considerations. The thing is, at any given time, in any given
situation, there's usually more than one primary consideration, and they
often compete with each other. If you choose one, it's probably at the
detriment of another. There is a balance to try to reach.

It has been helpful to me to simply have an awareness that conflict
is going to happen around important things. Our money, our time, our
energy, our reputation, our health, our office, all these are primary considerations. Every individual has his or her own set of primary considerations, and they are fluid, changing from day to day, year to year, and
sometimes moment to moment.

Some of the conflict is an extension of my last law about needing
proper procedures to avoid chaos, because chaos breeds conflict. Let's
get started.

My First Real Office

After working for four companies with different business cultures, my
wife and I started our own business. This meant, for the first time I got
to pick the location for my office. We were on a very tight budget, so I
rented something inexpensive. That first office was quite an experience to
say the least. Some might call it an "out-of-this-world experience."

Located within an office supplies outlet, in Longmont, CO, I soon found out there was no shortage of "interesting and odd" people all around me. It was quite an adjustment when I learned the office was filled with employees who believed with their whole being that they were living proof of the idea of "reincarnation." For those of you who are unfamiliar with this particular theory, it is the belief that the soul and spirit after death begin life in a new body.

Within this office complex, certain employees, ones that I came in contact with regularly, took it a step further. They believed they once lived in the legendary city of Atlantis in its prime. Hey, I'm not kidding you about this! The idea was new to me, so I listened with interest to their ideas and practices.

They spoke to me about how they had this psychic mind that allowed them to look into their past lives and connect with the person they once were. I would not say I bought all of what they were selling, but I kept an open mind. That is until there was one connection I was just unable to make. On my journey of understanding where these people were coming from, one particular gentleman and his girlfriend led me astray.

He believed he was a man with a great past. After his adventures through Atlantis, he then was a great monk. Not only was he a monk, but his girlfriend at the time also traveled through this journey with him. She was a monk, too. As he told me this story, he stared at my confused look and just smirked. He thought I was confused about how he and his girlfriend came to meet again. In actuality, I was trying to picture how the woman he loved was once a monk. She was an unusual individual with furry legs, long armpit hair, and a face that was anything but peaceful. Maybe she got tired of her calm, disciplined life as a monk, so this time 'round she chose to be a little less, shall we say, put together.

As I was trying to picture what the days might have been like with his girlfriend as a monk, he began to explain how they were meant for each other because there is one sex in that universe and no physical difference between people.

I smiled. This was too much for me. I had work to do, kids to support. Those were my primary considerations. He truly thought I was buying into his story. That was his primary consideration.

Perhaps I could have exploded and told him to keep away from me. There was some conflict inside of me. I decided on a calmer approach. I would try to tell him what I really thought in the most respectful way possible.

After he had told me all this, I nodded my head as if I agreed. He looked at me pleased, as if he had turned yet another person on to his beliefs. Yikes, I wouldn't be able to come home to Sugar if that were the case. With one simple sentence, I indicated to him and others in that office just what I thought of their ideas.

I told the gentleman, "You know, it must be my psychic mind block, but I'm just not seeing how you went from being a man in Atlantis, to a great monk, to a salesman in Longmont, CO, selling office supplies; maybe reincarnation is trying to humble you."

As I walked away with a giggle and a smile, I could feel the glares burning through the back of my shirt. But hey, enough is enough.

Ketchup Bottle Effect— Memorable Moment #72

Sometime later, I was able to buy a commercial building after proving to my banker it was a cheaper financial option than my continuing to rent. It took many meetings to convince the bank. My primary considerations were not necessarily the same as the bank's primary considerations. In the end, the bank agreed to finance the principal. I was on my way to becoming a real estate tycoon.

The space was bigger than my company actually needed. Early on I had one tenant who stayed for about five years before he gave a six-month notice not to renew his lease. He requested an early vacancy without any rent adjustment. That was his primary consideration. This was OK with me since I thought there was more than adequate time to list and rent his unit. I felt that I would be able to release him early from any remaining rent due, and I did.

After listing the unit with an "expert commercial agent," I experienced the "ketchup bottle effect." You are probably familiar with the phenomenon. You turn the bottle over and nothing comes out because the ketchup is too thick. So you shake or pound the bottle and everything comes out at once.

Four months went by without any action on my unit. I inquired why there weren't any prospects for leasing my building. Well, the agent shook the bottle and had a surge of potential clients come forward, but he was quite sure I would not consider them as desirable tenants.

He listed the potential renters that had come forward:

1. A game arcade to be open 7 days a week, 24 hours a day.

2. A dog daycare center.

3. A porno studio.

For that last one, can you imagine me coming to work and greeting these hard-working ladies, "Good morning ladies!" No doubt I would get a smile and response, "How are they hanging?" I gotta move on, Sugar is going to read this.

Eve Arden the actress once said, "Life is full of miracles, but they're not always the ones we pray for."

Well after that, a small church rented the space from us, but unfortunately the leadership of that church was not good with paying rent. And then they just left all together. Eventually we rented the space to just the right client.

I would like to offer a little advice here about business and primary considerations. It makes sense to buy your own building as quickly as you can. Otherwise, you are stuck with landlords who want you to pay the most possible when you want to pay the least possible. It is my experience that life is a whole lot better when you are not answering to the bank every month.

Let me share one more idea on why it makes sound financial sense to own your own building. We have important data that needs to be backed up. Almost every business does. This is a primary consideration. What do you do if the power goes out? Now there's some conflict for you. Well, you need a backup generator. Why would you spend $70,000 for a backup generator if it weren't your own building? And how could you do business without it?

If you want to own your own business, make owning your own building one of your primary considerations. Making that a reality will no doubt require many challenges. I heard this quote from sales guru Zig Ziglar, "May you see sunshine where others see shadows and opportunities where others see obstacles."

Quality Hire

In 1975 at IBM I was asked to meet corporate hiring objectives. On the one hand, it was ivy leaguers with at least a 3.2 GPA. On the other, it was achieving a certain percentage of women and minorities. Our field sales managers were old-school white men with little experience in hiring candidates outside their personal experiences or prejudices.

Yes, there was conflict around this. After all, primary considerations were involved. Part of my job was to help the company move away from the conflict by creating a solid method of hiring a diverse workforce.

I solicited a human resource director named Samuel, who was a minority himself, to help me develop an interview form consisting of three sections with multiple remarks for each question. This would be used as a measurement tool in the interview process. This approach would aid the old-school management in selecting the right candidates to help transform our company. In each section, the evaluator only had to check the definition, which best described the candidate's answer; the scoring was 1 to 3. The overall score gave a strong indication of whether this was a quality candidate.

Samuel had moved up the management ranks not because he was black, but because he was experienced and competent. His disposition and temperament enabled him to perform in this changing work environment exceptionally well.

One Monday morning I met with him in his office to put the finishing touches on our interview questionnaire. Obviously, we had to avoid profiling since the government had strict rules about it. Samuel was in a particularly good mood that morning. With a little coaxing, he shared with me his weekend experience. He lived in an expensive neighborhood and enjoyed working in his yard. Saturday morning, he was cutting his lawn when a woman stopped her car, opened the window, and asked how much he charged. He replied, "I get to sleep with the lady of the house." Up went the window and off that lady drove. Samuel and I looked at each other and burst out laughing. That was a good one!

Later that afternoon I wondered if Samuel was putting me on with that story. I did a search for it and found it in a joke book. The whole interchange reminded me of something the author Roald Dahl said, "A little nonsense now and then is relished by the wisest men."

Melba Colgrove, the psychologist, once said, "Joy is the feeling of grinning inside."

Just because there is conflict does not mean that you can't work with people. Look to work with people who have the conduct and the character that you admire. That should be a primary consideration for all of us. Samuel was one of my favorites.

Experiences

Let me share a bit about some experiences I think we all have in one way or another, whether it is in business or in our personal lives.

- Experience 1: You will work and live with many unique individuals throughout your career, who will offer challenges. And hopefully laughs!

- Experience 2: The more promotions you get, or the older you are, the better the odds that those unique individuals will work for you, or be part of your care.

- Experience 3: Make sure your company, department, or household has a detailed employee handbook, which covers every possible foreseeable situation. I think you should review it annually and keep it updated with current government regulations. Avoiding difficult situations is like dodging rain-drops! Get yourself a good umbrella, or somebody is going to take you to the cleaners.

- Experience 4: If you're at the vice president or higher level, for instance, great grandfather level, and you're involved in a harmless meeting where somebody wants to detail a series of pie charts and hand out a thick report, write the name of a subordinate in the upper-left hand corner. Share the wealth and give someone else the opportunity to curse that report.

Attorneys

What chapter about primary considerations and conflict would be complete without bringing lawyers into the discussion? Let me start with the funny story of the grandma who went to court. There is a lot of truth in this story! I have adapted it from the version you could read about on Snopes.com.

It seems during a trial, a Southern small-town prosecuting attorney called his first witness, a grandmotherly woman, to the stand. He approached her and asked, "Mrs. Jones, do you know me?" She responded, 'Why, yes, I do know you, Mr. Williams. I've known you since you were a boy, and frankly, you've been a big disappointment to me. You lie, you cheat on your wife, and you manipulate people and talk about them behind their backs. You think you're a big shot when you haven't the brains to realize you'll never amount to anything more than a two-bit paper pusher. Yes, I know you."

The lawyer was stunned. Not knowing what else to do, he pointed across the room and asked, "Mrs. Jones, do you know the defense attorney?"

She again replied, "Why yes, I do. I've known Mr. Bradley since he was a youngster, too. He's lazy, bigoted, and he has a drinking problem. He can't build a normal relationship with anyone. His law practice is one of the worst in the entire state. But he's better than you in at least one way. He cheated on his wife with THREE different women. You may be surprised to learn one of them was your wife. Yes, I know him."

The defense attorney slumped in his chair and snapped his pencil in half.

The judge ordered both counselors to approach the bench, and in a very quiet voice, said, "If either of you idiots asks her if she knows me, I'll send you both to the electric chair!"

This little story explains why attorneys never provide or allow any answers without first doing billable research. After extensive careful research, expect them to recommend to you another attorney who "specializes" in that particular area of the law. So that you can add additional insult to injury, you should know that the common Latin phrase used by attorneys "res ipsa loquitor" really means "be prepared to pay a retainer." That's the truth of the matter, even if others say it is attorney jargon for, "The thing speaks for itself."

The Case I Lost

The story you are about to read is true. It hasn't been circulated on the Internet. The names have been changed to protect against possible litigation.

It all started when I sold 300, high-priced, multi-function printers to a discount store in Chicago. This was a small percentage of a large barter deal I did with Xerox. Mr. G., president of the company that bought the units, called me and said he was having problems selling the product. He asked if I could help him out. He wanted to do a price-discounted return. I agreed, but offered to buy the printers back for $430 each.

I originally sold them to Mr. G. for $390 each. I had done business with Mr. G in the past and felt a close business relationship. I felt this was an opportunity to strengthen that relationship. Peter Abrahams once said, "To get where you want to go, you can't only do what you like." Sure, I could have bought back the computers at a large discount, but I knew I could resell them again for at least $490 each. In a way, I split my profit with Mr. G. One way to look at this is I set my eyes on the long-term primary consideration, which was strengthening a relationship with a great client, not the short-term quick-profit primary consideration.

I sent ZA Trucking to pick up the printers at Mr. G's warehouse and return them to me in Denver. I took complete responsibility as both the assignee and the consignor of this shipment.

The freight quote was $760. After delivery, I received a bill for $1,100 from the freight company. I immediately called to get an adjustment, and ZA Trucking agreed the correct charge was $760.

We sent ZA trucking company a check for $760 and thought everything was okay until a few months later when Mr. G. called complaining he was being billed for freight for an additional amount. I explained the invoice had been adjusted to the price of the original quote and was paid in full. Mr. G. called back a couple more times and finally complained the freight company had submitted this payable to collections and Dunn & Bradstreet was listing his company with a payment delinquency. I called the headquarters of this freight company two or three times without any success. I made one last phone call and emphatically told them Mr. G. had nothing to do with this delivery, and the corrected invoice was paid in full.

I may have added in a couple other choice words, just to be sure they got the full message.

After four months (can you believe this?) Mr. G. continued to be harassed. I again called and this time I got all the way to their president. I calmly explained the details. He was not favorably inclined to take any actions to resolve this dispute. If you wonder why I have heart problems, read on.

I then suggested all further collection actions should be against me, not Mr. G. Before this case I was 11 for 11 in court hearings and felt "invincible." Guess what? They sued me for more than $1,700. I guess they thought I was a pushover. Perhaps I had been too calm in my phone calls with them, but they were about to learn who I really was. Soon it would be 12 for 12.

At the court hearing, ZA Trucking was represented by Mr. Nelson. I represented my company as president. Once the hearing started, I noticed the judge was also named Nelson. I asked the judge if this was a possible conflict of interest and whether he was related to the plaintiff. He denied knowing the freight company representative. I am not so sure that was the case, though.

Nelson responded with a challenge as to proper corporate representation. I had prepared myself for this expected tactic and submitted the corporate resolution authorizing me as the corporate designate. The judge overruled the plaintiff's objection and instructed the plaintiff to proceed with his case.

Nelson was first to testify and pleaded the excessive billing was legal because of Interstate Commerce Law allowing full-load billing when fifteen feet of space is exceeded even if it was a partial load. He then rested his case.

Judge Nelson then asked attorney Calabria, hey that's me, if he wanted to cross-examine the plaintiff. "Yes, your honor," I responded.

QUESTION: Were you present when the truck was loaded?
ANSWER: No
QUESTION: Were you present when the truck was unloaded?
ANSWER: No
QUESTION: How many pallets were included in this shipment?
ANSWER: 12
QUESTION: Were the pallets double stacked?
ANSWER: Don't know
QUESTION: What is the size of a pallet?
ANSWER: 4 feet 3 inches by 3 foot 1 inches.
This witness is dismissed!

Attorney Calabria then called Mr. Calabria (hey, they are both me) to the stand:

QUESTION: Were you present when the truck was unloaded?
ANSWER: Yes
QUESTION: How many pallets were unloaded?
ANSWER: 12
QUESTION: Were the pallets double stacked?
ANSWER: Yes

QUESTION: Were the pallets side by side with four pallets per row?
ANSWER: Yes
QUESTION: Was the length and width of the each of the pallets 4 feet 3 inches in length by 3 feet 1 inch in width?
ANSWER: Yes
QUESTION: Were there three rows of pallets stacked flush against each other?
ANSWER: Yes
QUESTION: Would that add up to 4 feet 3 inches, plus 4 feet 3 inches, plus 4 feet 3 inches, for a total of 12 feet 9 inches?
ANSWER: Yes
QUESTION: So the total length was less than 15 feet?
ANSWER: Yes

Attorney Calabria then said to Mr. Calabria, "You may step down." It was easy to see why I had won my last 11 cases!

Judge Nelson picked up his gavel and smacked it down. "I rule in favor of the plaintiff and hereby order Mr. Calabria to pay the $1,700 invoice, plus interest." I said, "Your honor, I must take exception to your ruling. It's obvious the freight was stored within 15 feet from the front of the truck to the end of the third row of pallets."

The Judge replied, "You never said you used a tape measure to measure the distance from the front of the trailer to the end of the third row of pallets."

I was blown away, and started to feel the known risk factors of heart disease. I got sweaty. I could hear my heart pounding. I felt dizzy. My chest hurt.

The next day, I got an EKG for myself. I am a survivor, but my heart can't take many more of these! This judge now serves as a district judge in the Federal Court System.

The lesson I learned that day was that if I really wanted to be clever, I should have taken the judge to lunch, rather then pretend to know the law. I guess I'd say, if you want to avoid conflict when primary considerations are at stake, smooth the waters!

A Case I Won

In 1993, I hired the first of two brothers. I will refer to him as Brian Crook. This informal tag best describes his distinctive trademark. At this time in my business, I had two sales groups. The larger group sold ready-to-use and current computer products. The second group sold surplus computer parts. Each group had its unique compensation plan. One day, Brian who sold in the second group, approached me and asked to hire and partner with his brother, suggesting all commissions would go into a single account to be split evenly by the brothers. For this to take place, I would have to make an exception to our hiring policy.

First, we didn't hire multiple members of the same family. Second, and more importantly, never let them work in the same department. Unfortunately, I broke the code I had in place for eight years and let Brian hire his brother. After one year, they decided to file and litigate a claim against my company claiming more commissions were owed.

As you might imagine, my blood pressure skyrocketed! It should have been no surprise, because this is simply conflict around primary considerations. But it is still aggravating.

Their claim was based on a concoction of combining the commission plan from the first group with the commission plan of their group. They challenged the product cost basis and anything else they could muster up. The trial lasted four full days, and the judge ruled I was right and the brothers, their lawyer, and their erroneous exhibits were all wrong. Had their attorney been able to prove that even 1¢ was owed in commissions, he would have been awarded his legal fees, but since he was working on contingency of winning the case, he got nothing.

He couldn't even show that 1¢ was owed to the Crook brothers.

Not being one to give up a good fight, I then followed the closure of their suit with my own case against them. Action number one, I was litigating for legal fees. Action number two, I filed a grievance against their attorney. The brothers each declared bankruptcy. I ended up in the emergency room with a heart attack.

Luckily the on-call cardiologist was a specialist in non-invasive procedures, and he solved my problem with four stents. A stent is a little tube that is placed in a blood vessel to help blood flow.

On a follow-up visit, it was suggested I enroll in an 8-week program, which incorporated stress management, lectures, diet, exercise, circle discussions, and more. Through this program, I learned tofu was not a foot fungus, but an edible food. What I really wanted to hear was an order to go on an eight-week golf trip with my buddies, complete with a prescription for cigars, cognac, and casinos!

That wasn't in the cards, though, and I actually found value in the classes. Two weeks into the program, the state probe into the brother's attorney was rejected. It happened on a treatment day. We always started those treatment sessions with blood pressure and heart rate monitoring while exercising for forty minutes. I knew my test results would be high as I could feel my tension racing through my body. I started my walk but could only take a few steps before the monitor I was wearing started to send an alert message to me. After three attempts something amazing happened.

I looked up at the sky, and the danger signal lowered itself without me ceasing my exercise. I continued walking and went back to thinking about the state refusing to take punitive action on that scumbag lawyer. At that moment, I watched the monitor rise faster than any thermostat.

Again, I looked up at the peaceful blue sky. This time I focused on some birds flying about, gliding on the wind, circling through the sky. The meter immediately returned to the safe zone. I finished my exercise portion of my program raising and lowering my stress and tension level simply by focusing on the litigation and then the natural beauty in front of me. I learned on that day, and more thoroughly through the class, that I could certainly help manage my stress levels by where I chose to center my focus. That is one of the secrets, and I share it with you, to healthy, happy, living (HHL).

And that should be a primary consideration for all of us.

My Deposition

But hey, I'm a businessman, and my stories don't end there. I have lots more to tell. And many of them are about primary considerations! In 2006, I formed a real estate company and purchased an old Wal-Mart building. My intention was to build a gym for my son's business and convert the remaining unused space to commercial rental units. During construction, a dispute arose with the general contractor. Although a settlement agreement, which was to cost me significant dollars, was signed and witnessed, the general contractor reneged on his agreement. With the advice of a lawyer friend, he increased the claims by an excessive amount and, according to the terms of the contract, submitted the new claims to arbitration. After years of proceedings, the arbitrator made a lesser award of damages to the contractor. Short story, though, I was still going to have to pay big.

The construction contract was a "cost plus, not to exceed contract." Not to get too technical here, but a contract like this has an unmistakable meaning. All settlements, or changes on amounts due from any subcontractors, must be credited back to the real estate company. That's me.

Fast-forward to six years from the time all this began. My real estate company, Jomar Properties, LLC, formed a company called Subcontractor Recovery Fund (SRF) to purchase the claims of the contractor's unpaid subcontractors on the project. SRF purchased seven unpaid claims of the subcontractors at a reduced rate. This strategy had the potential to reduce the award against Jomar. Shortly after that, SRF was awarded the claims against the contractor. SRF moved to secure the assets of the contractor.

The contractor then filed Chapter 7 in Bankruptcy Court. Here's where the story seems to depart from reality. In other words, this will cause you to sit up and take notice of the flaws in our current legal system. And, yes, also make my stress levels soar.

A. The bankruptcy trustee brings an adversary proceeding to try to equitably resolve SRF's claims.

B. In the trustee's complaint against Jomar, the trustee states,

"Upon information and belief, SRF bullied the original owners of the unpaid subcontractor claims into selling the claims, made misrepresentations to induce them to sell their claims, and used boiler-room-style pressure tactics."

C. Trustee demands a deposition of the responsible member of SRF and asks him to admit to item "B." SRF's manager, hey that's me, is ordered to testify. I state I have no idea what "boiler-room-style pressure tactics" means.

D. The trustee attorney pressures the SRF manager into a response during this deposition hearing.

E. So SRF manager, remember that's me, responds in eloquent fashion to this unbelievable scenario about "boiler-room-style pressure tactics." I say, "It sounds like it would have some implication to a type of organized crime syndicate whose primary activities are protecting racketeering. I find your complaint to have, give, or imply some racial overtones. I'm Italian. My family was poor, and we worked hard to find success. When I was young, I had to endure accusations against my family that we were members of the Italian Mafia. I believe this is what your veiled language means."

The court reporter had a good chuckle, and the attorney went forward with a different line of questions. I won't go into it, but it is as Albert Einstein once said, "Logic will get you from A to Z: imagination will get you everywhere."

Enough said about this sorry saga. It has cost me dearly, and it should not have cost me anything. Life would be so much easier if people would just do what they say they are going to do. But each of us has his or her own agenda. I call them "primary considerations." The irony in this crazy deposition was the trustee got to charge the Bankruptcy Court his fees, while SRF had no legal standing to recover any of its legal fees or other costs. Unreal!

Plaintiff's Voluntary Dismissal

Just so we are clear. A plaintiff is someone who brings a case against another.

People try to make money in lots of ways. After all, making money is a primary consideration. But some of the ways people make money are clearly not right, yet they may be legal.

I remember one day enjoying my morning walk down our driveway to pick up the newspaper, which was rolled into a plastic bag. The driveway is made of colored pavers, which always remind me of happy smiles. What a great day it was! The birds and flowers added to the tranquil atmosphere. I actually remember thinking those paver smiles were helping us all kick start a beautiful autumn day.

Once back in my house, the doorbell rang. Looking out through the front door glass, I saw a bearded man in jeans holding a paper in his left hand. My happy mood quickly went away. It seemed obvious, he was trying to serve me court papers. His motorcycle was parked blocking the exit to our driveway. My first reaction was the concern that his cycle was pissing oil on my now frowning pavers. Next, I whispered to my wife, "Don't answer the door."

This whole scene had the clear scent of a process server, probably hired by some plaintiff I didn't know. I imagined there was some perceived wrongdoing of which I had no idea. Was I just becoming a paranoid business owner, fearing lawsuits around every corner, or in this case, in my driveway? I didn't know, but after a few quiet moments, biker guy remounted his leaky steed and road off into the sunrise.

The next day the biker returned. He rang the doorbell, and I didn't answer. After that, since he was clearly going to come by everyday, I decided to have some fun, so each of the following mornings, I substituted the previous day's newspaper into the present day's plastic sleeve and let them accumulate in our driveway. Later that day in the mail, I found enclosed in a plastic sleeve what I thought was a large "advertisement" package. As I picked it up, I thought my driveway pavers were smiling at me. However, as I started reading, I knew they were really laughing at me.

The "advertisement" was a four-page colored proposal and its first words were: "If you have already retained a lawyer for this matter, please disregard this letter." It further advised me in a generic documentation that: "According to the Federal Court System an American with Disabilities Act (ADA) lawsuit has recently been filed against you or your business. You may not yet be aware of this case, and we have therefore enclosed the first three pages of the lawsuit for you to review. We will be happy to provide a full copy of the lawsuit upon your request."

As John Green, one of my favorite authors, once wrote, "I just figured something out. The future is unpredictable." I would add that Green's epiphany is especially true for young entrepreneurs. Business is full of surprises, and there is a steep learning curve.

I figured out that the bearded motorcycle guy trying to serve me papers must not have left this advertisement. Indeed, he continued to come by the house at different times each day. Some days a woman took his place. She would look in the window, bang on the door, and then eventually leave in an agitated, rotten mood. It's no picnic knowing someone is home and refusing to answer the door for you, and if they don't open up, you don't get paid. Our primary considerations were clearly different.

I called the attorney who sent the advertisement to get the full filing of the lawsuit. It included the name of the scumbag, whose official title was "Serial Plaintiff Attorney," who filed the case. It described my alleged violation of the law. I wasn't surprised when the lawyer who provided this information to me included a representative contract to be signed by me and requested a retainer. I wasn't ready to sign it.

The actual violation in question was somewhat complicated, but appeared to be almost nothing for my business and easily correctable. Nonetheless, I had to take it seriously and follow legal channels.

My next call went to the local city attorney. I asked him the following: "First, tell me how an attorney 90 miles away is in charge of code enforcement for your city. Second, why is this going to Federal Court with no rights to a jury trial? And third, didn't I submit drawings from a registered architect, signed sealed and delivered to the city planning department for review before receiving a building permit, and didn't I complete inspections before a certificate of occupancy was issued?"

I guess my call raised some concern, for within a few days I was asked if I was going to include the city in this litigation. The city's attorney explained the city didn't have the budget to cover all the past, present, and future cases for which this scumbag was going to initiate legal proceedings. He did say the city had also been sued and it cost the city $130,000 in fees and corrective actions. He suggested the city's outside council was experienced and knowledgeable in these matters and could accomplish a quick and less costly conclusion for me.

I did call the attorney who represented the city, and he agreed to inspect my property and report back to me. I told him I had called the scumbag who had brought the case against me, and we had discussed the fact that I only had title to part of the location in question. The scumbag's complaint was amended within one day to include the owner of the remaining portion of the property.

The inspection by my attorney went well. Only a few minor issues were discovered, i.e. faded paint on the handicapped parking spaces. My attorney called the scumbag back and reported his claims were generic without evidence and convinced him to dismiss any claims against my property.

In the meantime, each morning I had continued to avoid the process server. My pavers were starting to smile again. I had the handicapped spaces restriped to meet the strictest requirements of the law. I also added the signs shown in this picture to my parking lot.

My version of maximum compliance for our handicapped space

And finally, to finish this happy story, my bearded, motorcycle friend left me a card on my door one morning. A handwritten note on the back said, "Please call John at this number. I have some docs for you." Talk about wishful thinking! I framed the business card from "Quality Process Servers" and smile every time I see it.

I know that was a lot to share, legally speaking. Conflict is part of every business and every individual's life. We have to have primary considerations. We must know what is most important in our lives, and we must make decisions that come at us in a seemingly ever-increasing speed. Read on to get my advice on what to do when you are uncertain about your next decision.

CHAPTER SEVEN

Calabria's Law Number 4

When in doubt...
...Hesitate

S OMETIMES, WE KNOW EXACTLY WHAT IS RIGHT. IT STARES US IN the eyes. We don't hesitate. We grab the bull by the horns and seize the moment.

Many others times, though, things are complicated. I have found myself unsure what to do, what to decide, where to go. I am guessing you are like me. You don't always know what is the best course of action to take.

When I am in doubt, I have learned to hesitate, to pause, to let things sink in. Many a time I thought I knew what was best, but I had a lingering doubt, so I decided to sleep on the decision. The next day, I woke up with 14 questions that needed to be answered before I could truly make an informed decision.

Hesitation doesn't mean that you are indecisive. Often, hesitation can be your saving grace. People need to understand that. In my time, I have served on many boards and committees. It is not uncommon to receive information just moments before we vote on important issues. That's wrong. Some hesitation is necessary.

Let's take a look at some stories to explore this concept.

Dealing With the Government

Warning! I may rant a little bit here. Saying the word "government" can do that to me.

We are taxed on what we build, what we buy, what we sell, what we drink, and where we travel. We are taxed on our desks at work, our supplies in the office closet, and our homes. And let's not forget that we are taxed when we die. Aren't they supposed to be separate, death and taxes? But, no, it's more like death from taxes!

For me, it all came to a head when the city decided to put a water usage tax in place. It started with a reduced quota of 70% of my 2001 water usage as a base. At the time, 2001 was five years prior, and my water usage had climbed steadily as my company had grown. But above that unrealistic, reduced threshold, we got a rate surcharge. I must admit this situation brought my stress level high enough to give me another heart attack. But laughter is good medicine. Sometimes laughter is the only thing that keeps me functioning. It can be a surefire way to hesitate in a healthy way. It can allow me, and you, the time to calm ourselves before we do something we will regret, like try to cheat the government.

These days, absurdity is known as reality. As I think about some of the governmental taxes, it feels to me like trying to cure insomnia by ordering people to sleep more.

Here's what happened. After getting through on the phone to the "Director of City Water," whose best descriptor would be a ravenous wolf, and without gaining any sympathy for my situation, I invited him for a visit to our office. An hour or two went by, and the water representative finally arrived. I waited at the front desk for him to come in, just to see the look on his face when he read my new sign on the front door. As he read, I watched his arrogant smile slip from his face. The sign said:

DUE TO THE CITY CHARGING ME EXTRA ON
MY WATER BILL, VISITORS WILL NO LONGER
BE ALLOWED USE OF OUR FACILITIES.

FURTHERMORE, EMPLOYEES WILL BE PROVIDED A USAGE SCHEDULE TO EFFECTIVELY SHRINK OUR WATER BILL.

As I led him back to the conference room, we walked by the employee bathrooms. The employee schedule read as follows:

THOSE WHOSE NAMES BEGIN WITH LETTERS A THROUGH M WILL BE ALLOTTED TWO BATHROOM VISITS ON MONDAY, WEDNESDAY, AND FRIDAY. IF YOUR NAME BEGINS WITH LETTERS N THROUGH Z, YOU WILL BE ALOTTED TWO BATHROOM VISITS ON TUESDAY, THURSDAY, AND ON SATURDAY, IF YOU SHOULD DECIDE TO COME TO WORK TO USE THE TOILET.

I could see the hesitation mixed with confusion stirring in his eyes. I held back my laughter as he fidgeted in his seat, his discomfort engulfing his confidence with each passing second.

In fact, I was enjoying the situation so much, that I decided to amplify it. I asked, "So what do you think of my sign?"

He mustered up his best smile and replied, "What do they do if it's not their day to use the facilities?"

"I was hoping you'd ask that because, you see, that is the BEST part! Each day we will have a school bus come at 10 a.m. and again at 2:30 p.m. to escort our employees, who are not allotted restroom use on that day, down to city hall where they will be allowed 15 minutes to use *your* facilities."

I paused to let that thought sink in for a moment. "Once they're finished, they'll be brought back to continue their work day." I grinned and waited for a response.

After sizing me up, he said, "You're joking, right?"

"In fact, I'm not. I'm doing this because your division has hiked up my water price with a $3.11 surcharge per 1,000 gallons for usage between

7,170 and 10,070 gallons. If we hire more employees, the surcharge increases to $6.71 per 1,000 gallons over 2001's 100% usage. I'll need to cut back the usage around here. We are a business after all. Financial management is extraordinarily important for a business owner."

"Say your employees need to go to the bathroom before the scheduled bus arrives, what then?"

"We are installing a credit and debit usage meter, developed by one of our partners, that will monitor each flush. They are developing what they call "cheek recognition," so the user won't need to swipe a card, or enter a code. When a toilet is flushed in the building, the system will register the flusher and automatically pull a per flush payment from their home account." Again, a small grin twitched about my lips.

"You don't find this inhumane?"

"Not at all, my employees understand the cost of business. Now their personal business can be counted as a business write off at the end of the year. You see, when all is said and done, those who are costing me more for water will be effectively paying my water bills." I laughed as this notion crossed his mind.

After another brief silence, he asked, "And how long will this last?"

Again I chuckled out loud as I said, "Forever, or at least until this tax is repealed. Now sir, if you'll excuse me, I have a 2 o'clock appointment." And as quickly as he was here, he was gone.

As a little side note, I told this story to two financial personnel on their annual visit. As they were leaving, the CFO was cautioned by his subordinate not to use our restroom. She understood the cost implications, but I digress. Let's just say this was a creative way to manage escalation costs, which became my Memorable Moment #60.

I guess this begs the question: Should democracy be something more than three wolves and a sheep voting on what to have for dinner? Of course you realize, that in my world, the three wolves are local, state, and federal tax leviers. The sheep is me, and you.

Taxes

Sometimes I think the avoidance, or the "hesitation," of paying taxes is the only intellectual pursuit that carries a reward. Our business model has been successful in selling to the federal government as a one-stop vendor. In other words, we often combine a diverse set of products into a single purchase. We mainly sell computers and associated components, but sometimes we include odd additions such as TVs, refrigerators, or power tools.

Occasionally that leads to returns and overtime from our warehouse employees dealing with sorting unusual inventory. Here is a hypothetical example, which may seem strange, but remember, reality is stranger than fiction. Let's say we once had returns from the Pentagon (four hammers sold for $171 each), NASA (six toilet seats sold for $600 each), and HUD (one 1.5" screw valued at $22).

Let's pretend that same year, I discovered that I had underpaid my federal taxes to a tune of $4,284 still due. So I boxed up the returned inventory, which had a total value of $4,306, and attached it to my tax return and sent it to the IRS. In my mind, I included this note to the IRS.

"Please apply this overpayment of $22 as a carry forward credit to next year's tax return."

This helped reconcile my gross habits with my net instability.

OK, I am only joking about this one, but you've got to admit, a bit of humor is needed when at least half of your income disappears every year into the tax abyss. That is no joke. That happens to me every year.

Beating the Dreaded IRS Audit

The IRS likes me. They like to meet with me, and my staff, regularly. They want to get close enough to learn everything about me and my business. They call it an audit, but I think of it more as a "date." One of these days I hope to get lucky. I have certainly paid for dinner and a movie. Here are my takeaways from dealing with audits:

- Never meet the IRS agent in person. Make them document all questions and allow yourself time to digest and find "documentation" to contradict their position.

- Always ask for an extension, which is normal government practice when the IRS doesn't like the situation. In this chapter we call it "hesitating" when unsure.

- Treat the audit like any other business objective. Don't compromise unless absolutely necessary. Never agree to a small settlement just to be done with it. Only a "no charge" is acceptable.

- Use the old lawyer's trick: you talk; he delivers his response. You ask a question; he then explains his points, and you deliver your response, which starts the cycle once again. This can repeat for a long time.

Following these rules, we once spent a full year on an IRS company audit. When you do that, it is my experience they are ready to be done with it. Here is an example case. An IRS agent sent a final draft letter disqualifying certain expenditures as discretionary and taxable. These included salary payments to employees who were no longer living in Colorado.

Really? Salary payments are discretionary simply because someone is not living in the same state as the business!

My first reaction was to allow the IRS agent to finalize his report and then appeal his decision. After some reflection, I decided to save him embarrassment and explain what I thought was his error. After all, no one wants to see "how the sausage gets made," and no one wants to waste unnecessary time dealing with the IRS.

In my response, I explained that my first employee in question was now a former employee living in Washington, D.C. The move was one he requested to accommodate his family for medical reasons. We paid him the rest of his salary throughout his transition to the new location. Had we not agreed, he would have applied for unemployment benefits, which would have increased our rates and been bad for everyone.

Our second employee challenged by the IRS was still employed by our company and was living in Houston, necessitated because of a career move by her husband. Being concerned citizens, we worked out a way for her to keep her job and stay off unemployment. After all, if she filed for unemployment, our rate would have increased yet again. After receiving my letter, the IRS agent saw the light, relinquished his bonus opportunity, and sent a "no charge" letter.

After all was said and done, I hesitated for more than a year, reluctant to write another check to the IRS. I was doubtful that they deserved more money. That worked out just the way it should—no taxes due. Sometimes hesitating pays.

My Tax Auditor

My business needs to be audited, even when the IRS isn't involved. I have been searching for an auditor who only needed two numbers to sign off on my financials. After all, how difficult can that audit exercise be? The top number is actual revenue achieved, and the bottom number translates to taxes due.

What I would like is to have the auditor who reveals that bottom number is zero! That would be "no taxes due" and my Memorable Moment #59 every time it occurs.

It would be possible as long as everything in between the top and bottom numbers is a credit or debit. I think it is worth hesitating long enough to figure out how to make that happen. Someone once told me the tax code states you are responsible to pay the minimum amount of taxes due. However, it is your responsibility to determine that minimum amount due. Zero is the minimum I'd like to pay.

I have learned I can't rush my auditor to complete the job, even if he already drinks my coffee all day.

I asked my auditor, "What would it take to switch jobs with you? I am envious of how you spend time in such a relaxed manner, sipping your coffee morning, noon, and night."

He shot back, "You could never do my job. You wouldn't know the correct mixture of milk and sugar to make the perfect blend."

Last year's billing for the audit exceeded my worst nightmare. The increase in fee was because my auditor had completed newly required special certification. It took three years and is called "wasted nothing." It consists of a mandatory peer review. That is another auditor that I am paying to look at my auditor's work. That is a lot of coffee, let me tell you.

I think it is one more ridiculous government regulation too bizarre to believe. Your banking leaders required the audits, and I incur the cost. The government requires peer reviews, and I incur the cost. Of course, once the auditor completed the 3-year exercise, he was worth the extra fee, and I incur more costs! It translated to having an auditor reviewing an auditor reviewing our precise, carefully prepared, detailed books.

My auditor was a master at hesitation, but I have to admit I didn't like it. He had a variety of excuses for his delays in the finished documents. The one most memorable to me was when he took his grandson to Disney World for two weeks and wrote off his trip, because I owned a property just south of Orlando. He claimed he needed to see that property, because certain of my expenses were related to it in his audits. I agree with author Tom Clancy who said, "The difference between reality and fiction is that fiction has to make sense."

I'll tell you this. His productivity wasn't based on seating comfort. Couches versus office chairs did not make him more or less productive. He lounged in all of them. Over time, I realized that free coffee was the best solution to keep him chugging along. Although I didn't do it, I gave some serious thought to listing his coffee as a deduction!

Otrona

In 1983 I joined a computer start-up company named Otrona. Owning stock in a start-up company—Memorable Moment #97. In fact, I still have over fifty thousand stock options, which were issued to me at 10¢ each. I admit to having the Phoenix dream that its value will one day rise up from the ashes and soar to new heights. I'd be happy with $1 per share. I'll share that dream with you. Since you have gotten this far in reading my story, I'm willing to sell my options for 5¢ each as a reward for your perseverance.

In late December of 1983, I was visiting a client in Cleveland, OH. The owner invited me to lunch, and although it meant a close timeline to make my return flight home, I accepted. Halfway through the meal he pulled an envelope out of his jacket pocket and gave me a quick glimpse of a million-dollar check. That was the first time I viewed eight zeros, six in front and two after the decimal point.

He said his check was for two million, while his minority partner was to receive a check for only one million. I was taught fractions in Catholic grade school. A small percentage of a large monetary number is still a big number.

Calabria Named Marketing V.P.

James Lindner, Otrona president and chief executive officer, has announced the appointment of Joseph M. Calabria, Jr. as vice president of marketing. Calabria is responsible for directing the company's sales and marketing functions.

Calabria formerly was director of marketing operations for Exxon Office Systems, headquartered in Stamford, Conn., where he had overall responsibility for marketing

support services, field training, product launch and product marketing.

"We are very pleased to hav someone with Joe's professional experience and achiev ments joining Otrona, parti ularly at this stage of our growth," said Lindner. "He uniquely qualified for the critical role of managing our sales and marketing activities."

Prior to heading marketing operations for Exxon Office Systems, Calabria was grou director of marketing for Olivetti. Before that, he hel various sales and management positions with IBM fo nearly 15 years.

My promotion announcement

My mind figured if I netted two million dollars after taxes for the stock options I owned, and invested the principal at 5%, I wouldn't have to work another day in my life. My wife and I would be able to retire. I never described myself as someone in high society, or with a glamorous life. I had no plans on changing into a jet setter, but I must admit I liked the idea of the freedom to not have to work.

I worked my butt off for the next 10 months to make that happen. Our company was poised to hit the big time. I had a deal in hand. The contract was drawn up. But we had a cash-flow crisis.

On a rain-filled day in October 1984, the board of directors decided to pull the plug on Otrona. If the board members had waited two more days, Compaq, still in its infantile stage, would have had fierce competition. Two future Goliaths would have been pitted against one another. Two days after our removal by the board as a viable business, the local newspaper captured employees exiting from our building with their walking papers, while executives from a large German company were trying to enter to sign a 35-million-dollar agreement to have the right to manufacture our equipment. I had this agreement prepared and ready for a signature.

I was unable to convince the board that Sunday afternoon to consider this opportunity. The board treated its recent decision as ironclad and irrevocable. The members were not willing to extend a two-week bridge loan to close the deal I had set up. It was too bad there wasn't someone of Polish descent on the board who would be able to quote the Polish proverb, "A reed need not be afraid when the winds uproot the oak."

The board members were filled with doubt, but they did not hesitate to close the company. If they had hesitated, and followed my fourth law, one of the best deals of their lives would have dropped into their laps.

CHAPTER EIGHT

Calabria's Law Number 5

Everything is negotiable…
       …*Except failure*

W HEN YOU START SOMETHING, YOU START IT FOR A REASON. Remember that reason and work for it. If you don't hit your goal, you fail. Don't fail. Find a way to achieve your goal no matter what it takes.

Take marriage as an example. Lots of marriages fail. I am not here to judge, but I will say this. Pick a clear goal to work toward. If you start by saying that maybe you'll stay married, or maybe you won't, that is not a clear goal, and your marriage is far more likely to fail than if you enter into marriage with the traditional view that you are sticking with each other "through good times and bad, sickness and health, until death do us part." It is one thing to say the words; it's another thing to live them.

Of course, not all marriages survive. When abuse is involved, people need to save their own life. Yet, many problems in a marriage are natural and predictable. Every married couple has challenges.

Author Barbara Johnson offered wisdom on this subject, "Never let a problem to be solved become more important than a person to be loved."

So, I am saying, "Go for it." Set strong goals and go after them. Set goals you believe in and are willing to work hard to achieve. Find what you care about and go after it. Everything along the way is negotiable, but you have to reach that goal.

Obviously I have not reached every one of my goals. I just told you about the failure of Otrona, where a 35-million-dollar deal went down the tubes. But I have to look at the big picture, and so do you. Yes,

Otrona failed, but I didn't. I worked hard, and when the company went under, I continued to work hard. For you see, my real goal was to be successful, and I learned a lot along the way with Otrona. It helped me to start my own business that next year and take me to the point I am at right now. I have succeeded and so can you. Don't let the hiccups along the way stop you!

The Edge

Little wins can build up our self-esteem. So it is important to pick some small goals now and then. You never know which one is going to teach you a bigger lesson in life. Back in my early years, my IBM office was located at the same intersection as one of the branches of the biggest bank in town. With banking convenience a major selling point, I opened a checking account and always used the drive through for its ease of deposits of my checks.

The regular teller who worked the window looked like she could have been a model, but she also had a lack of what I would label "friendly customer service."

Most successful sales representatives wore their confidence level on their coat lapel. I certainly filled the youthful version and considered it a challenge to gain some "respect" from this teller. I just had to figure out what to do.

Since money talks, I got an idea. But first let me share some background information. One month, I challenged the rest of the office staff, me against all of them, to a sales contest. The losers would have to pay for a high-end picnic to take place at the boss' backyard.

I led the sales results through the first twenty-nine days of the month. To be sure, there was bad mouthing, inappropriate gestures, and verbal jabs every morning and again when we gathered at the close of business. I guess I got under their skin, because they finally edged me out on the last day of the month. It cost a lot to pay for the party, but there were two real benefits for me. First, my next month's paycheck was equivalent to my last year's W-2 pay!

The second benefit was that I got to visit my favorite, albeit aloof, teller with my check. I had an idea on how to impress her. At the window, I tried to control my excitement of depositing the big check, giving only a hint of a side-eyed glance to see if she was impressed. When she asked for instructions for cashing or depositing my check, I answered, "I want it all in cash." She asked what kind of bills I wanted. I responded, "Hundreds only! I'm heading to Vegas for the weekend."

It took some time to assemble the stack of hundred dollar bills, but she passed them to me with a smile. I drove off, and without closing the window of my car, I accelerated around the corner of the bank building, and quickly slipped into a parking space at the front of the bank. I got out of the car and went into the bank through the front door. I was careful not to be seen by the teller and deposited the money into my wife's and my joint account.

Tiptoeing out of the bank, I had a huge grin on my face and realized successful sales are dependent on what I came to call "The Edge." It is an outgoing and daring attitude in life. It is also my Memorable Moment #35.

From that day on, the teller was both courteous and friendly, always flashing a blinding smile when I made future deposits with the bank. It pays to reach your goals. Keep your edge.

My First Country Club Membership

No one in my extended family had ever been invited to join a country club. After returning home with a diploma from Providence College and securing a job with IBM, my next goal was to make Memorable Moment #13, which was to enjoy the privileges of membership in a country club. As they say, "Timing is everything," and it was perfect timing to join the Berkshire Country Club.

The club's membership was aging and consequently dwindling, and they were looking to add a limited number of young members at a reduced entry fee. Up to this time, the club hadn't allowed Italians (or other select groups) to join.

One of my friends asked, "Why would you consider joining a club whose membership was intolerant towards, or discriminated against, certain groups including your own?"

I told him, "I believe it's easier to change from within, rather than from the outside. I want to be on the fairway, not behind the spectator ropes. Plus, if I find the members to be a bunch of old bogies, I can always resign!"

My first day at the club, I was living out the lyrics of Travis Tritt's album, Country Club, "Well I'm a member of a country club, country music is what I love, I drive an old Ford pickup truck, I do my drinking from a Dixie cup."

I felt out of place. I was not showing my normal confidence and was having trouble remembering the names of the members to whom I had been introduced. I soon discovered, I could address all the members without remembering their names just by calling them "sir" or "madam." To my amazement, the membership accepted my greetings as very cordial.

I wasn't a good golfer and didn't own any of the newest or most recognized brands of clubs. In fact, mine were a collection of throw-away clubs which probably wouldn't have sold even at the lowest of discount prices at the cheapest of closeout stores. But they were my clubs. At least I had some.

Early on, I met an old member (both in age and number of years at the club) who was a considerably worse golfer than even me. Let's call him "Ed" for the sake of protecting his dignity. Ed had no financial problems; his junkyard business was a cash cow. Ed would always have a companion, or a young female escort with him.

One day, we were both playing in the last flight of the club championship. As most members probably expected, Ed and I were tied for last place, and Ed was insisting on a playoff. I wanted no part of any playoff, since everyone else had already finished their round of golf. I thought it was a "lose, lose" situation. I had nothing to gain except possibly the bragging rights to say that I was only the second worst player!

But hey, what the heck, I was creating relationships and becoming known to all the other members. I was willing to negotiate a bit to reach my goal to be a real country club member. In this instance, I offered up my pride to close the deal.

So, off Ed and I went on the first playoff hole. Ed and his beautiful and charming young escort, drinks in hand, out in front, with me for-lornly following behind, carrying only my golf bag of mismatched clubs. It was already clear who was the real loser. That pissed me off. I am prone to that. I'm emotional. I'm Italian. No wonder today I have 21 stents to keep the old ticker ticking.

Anyway, back to Ed, his honey, and me. On the first playoff hole, I made a 7-foot putt, with a confident steady putting stroke. It dropped into the cup with a satisfying plop. The only problem was the nine strokes before that putt. I got a 10 for that hole! Perhaps I had been distracted by Ed's beautiful escort? Miracle of miracles, we tied on that hole. Apparently, Ed couldn't keep his mind off his escort either.

We proceeded to the next hole. As we approached the green, the golf pro arrived to witness the results. At that point, I couldn't take the embarrassment anymore. I surrendered and told the pro that Ed had won. I walked quickly to the parking lot and left the club.

It turned out that it wasn't the end of the world. There were other bad golfers and other people who had bad days. Little by little, I began to fit in. I saw that these country club members were ordinary people in all the ways that make us human. When the time came, I was able to help promote opening the club to a more diverse membership. We are all better because of it. Each time my wife and I moved our family to a new city, I joined a new country club. Today, I am one of the old members, both in age and number of years, at our club!

I have noticed that as the years have gone by, my country club experiences have become much more relaxing and less stressful. However, my scores haven't gotten any better.

Since I am talking about golf, and what we are willing to give up in order to achieve our goals, let me share another quick, memorable moment. Although, this one I have not put into my list, and frankly, I am trying to get the memory out of my head.

Several years back, my friend Billy was visiting me from Providence. I decided to take him to the club one afternoon and showed him around the facilities. He spotted a sign in the pro shop that said, "40% off all clothing." Next thing I knew, this crazy Irishman took off his shirt and dropped his drawers! I am glad it wasn't 100% off! I thought I was off to the hospital again, this time to get stent #22.

After all, we just don't do things like that at the club. Who lets people like that in, anyway?

I do!

Four Locations, Four Trains

Trains are a powerful and majestic metaphor of blazing down the tracks toward a goal. You can negotiate what kind of train to take, freight or passenger, coal or diesel. But you know when you are on a train, you are headed somewhere! That is what we want in business.

Believe it or not, each of the first four office locations of our new business had train tracks across the street from them. Each of these locations was within 30 miles of Denver, CO. With trains as a theme in both traditional and popular music since the first half of the 19th century, we decided to embrace the train as a metaphor for staying on track with our goals. One of the fun ways we did this was to put a sound bite of train noises on every one of our phone answering systems.

Next, I purchased a framed train picture for each location. One by one we added to our train collection. Howard Fogg, the famous American artist who specialized in railroad art, was known for startling detail and accuracy in his American locomotive series. Turns out he lived within a half mile of our home office. So, I purchased a set of his limited edition watercolor prints. Since only freight trains moved past our office, a sure sign of inexpensive rent, we initially only purchased pictures of freight trains. After a few years, I also purchased pictures of passenger trains such as the Carolina Special, a splendid passenger train, which ran from 1911 to 1968. It reminded me that we want to travel toward our goals in style.

The noise and vibration of the trains racing down the tracks next to our office allowed our employees extra coffee breaks. It was hard to do much else during those times of the day when the trains passed through. Finally, on my fifth try at securing an office location, we relocated and consolidated all our locations away from any train tracks. But then, what was I to do with all those pictures of trains?

The metaphor lives on. The trains no longer go past our office, but you can see them on our walls.

I like the Burt Lawlor quote, "Decisions and determination are the engineer and fireman of our train to opportunity and success."

I Became a Bean Counter

I knew running a business required a focus on finances, affectionately known as bean counting, but soon I learned it required me to take on a new and all-important job. My title became Chief Office Coffee Roaster (COCR). As a COCR, I purchased fresh coffee beans from around the world and tried to rotate my selections with the harvest seasons. I got coffee from Ethiopia, Costa Rica, and Colombia. I also paid attention to the decaffeination process without the use of chemicals.

Now what separated my company in those days from my competitors was our focus on quality with the infusion of ethics into our business practices. I ensured this focus carried through to our COCR as well. I believed then, and I believe now, there is a strong correlation between the quality of the coffee and the quality of the employee work environment. It helps employee morale to offer complementary coffee as good as the deep-flavored roast and rich experience they would expect from a local coffee shop. All pastries, for health reasons, were only offered on Fridays.

There is a certain mentality that I have tried to bring to my business. I am demanding of my staff. I want to stay on track with high goals, but I am willing to spend some money to reward them by having a nice environment, as well as good salaries. All things are negotiable, except failure.

A great idea, yes, but it was not so easy to sustain. Have you ever seen something for free, and thought, "It must not be very good?"

One example of this phenomenon is the free coffee we provided to our employees. After a while, people stopped valuing the free coffee. This nearly broke the heart of our COCR. To understand this point, pretend for a moment that we assigned a monetary value to each cup of coffee that you drink in a day. Go along with this even if you don't drink coffee. Since we are brewing it ourselves, let's say 75¢ is the value assigned to each cup of coffee. Every time you spill your coffee, you see 75¢ dripping off your desk. When you dump out your coffee because it got cold, you see your 75¢ slipping down the drain.

Now 75¢ is not a lot of money, but it's enough to make most of us appreciate what we have bought with it.

The idea is that when you throw away someone else's money, you don't appreciate it, but if you're throwing away your own money, you're far more cautious and appreciative of your nickels and dimes, let alone three quarters. My challenge was to try to find a way so that the coffee had a real value for everyone.

It is not easy to get people to care about a few quarters of someone else's money. People have to want to care. I experienced this once in Italy at the Trevi Fountain in Rome. People cheered as I made a wish and tossed a coin into the water. My quarter mattered to them, because they recognized the value of that gesture. That was Memorable Moment #26. How could I bring that same spirit into appreciating our office coffee?

After a number of years, I realized there were alternatives to our free coffee for our employees. McDonalds, which was located right across the street, sold a large cup of coffee for $1.06. In addition, Starbucks opened a store two doors away. Their universal mystique had a few employees paying $2.79 for their coffee, versus free coffee at my office. And yes, sometimes I was one of those employees! But, I didn't want to have this company perk's value diminished and decided to have a coffee survey. Somehow we needed to create ownership in the coffee we served.

In the meantime, I found a Starbucks coffee machine in the Marriott Concierge Lounge with a three-blend option and also hot water. Our actual cost would go from 21¢ per cup to 93¢ per cup, and we would be required to purchase from Aramark Coffee Service with a monthly minimum.

We launched the survey and reminded everyone that currently we were bringing in Italian Breakfast Blend in regular and decaffeinated, and French Roast, both bold coffees, plus exotic coffees from around the world. We asked how many were interested in a light coffee, a medium roast, a bold roast, a decaf, and did someone say flavored?

We asked everyone for input and stated all inputs would be

appreciated. We also added that if the employee was not a coffee drinker, but felt compelled to comment, knock yourself out. Everyone was welcome to voice his or her opinion.

The results showed what the people wanted was quite diverse and even more expensive than the upgraded alternatives I had been investigating. So the Chief Office Coffee Roaster checked in with the Chick In Charge, my wife. When I discussed these options with her, she reminded me that our employees were part of our extended family and that this extra expense was worthwhile since we were profitable. We agreed it's important to always reward our employees' time and effort. It's also important not to allow the value of our workers' paychecks to be cut because we didn't take the necessary steps to provide a competitive drink alternative.

Eventually, we found a machine that dispensed coffee, espresso, latte, and cappuccino, plus vanilla and chocolate flavored shots, and (drumroll please) hot water. In addition, it had single, double and triple shot options available! Our employees no longer found it necessary to stop at a specialty coffee shop on their way to work. This was our machine. There was a sense of joint ownership since everyone was in on the selection of it. Our machine was appropriately named "First Choice." A good COCR will make all this work. A good wife will make the good COCR work!

Office snack management is the second morale booster and helps employee camaraderie when they meet at the reception desk for a snack. We decided on healthy candy snacks to munch on and everyone agrees they are pretty much the most valuable player of the office. No trades or negotiations are necessary.

I spent a lot of time researching coffee and snacks. I had a goal in mind. Failure was not an option, but there was a lot of negotiating along the way. Getting the details correct makes a huge difference. As Leonard Nimoy, Mr. Spock from Star Trek, said, "Insufficient facts always invite damage."

CHAPTER NINE

Calabria's Law Number 6

Sacrifice today…
         …For tomorrow's reward

W HEN WE HAVE GOALS AND WE WORK HARD TOWARD THEM, it's not always a fun ride. We can try to make it fun, but some things are just plain tough. It takes sacrifice to get through, but it is worth it, because one day we will get our reward.

Achievements in Life

First formulated in college as goals for a successful life (later changed to Memorable Moments), I started becoming a true dreamer. I was dreaming of all the things I wanted to achieve in life, all the memorable moments and lasting relationships awaiting me. I wanted to find just the right woman to marry. I wanted to not only get a job, I wanted to provide jobs for others. I wanted my income to soar. I wanted to travel and see the world. I wanted to have kids and grandkids. I could close my eyes and see it all, especially that beautiful woman who was destined to come into my life!

I never really knew I was born poor until later in life. In case you aren't sure if you are poor, let me list some of the obvious signs of growing up poor. They include, but are not limited to, a dirt alley separating your backyard from your cousin's; a large garden swallowing up your back yard, and providing a big harvest in the fall; stewing and jarring the vegetables in a hot kitchen in late August; eating lentil soup once a week;

walking two miles one way to church on Sundays; and wearing hand-me-down clothes from relatives, including your uncles. This is especially true, if you're a girl.

In case you are wondering, no, I didn't have to walk through the snow in my bare feet uphill, both ways, five miles to school. I wasn't that poor.

One thing was for sure, though, I had an abundance of spirit, and I had no shortage of ambition. I was pretty much born ready to start working on making my dreams come true. Since I was short on funds, though, I started a business in college to help offset expenses. I like to mention this because it had such a big impact on the trajectory of my life. I worked two days a week at my start-up "laundry" business, taking and returning my classmates' clothes to the local, off-campus cleaners. I supplemented that little moneymaker with a somewhat chancier business, playing the horses! Between dirty shirts and fast horses, I was able to pay a big chunk of my college tuition.

Full details on the horseracing enterprise are available a little later in this chapter.

After college, one of my biggest dreams came true. I had been working toward it my whole life. I wanted to make $30,000 a year before I was thirty years old. I came in two years ahead of schedule. It was Memorable Moment #3. For all of you who think that was nothing, I'll just add that in today's dollars, it was more like earning $100,000! Pretty good for a guy who was 28 years old.

My First Triple-Double—
Memorable Moment #5

I love sports metaphors. Every basketball player wants a triple-double in which a player records three different double-digit total numbers, for instance, ten points, ten rebounds, ten assists, in a single basketball game.

Providence College has a strong sports tradition, with its graduates united and connected to players who were stars a long time ago. Rushing the court is a basketball tradition with a sketchy origin, but nonetheless, a tradition many students embrace after an important win. Those wins don't happen without a breakout performance by a player.

Although I was once "all-neighborhood" in basketball when I was 12 years old, I had no chance to go much further. At five foot, seven inches tall, and with a well-practiced three-inch vertical jump, I was not headed to playing Big East college basketball. I remember spending countless hours, with my right hand high above my head and as close to the cellar wall as possible, performing one jump after the other. But, sigh, I was never able to exceed the opposing forces of the four-inch barrier.

Despite this physical challenge, I applied to Providence College, with its strong basketball tradition. Was there still some way for me to get a triple-double? Well, I was "17" years old when I applied, and my ACT score was also "17." That's a double-double. Lo and behold, I graduated with a "1.7" GPA. As I see it, this qualified me for a triple-double! And I did it in the Big East. Many times, I have grabbed my favorite beverage and repeated my story. It is now remembered folklore, and my good friends tell me that I am their personal hero! Of course, that is after they have had a couple of their favorite beverages and are itching to rush the court. I remind them, it wasn't easy and that I had to bide my time through the rigors of college, but in the end, it all paid off.

The real learning point for me is that success is possible for someone with only average intelligence. We need the discipline of hard work. Even when our grades are not great, it is important to not get discouraged. One day you will be surprised with a college degree. My studies were very difficult for me, but as you know, I did get the degree. That took a lot of hard work and sacrifice, but the reward was a dream come true.

Happy Days Are Here Again

My parents taught me to work hard and save every penny I ever earned starting in 5th grade when I began cutting grass earning 10¢ an hour. I kept this job, but added a paper route. That's right, I had formed a conglomerate when I was just in 7th grade. It was then I began to realize the importance of customer relations. Inclement weather wasn't an acceptable excuse for a late newspaper delivery. By the time I got to college, I had enough saved to pay for one and a half years of college. The bulk of that didn't come from cutting lawns. Thank the Lord for my after-school job as a stock boy at Lobel's, our local clothing store. The summer between my first and second year, I was able to get my old job back and supplement my savings, so I was OK for my second year as well. It wasn't easy, but I didn't mind it. It was a necessary difficulty so that I could keep on track with my many emerging dreams for my life.

I sold cookware the summer between my second and third year, made eighteen hundred dollars, and paid the tuition plus room and board for my third year. I'll tell more about that later. The last summer I only earned enough for part of my final year's cost. No problem, my racetrack algorithm took care of all remaining amounts due. Do you hear that horn in the distance? That's the fanfare for my much-anticipated explanation of my racetrack winnings.

Winning at the Track— Memorable Moment #6

The first time I went to the track, I had no idea how the racetrack worked. Did the horses race with their heads forward? How many legs did a horse have anyway?

I only had ten dollars and my friend suggested we play the daily double. I soon learned that meant to place a bet on one horse in the first race linked to a bet with another horse in the second race. What we did was we bought 10 daily double tickets. Every bet was the same horse for the first race, but we bet a ticket on each of the horses in the second race. That way, if we won in the first race, we were assured a win in the second race.

In that first race, our horse out-distanced the field, and we became winners. All that was left was determining how much I would win. We were hoping for one of the long-shot horses to win in the second race, and we got our wish! I could hardly talk the rest of the day, because I screamed so loud as that beautiful horse crossed the wire! My split of the winnings was $31! My $10 had magically transformed into $31. I was hooked! Back in my dorm, I was feeling unrestrained, copious, and over-flowing confidence. I felt I had found the answer to negotiating the financial gauntlet that was my tuition payments. They were past due.

There was something else going on in my life. My father had lost his job. There was no way my parents could help with my tuition payments. I wanted to leave school and go back home to help out at the house. My father wouldn't hear of it. I had to find a way to pay my tuition bills. I couldn't let my parents down. The laundry business I had going was helpful, but it wasn't enough. I couldn't make enough at another job. I needed something else. And I should add, classes were tougher than ever, and I was just managing to keep my head above water.

The track was closed Sunday, but Monday I was there ready to bring the track to its knees. I was going to squeeze every dollar out of it that I could!

That day I learned Track Mistake #1, don't waste your money on a handicap card. It is supposed to be an informed cheat sheet legally available for a small price. I soon understood that if the handicapper selling you the card was that good, he wouldn't need to work. But hey, I bought the card and was surprised to see two horses listed in every race. How was I supposed to know which one was going to win? I didn't have the money to bet twice on every race.

Mistake #2, never bet against yourself. I learned this the hard way. First I won, then I spent a long period of time emptying my pockets learning my lesson. I started that day by betting on only one horse for each of the first eight races. Eight losses! Maybe horseracing wasn't that much fun? I took a last look at the card. The card listed two horses for the ninth race. I split my last twenty dollars on the two recommended horses in the ninth race. The first horse, which went off at 9:2 odds, won, and I rode the bus back to campus feeling like I had reached the blue vault of heaven.

I went every day after that, and lost every time I went. I slowly learned the lesson to not bet against myself. One day I brought back with me the Morning Telegraph, which was a racing newspaper, affectionately known as "the rag." I began to study the statistics listed in the paper. I was looking for patterns and other indicators that would help me make informed bets. I started to build "my algorithm" that would factor in variables like the length of the race, condition of the track, the experience of the jockey, weather, and, of course, the horse's previous record.

I built my algorithm with these variables, and I started winning. In a five-day stretch, I got to the final race in the twin double (win the fifth race and sixth race, trade your ticket in with your picks for the eighth and ninth races) three times and twice won the twin double. The second time I won, I went out and celebrated. I remember calling my mother from Brad's Bar, and in an emotional and animated outburst telling her I had the money to pay off my tuition bill.

I got her authoritarian instructions, "Rush back to your room, put the money under your mattress, and be first in line at the college bursar's office tomorrow morning." I had a couple more drinks and then followed my mother's instructions. I got my degree without debt, which was Memorable Moment #15. Of course, there was a trade-off between spending so much time at the track and my grades. That last semester, I scored five Ds and one C, but I had already secured a job with IBM and I did graduate on schedule.

Always remember the advice of Lou Holtz, "Motivation is nothing more than a sense of purpose."

This is my first and probably most important racing story, but it only tells one of many subplots in my track experiences. Some friends who have learned my story have compared my algorithm to card counting, a casino card-game strategy used by certain gamblers with great memories to keep track of every card played. One of those friends said, "You've created a horse-racing algorithm that counts every variable in any given race. You're no better than a card counter."

I fired back, "I am too better. First, there is no way to count every variable in a horserace. And second, in the casino you're forced to breathe the air in those smoky rooms. With my algorithm, I am outside breathing fresh air."

But on second thought, I always did best when I was close enough to smell the horses, and that was not what I would call fresh air, although, there was something "fresh" in the air. I better end this debate before I step in it.

To sum up, obviously not perfect, my algorithm reduced the element of luck and improved the betting odds in my favor. However, as I've learned throughout my life, in every success there's always some luck involved.

Photo Finish

One Saturday, during my college days, I was going to the track (by bus with two transfers required) wearing my black Fedora hat. I also carried my Cohiba cigar. In those days Red Auerbach was the coach of the Boston Celtics and was well known for smoking a cigar when he thought a victory was at hand. Red had the resources to afford the Cohiba Limited Edition Double Corona. Me? I just smoked the cheapest Cohiba, but what the hey, I wanted to be a winner like Red, even if I could only do it on the cheap!

When I finally arrived at the track, I had to quickly place my first bet. As usual, I was sitting at the finish line close enough to smell the horses as they raced to the finish line. After the first three races, I had three winners. It became obvious to those in the stands around me that I was on a winning streak. After six races and six wins, I was getting excited about the notion of a sweep. After the eighth race, I had eight consecutive winners!

I reviewed my horse race calculator (algorithm) for the last race. It showed a two-horse race with the best horse having a jockey with rumors of fixing races, and the second-rated horse ridden by today's five-time winning jockey. I bet on the best horse based on my analysis. I had to hope the rumors about its jockey weren't a factor. The amount I bet was the cumulative winnings for the day, $2,400. That was a gigantic amount of money back then. Before the start of the race I lit my cheap Cohiba cigar. Winning big was in the air. The race wasn't over and the winner wasn't announced, but I thought I had a win.

The gates opened and the horses were off. My horse led easily through most of the race, even when my jockey took a grandstand turn on the final lap. That's when you take your focus off the race and look around at what's behind you. The jockey then slowed down and allowed the other horse to pull up to him on the inside part of the track next to the rail. The race ended in a dead heat, and it seemed like an eternity till the winner was announced. Then the photo-finish appeared on the large display screen. I lost by a whisker! If only I had had one of those expensive Cohibas! Then I would have been a winner. Looking into the sky, through the smoke of my cheap Cohiba, I saw hundreds of $100 bills with wings, apparently flying into other gents' pockets. I would have won more than $10,000 if my horse had been first. Easy come, but nothing easy about going, going, gone. Sacrifice can be painful. I was willing to sacrifice my accumulated winnings for the big payoff.

Class Ring

Of course my epic loss was not enough to stop me. When you win eight races in a row, you want more. I didn't just want it for myself. My roommate in my senior year, Robert, was a pre-med major studying with a full scholarship. It was this scholarship, along with a tight financial aid package, that allowed Robert to attend Providence and, fortunately for him, end up as my roommate. Often, as Robert was diligently studying his books to keep his scholarship and aid package, I also was studying diligently. But, I had a cigar in my mouth and was studying my racing rag to keep my algorithm up to date. This was the only way for me to keep my financial aid package, which came straight from the racetrack!

He studied 50 hours a week. Sometimes his classes were so intense, he wouldn't even sleep to keep up with all the work. He would occasionally encourage me to spend more time at my college studies. I kidded him that even though he'd be a doctor, he'd be dead in 50 years, but I'd be rich and live 'til 90.

I'm sorry to say, at our 50-year reunion, I learned he had passed away. Let's hope my ticker makes it 'til 90.

One day, I was studying a filly, that is a female horse less than 4 years old. Her name was Young Mary Jane. This filly had run and lost one short race after another. These were five to seven furlong races. A furlong is 1/8th of a mile. So up to this point, her longer races weren't even a mile long. She always had a strong finish. Finally, she was entered in a twelve-furlong race. This was a mile and a half long. This filly had a history of racing last until the final two or three furlongs and then sprinting to the finish line, often passing half of the field. My algorithm showed this race with Young Mary Jane was the perfect chance to get good odds and win a bundle.

I left Robert a note, "Leave me $10 and I'll win you enough money to buy a class ring." Robert wanted a ring but didn't have the money available to get it. This was a chance for me to experience the joy of helping someone every day. That was a life achievement I set in motion while I was still in college. I call it Memorable Moment #16, help someone every day. Before I left for the track, I went back to my room. I was somewhat astonished when I saw tight-fisted, study-all-the-time Robert had not only read my note, but he actually left me $10. The pressure was on for me to deliver on my promise.

Young Mary Jane was running in the fifth race. That was a rough day for me. You might think that my algorithm ensured success on every race. Well, it didn't. This was one of those days that I was losing big. What would I tell Robert if I also lost this race? Should I just give him enough money for his ring? What if he checked out the race results? Should I just say I didn't get the tickets in time and return his $10 investment? Never one to shy away from risk, I went forward with my plan.

During the race, I sweated excessively, my conscience pouring water out of my armpits. As predicted, Young Mary Jane lagged behind. Unfortunately for my shirt, which I was about to lose, she stayed behind.

But then, from the back of the pack she made her move. This time she had time to continue her blazing sprint all the way to the finish, passing every other horse in the process!

Only when I saw my filly finish first did I breathe a sigh of relief. Robert had more than enough to buy his ring. He was so excited he decided to bet some more with me. I refused Robert's request to continue betting with his money. Robert got his class ring free, courtesy of Young Mary Jane. That was what he needed and that was enough.

I want to take a minute to address some questions you probably have. Many people wonder why I didn't continue to go to the track. After all, I had the winning algorithm. As I mentioned earlier in the book, my mother set me straight as I was finishing college. She made sure that I chose the respectable route of accepting a job with IBM, not to embrace a life of gambling.

There was more than that going on, though. Some of it was just logistical. After college, I wasn't close to the track, so it didn't make sense to try to go to the track everyday. My algorithm doesn't work without being at the track, seeing the horses, smelling what's going on, taking the time to notice every little detail that might affect the race. And before long I was married, and then we had kids. My priorities were to spend time with my family, not at the track. Yet, I would also like to admit that there is a draw to the track that is not healthy. What starts as fun and excitement can develop into an addiction. I could feel that pull, and I knew it was time to break away from it.

One more thing, I believe in Providence. During this period of winning at the track I was up against a wall. I didn't know where my tuition payments were going to come from. My family needed help. Oddly enough, my education, the mathematics and physics of it all, showed me how I could win at the track, or at the least, improve my odds of winning. Insight came to me. I think of it as Providence working in my life. Then the time came when I no longer needed the money. I knew that was the time to let it go and move on. It was a sacrifice for later rewards. I have never regretted it. Enough said. Let's move on to some of the other things that have motivated me to make sacrifices to achieve later rewards.

Own a Second Home at the Ocean— Memorable Moment #31

Some people think the idea of sacrificing today for rewards tomorrow is only a long-term strategy. In other words, save your whole life so that you can have a great retirement. That is part of it for me, but the short-term successes are just as important. We need to experience some of the rewards along the way.

Growing up, my family didn't have a lot of money, but we did take time to have some fun. When I was very young, my parents took us to Sea Isle City, NJ. We shared a rental unit with other relatives. The rentals were two to three blocks from the ocean, but we never complained about walking to the sandy beach. We spent the entire day playing in the sand and jumping in the salty water. Once I started my career, I made it a point to rent a place on the beach. My wife and I always invited our parents to spend the week with us. We had many a-ha moments during those summer retreats. One which stands out for me was July 16, 1977.

#III

A.W. Laricks Agency rented us the home at 5 81st St. in Sea Isle for $500. Today we would need to add at least one more zero to the price!

Fishing for flounder was one of the highlights that year. I had my father and 7-year-old son with me. We were fishing in the morning at an ocean inlet. So we had Joe # I, # II, hey that's me, and # III all fishing! That in itself was a reward worth remembering. Back then, I had no idea what bait and tackle to use. I started out with live minnows, but the water wasn't very deep and dragging the minnows across the bottom after each cast made them fall off the hook. It wasn't too long before we were out of minnows and had to switch to artificial bait. I've since learned silver and yellow grub-tailed jigs work best. That's a free tip, no charge.

My son wasn't happy. He hadn't felt a single strike for his bait. Finally, he gave up. At just that time, I felt a subtle strike on my line. I quickly passed my rod to him. "Take my rod," I said. "There's a big one in the water that I just saw!"

"Dad, I'm never going to get it." A few seconds later, not knowing at the time a 5 to 10 second pause was necessary, he hooked the flounder. The fight ensued. My son screamed with delight.

"I've got one. I've got the big one. It's huge. It's nearly pulling me into the water!" When we finally got it in the net, it wasn't bigger than two pounds, but it was the biggest catch he ever had. He ran all the way back holding up the fish yelling and telling everyone he caught a monster fish. My mother freely offered to clean and cook the monster fish. Life doesn't get much better than the taste of that fish, and three generations enjoyed it! What a thrill watching him tell everyone about the catch. That was a reward worth working for, and waiting for. But it was a short-term goal.

My long-term goal was to be able to buy a house on the beach. It took us thirty-five years of hard work before I achieved my Memorable Moment #31, owning a house on the beach. It makes me think of all the special moments my wife and I have enjoyed with family. My father-in-law loved the sun, a beer, and golf. What a great man! Having family that you love is what makes working worthwhile.

As a side note, I want to share that in a weak moment, as I was finishing my first draft, I told my wife I had included a picture of her father in my book. "What!!" she was quick to respond. "I should pick out my father's picture! Where did you find the picture? How do I know if I like the picture?"

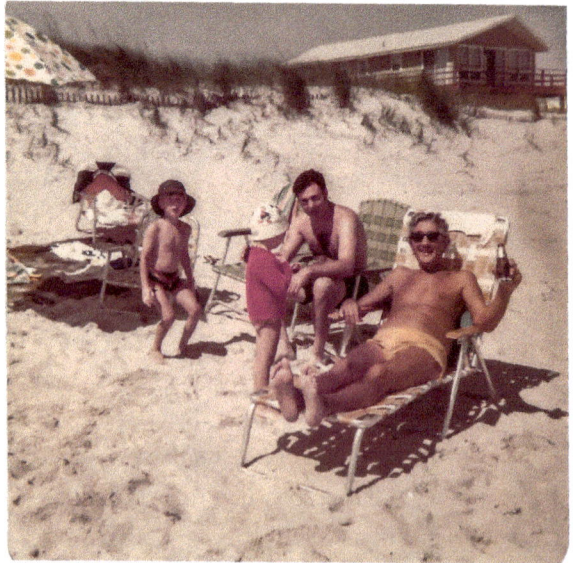

Our vacation rental

She paused for a short second to catch her breath. I seized the moment. "Number 1, would you like to see the picture?" She didn't respond. I knew she didn't want to see the book until it was completed. "Number 2, I found it in our archive of historical family pictures." She gave me the universal marriage sign for genuine doubt, head down but tilted slightly, mouth pursed, and eyes wide. "And finally, it's my book."

I quickly slipped out of the house and returned with a rose and note, "I love you." When it comes time for her to read the whole book, I am pretty sure I better have at least a dozens roses and a box of chocolates handy. Just in case she hasn't read it yet, wish me luck! And send champagne.

The Unlimited Budget— Memorable Moment #10

Speaking of my beautiful wife, here is another story about the rewards that we have worked so hard to achieve. For twenty-five years we experienced limited flexible spending as we moved from Pennsylvania to New Jersey to Connecticut and finally to Colorado. All the while, we were pursuing a career path that we were hoping would finally provide us some financial independence. We worked hard to stay out of debt and to send our children to college. After they both graduated and got married, I realized it was now time to reward my wife for all her sacrifices. She had worked incredibly hard for the sake of our children's education, and so they could enjoy sports, and so that they would have a stable home conducive to preparing themselves for college.

There were many home improvements that I knew my wife wanted to make. One day I took a long deep breath and said, "Honey, you have an unlimited budget for any and all home improvements."

Nudge me when this story is done. It's almost too much for me to take!

My wife took to it like a grasshopper takes to the air. She spent years on these home improvements. Finally, the amount of the unlimited budget was set. The last project was scheduled. But just when the contractor knew exactly what my wife wanted and had given us the final price of the unlimited budget, the vision expanded again and again. In the end, when the last power tool was put away, she had vaulted ceilings, her own dedicated laundry room, a floating fireplace mantel mixed with marble and granite, and many other unique additions in our home. I was especially proud of the extraordinary job she did in conveying what she wanted, and her superior, even exceptional, skill that she displayed in the fine details of this project. But most of all, I was proud, to the point of tears, she was able to exceed her "unlimited budget."

Dress Code

We all know that appearances matter. Let's take a look at how this has been a thread in my life's story. At times, it has definitely involved sacrifice on my part. Approximately two weeks into work at IBM, I got a call from the manager asking me to come to his office.

I got into the office, shut the door and sat down. I thought he was bringing me in to say that I was doing a great job. That wasn't the case. He told me, "I think I have made a mistake in hiring you."

My palms began to sprinkle like a garden hose. I asked, "How did you ever come to that conclusion?"

He walked across the room and opened the door to the bullpen. That is what we called the main room of the office where most people worked. "What do you observe out there?"

I looked out into the bullpen, where 15 sales reps and 25 system engineers were working away. I said, "Well, I think there are about 40 people out there."

"That's not what I am talking about. That is not an astute observation."

It seemed like this was another rhetorical question that a college professor would ask. Having just graduated, and having just spent these first weeks at IBM studying the numerous books on programming, which I found quite challenging, I wasn't in the mood for games. I took issue with his remark. "Sir, I don't know what you want me to see. What do you see out there?"

"I'll tell you exactly what I see. Take a look at what people are wearing.

Every single person in this room is in business attire except one. See if you can find the one person who doesn't fit in."

I must have looked perplexed and gazed out into the room. He coughed and gestured to me. "You are wearing a sports jacket, and everyone else in the room is in a suit and wearing a white shirt!"

Being kind of poor at the time, I didn't even own a suit. He gave me the afternoon off to buy appropriate clothes. I left the office in a panic and went to a clothing store and bought three suits. Luckily the owner of the shop was from Italy and knew my parents. He gave me credit, without which I wouldn't have been able to buy those suits. The irony of the story is that it was mid-summer, and so these were summer suits, with small lapels, and made with a sharkskin material. Within four months, I needed to go back to get fitted for winter suits.

That first year of suit buying was bad enough, but the second year was terrible. It was then that I realized everyone else wore 3-piece conservative suits. My "new" suits were now "old." Two years later, I was still paying off my suits and too embarrassed to wear them.

In the big scope of things, these were little problems, little sacrifices, that I knew I had to make in order to continue to work toward making my dreams come true. I wanted to live my memorable moments, and I wasn't going to let a dress code keep me from them.

Years later, I had a buddy arguing with me about the company dress code. He couldn't understand why a college graduate would have to be told what color shirt to wear. I explained to him that he had a job that would provide him and his wife a home, a car, food, and education for their children. It's a good job that pays big bucks. And you want to argue about the color of the shirt you have to wear? Give me a break. My take on all of this is that in any company you should not attack small issues, only the big ones. Of course, the men at my office are required to wear shirts, ties, and coats, but they don't have to wear suits. Although, if any of them would like a classic suit, I still have a few of my early ones in my closet. I'd let them go for a good price.

As Frances Willard, the famous 19th Century suffragist, once said, "I would not waste my life in friction, when it could be turned into momentum."

Now let's look at another story about clothes. They can't make the man, but they can sure help. Jim was an exceptional, well-paid IBM salesman who liked to party. I often witnessed his arrival back in the office after a venturesome, intrepid experience. The first thing Jim would do was open his top desk drawer and pull out a travel kit filled with razor, toothpaste, hairbrush, and aftershave. From his bottom drawer, he would grab a clean shirt wrapped from his cleaner. Off he would go to the men's room with a new tie in hand. It wasn't long before he returned, looking dapper, well groomed even, and ready to work.

The lesson I learned from watching Jim made an impact on me. I learned to think ahead. Take the time to get together what you may need for any given scenario in the future. Not all of us need a shaving kit and some clean clothes in our office or car, but some of us do, especially when we are working for a button-downed company like IBM. Think about what you need. Take the time and make the sacrifice to be prepared. Then when the time is right, you'll be ready.

I'd say shirts and shoes (S&S) are the keys to raising, uplifting, or escalating your appearance above your peers. For example, since my earliest days as a salesman, my shirts have always been custom fitted with added accents and detail. I get monogramed cuffs, no shirt pockets, and double sleeve buttons. Add the button-down collar with vivid colors and a body-fit design, and you have a psychological edge as you start your business meetings or make your sales calls.

A pair of high-end designer shoes like those made by Bally provide the knockout appearance punch. People go topsy-turvy with their eye contact. They look at your shirt, and then your shoes. And they are impressed, not overwhelmed, but favorably influenced. Shirt and shoes, shirt and shoes, say that three times fast, and remember it. I'm serious. It can give you a psychological edge that leads to a valuable and profitable advantage. I think it is worth the investment, and you won't know if it makes a difference until you try it yourself. Give it a try. Invest in your appearance. You may have to sacrifice for a couple of months, maybe even years, but I believe it's worth it.

Sacrifice now for rewards later, but please, have some fun through it all.

I want to spend a little more time on this subject. It is important to know where you want to end up, which is why you're making your sacrifices. What you want on your gravestone is a good question to ask.

A Cowboy Tombstone

Cowboy wisdom from Russell J. Larsen

I got a kick out of this one and wanted to share it. The Internet purports that Russell J. Larsen had the below inscribed on his headstone not knowing that he would someday win the "coolest headstone" contest.

On his headstone he listed the five rules for men to follow for a happy life:

1. It's important to have a woman who helps at home, cooks from time to time, cleans up, and has a job.

2. It's important to have a woman who can make you laugh.

3. It's important to have a woman you can trust, and doesn't lie to you.

4. It's important to have a woman who is good in bed, and likes to be with you.

5. It's very important that these four women do not know each other or you can end up dead like me.

Boulder or Aruba

New Orleans cemeteries are known by the nickname of "Cities of the Dead." There are dozens of cemeteries throughout this city, but most organized tours will take you through St. Louis Cemetery #1. My wife and I took a tour, and we decided we didn't want a plot in a creepy, haunted, above-ground cemetery. We decided on either Sacred Heart of Mary in Boulder, where we live, or St. Ann's in Aruba, one of the most beautiful places on earth. It will be Memorable Moment #75, to pick the perfect plot. My friends might prefer to visit Aruba. It is important to think of others. It's like Yogi Berra precisely phrased, "You should always go to other people's funerals, otherwise they won't come to yours."

Keep that in mind. Often we feel like we are too busy to make it to yet another funeral. We would rather work. Think again.

Spend some time thinking about how you want to die. What does a happy death mean to you? I was thinking I would like to reward the people who stop by my grave. Perhaps I could install in the tombstone a digital safe. I would pre-arrange that my friends would have the correct combination. Hours of operation would be inscribed on the stone. Once my friends open the safe, they would find a supply of fine cigars, along with a box of matches that has printed on the cover, "Have one on me!"

My friend Bret recently exclaimed, "I want to die like my grandfather did, peacefully and in my sleep...unlike the screaming people who were with him in his car."

Albuquerque International Balloon Fiesta

This was Memorable Moment #40 for me. Still speaking of death and the sacrifices we make for the things we dream of doing, let me add a note about hot air balloons. The Albuquerque International Balloon Fiesta has been a world-renowned attraction and destination for more than four decades. I always wanted to go there. My wife and I finally got the chance to go.

Walking among the magical moving picture show of hot-air balloons lifting gently through the crisp, fall air was a once-in-a-lifetime experience that we had to repeat. We watched 500+ balloons lift off from Fiesta Park in 2010 and again in 2012.

Any thoughts for generating additional memories of being a balloon passenger vanished, as I walked among the balloons awaiting their turn to launch. The balloon baskets looked claustrophobically crowded, and I immediately got a double dose of fear. First, I would be crowded into a flammable wicker basket below a raging gas furnace. Second, I'd be 500 feet in the air! I didn't want my tombstone to read "Horrible Fiery Plunging Death." No thanks. That is not what I sacrificially work toward.

Now, here in Boulder, CO, I look out my window at the six or eight balloon rides taking off from a field a few blocks from our backyard. It's usually before 7 a.m. on a sleepy weekend day as they pass above our neighborhood. When it happens every dog in the neighborhood starts barking. Apparently, their ears are very sensitive to the sound of the gas burners. Several neighbors come outside in their pajamas to either wave, or shake their fist at the sky! Every time, I am glad I made my choice not to be a rider in these fire-powered chariots.

Sacrifices involve choices. Be clear with what you want, and how much of it. Let me finish this chapter with one final image of what I live for, and what I have sacrificed to achieve.

My Pirate Treasure Chest— Memorable Moment #43

In my home, I have a treasure chest just for fun! It is a beautiful mixture of colorful gems, but no rubies, emeralds, or pearls. It is quite heavy. It can pull your back out of whack if you try to lift it! The weight of the chest worried me, so I reinforced the floor during one of our home remodels.

The chest is designed pirate style with a rounded hinged lid and a double lock system. It bolts shut and locks with an overlap padlock. "Aye matie, I keep me treasure under lock and key."

It is not for me, though. One of the greatest joys in life, and one of the best reasons to sacrifice is so that you can help others, and in this case, have fun with my grandchildren.

I tell the grandkids, "In me younger days, I sailed the seas with Long John Silver. He was a cunning and opportunistic pirate, who later opened a chain of fast food seafood stores. Someday when you are good, I'll take you to one of his shops."

Then I grin and shout, "ARRRR."

I continue the story, "Me and Long John Silver sailed with the notorious Captain Flint. He was hard as stone, and if you rubbed up side of him, sparks flew off! At night it was a might pretty sight, but just be sure you weren't next to a cannon with powder packed and fuse awaiting a light. I learned that the hard way and blew a hole through an innocent coconut tree."

You just might find your treasure

The yarn continues to spin, "We sailed the Caribbean and routes along the coastlines of Africa and North America. And all the while we collected treasure!" They still believe I went back to the southern most point of Florida, 90 miles North of Cuba, to retrieve the buried treasure. I tell my grandkids the famous Chinese proverb that I learned while sailing across the world, "Pearls don't lie on the seashore; if you want one, you must dive for it."

They all have a mini pirate treasure chest. When we open up our treasure chests we yell, "Yo Ho, Yo Ho!" I enjoy my grandkids and the

A treasure map

stories I tell them about my pirate adventures. Of course, the mermaid stories I can't tell the kids. They are too intense. I save those for my golfing buddies.

The stories would never fly if I didn't back up my tales with a treasure map. I keep one by my treasure chest. Now, you might not have a treasure chest, or grandkids, but we all have something to work towards. Hopefully you have dreams that you are willing to sacrifice for now so that they can happen in the future. We don't have to do it all at once. You don't have to be rich to save for something special.

Let me finish with a Ukrainian proverb that I also heard in my pirate days, "With patience, it is possible to dig a well with a teaspoon."

And while you're at it, you just might find your treasure!

CHAPTER TEN

Calabria's Law Number 7

When you're fast and efficient…

…You don't go unnoticed

MOST OF US WANT TO BE NOTICED. WE WANT TO STAND OUT from the crowd. We want to get the job, get the promotion, and get the sale. I think the secret of this is not to blow a horn and shout, "Look at me, look at me!" The secret is to be fast and efficient. Do that and people will take notice.

My Best Summer Job

I was born to sell. I heard that the number one rule of being happy in life was to do what you love. Selling made me happy, and still does. It is now time to share with you the story of how one summer in college I became the top cookware salesperson in the nation. It was all about being fast and efficient.

The summer after my second year of college, I found it almost impossible to find employment. Near panic, since I was already out of my savings for college, I took a job selling cookware. My parents weren't too thrilled. It meant I was on commission and had nothing guaranteed. My folks wanted me to take a salaried job, but the only one I could find was on the floor of the Birdsboro Steel Mill, working as a laborer moving iron ore to and from the red-hot labor molders. It was dangerous work. Plus, it would have been difficult to get to Birdsboro, since it was 25 miles from our home.

If I sold cookware in Reading, where we lived, I could drive my dad to work, use his car to make my sales calls, then pick my dad up at the end of his shift. Everything was arranged and I dropped my dad off that first Saturday. I made three calls that day and I made three sales. But it took longer than I thought. I picked my dad up an hour late.

When I drove up to get my dad, I could tell by his face that he was furious. When he got in the car he let me have it. He really gave me a piece of his mind. He said, "It's hard enough to work all day without having to wait for your son for an hour before he decides to pick you up. Where the hell were you?"

"Well, I made three calls today, and all three ladies placed an order with me. Three calls, three sales, I'm batting 100%. I'm sorry I'm late. It took longer than I thought. Those ladies can talk and talk and talk."

In the snap of a finger, my dad went from anger to happiness. I had just made more money that day than he had. From that day forward, he was my biggest fan, but he didn't like me to be late. I worked to become fast and efficient and pick my dad up on time.

When we got home and I told my mother about my day, I was so excited I couldn't stop my socks from running up and down my legs. What a way to officially start my sales career! In fact, I ended the summer with thirty sales, more than enough to pay my second year's college costs. I made $1,800 that summer.

I learned a lot about the benefits of being a business professional, which I somehow thought I instantly was. First, there was the early morning sales meeting. I always arrived with a valid excuse that I was hungry, and we should conduct the meeting over breakfast (at the sales manager's expense). A free breakfast subsidized my growing college tuition fund.

Prospecting for leads was next on the day's scheduled activities, but I didn't like the sales manager's suggestions on how to get leads. So, I always had an excuse to skip these sessions, because, for instance, I had another doctors' appointment (really). Why would I want to follow the sales manager's dodgy advice anyway? He suggested we should knock on neighborhood doors all day or try stopping young females on a downtown street with a gimmick promise of free gifts for allowing me to demonstrate cookware.

So, you're wondering where I spent my time instead of attending the meetings. Well, I went swimming until approximately 3:00 p.m., hurried home to change, pick up my dad from work, and then make my first sales pitch by 5:00 p.m. I worked until about 8:30 or 9:00 p.m. This was my schedule on Monday, Tuesday, Thursday, and Friday. On Saturdays, I worked in the morning until noon. My dad also worked a half-day on Saturdays, finishing at noon. After picking him up, I could have gone back out, but I didn't want to overexert myself. I never worked on Wednesday since I naively thought of myself as a professional and figured that since other professionals like doctors, lawyers, and CEOs took Wednesdays off to play golf, why not me? However, since I didn't have golf clubs, I went to the pool instead.

Of course, I have already told you that I was successful, but here is how I did it. The swimming pool was a natural place to meet prospects. Lots of young ladies were there every day. I would talk to them. I would find out who was about to get married, who was in the wedding party, and who had just gotten their own apartment. I'd tell them about my business and schedule appointments.

When it came time for the appointments, I would show up on time and dress to impress. I was always a good listener. The ability to hear what people were really saying was easy for me. Even when it seemed like I wasn't listening to what the ladies were saying, I was listening and registering selling points that I could use to persuade them to buy.

There was one thing that my sales manager had told me that I used quite frequently. He had said that our product could cook a potato without water.

"Excuse me, would you happen to have a potato in the house? The reason is, I would love to show you how well our stainless steel pot works. You can cook a potato even without water."

A few minutes later I would serve that potato to my client. It really did a nice job of cooking potatoes. I'd watch her try it. Then, I'd say, "Do you mind if I have a bite? It looks so good."

The thing is, it was delicious. I didn't have to fake it. When it came time to ask for the sale, I was persistent. I didn't take "no" for an answer. When a client turned me down, sometimes I would plead poverty. I'd tell my story that I was trying to make my way through college and without this money I wouldn't be able to go back to school. It was the truth, and people bought from me.

I loved sales. Because I was one of the leading salesmen that summer, I won a special set of knives. Then I earned the top salesman position in the entire nation. I got rewarded with an all-expenses-paid trip to New York.

In addition to allowing me to choose my own work hours, I found this job also allowed me to meet many young women, spending time chatting with them in their homes or apartments and at the pool. In addition to getting free breakfasts from my boss, sometimes I was lucky enough to get free suppers from my customers. After all, we had already cooked a potato!

The benefits didn't stop there. After business was completed, occasionally I would ask the young ladies out on a date, Dutch treat style, and quite a few accepted my offer. I was beginning to learn about the Universal Laws of Nature. You go with the flow. Don't swim upstream knocking on random doors of people you don't know. Swim downstream. Let the current take you to the swimming pool where people could look you in the eye and decide if they wanted to talk to you.

There is an Italian saying, "I would never dream of separating business from pleasure." I bought into that phrase lock, stock, and barrel. Selling cookware combined business with pleasure opportunities. I went on a lot of dates that summer, but I never dated the same girl twice. Of course, I tried a few times, but they all said once was more than enough! Plus, I wasn't ready to stamp the passport of my heart.

I should mention that one of the young women with whom I made an appointment to sell my cookware was my future wife. She didn't know it at the time. She was one of the few young ladies who refused to buy from me. So then I had no choice, but to turn up my charm, my Italian charm, so that she would at least go on a date with me. You know what she said, don't you?

She said, "No." So we talked some more and I asked her again. She smiled and said, "No." Being a sales professional, I was not dissuaded. A moment later, I asked her a third time.

I can still remember her melodic voice as she sweetly responded to me. Batting her eyes lashes she said, "I already told you no, and now I need you to leave."

It took a couple of years, but I eventually got that sale, and it's been the best deal of my life. She gives me a potato for dinner every night.

Recruiting

Since the success of our company is such a big part of my life, I want to spend a little time discussing the cultivation of our most important resource, our employees. We put a lot of effort into hiring high-quality employees.

The facts are out. Experts say only 5% of new hires are outstanding. It doesn't matter if it's in business, sports, medicine, or any other profession. The next 20% are good. They don't make excuses and perform to acceptable norms. Scientists claim the world is made up of protons, neutrons, and electrons. They forgot morons. It is that remaining 75% who lead to lost business revenue.

That last group is easy to identify. Simply add their shoe size with their IQ score, and if it falls below 85 they are definitely one of the 75%. Fortunately for me, I have big Italian feet, so I easily graduated to the higher level. Why include shoe size you might ask? Well, because if you are looking for someone who can fill some big shoes, it just makes sense. Hey, before you go criticizing my ideas, walk a mile in my shoes.

In the case of sports, this 75% often results in losses and low league position. Business losses can take longer to recognize and are harder to overcome. To make my company fast and efficient, I have what I call Calabria's "Curve of Employee Productivity." This formula requires new hires to have potential to be placed in the top 5% category. In other words, my aim is to only hire in the top 5%. My company measurement is revenue per employee. We have an objective to operate at three times the industry standard.

The way this works is to first consider the industry average, then compare to your fiercest competitors, and finally, set your own objective. Since we are a complex sales organization, I can't affect productivity with artificially manufactured personnel (robots). As a result, a great hire will make a critical difference both in terms of revenue and office morale. In order to achieve and maintain a company of high-performing employees, I place emphasis on the following:

1. Employee Tenure—I keep my people at our company longer by training and promoting from within our organization whenever possible, versus looking for new hires from outside of our company. Most employees can become strategic thinkers and appreciate the opportunity to train on the proper mechanics for higher positions of increased responsibility. If I find an individual to be honest and hardworking, I want to keep him or her and promote them to the next level when appropriate.

2. Profit Sharing—It makes a big difference when people get a share of the profits. They work extra hard to ensure that the company makes money. We pay bonuses and commissions based on financial benefit to the company.

3. Professional Level for Each Company Position—I want my people to have the best training. We try to train all technical personnel as if they were consultants coming to us, versus a simple dead-end technician. We want the training to include product certifications and our employees to receive appropriate titles for their expertise.

4. Recognition—I look for people who are working hard and are fast and efficient. We try to recognize good performance in the monthly company newsletter, at meetings, in one-on-one opportunities, and during the annual recognition awards.

5. Inclusion—It's important to ensure employees participate and have input into all strategic planning meetings. Our management must know the reality of business cycles. It is not enough for the owner or CEO to have the big picture. The more people who see it, the stronger the company. Explain cost control

and strategic investment. Let people in on the decisions to embrace new products, markets, and technologies.

6. Empowerment—I believe employees should be able to make many of their own decisions. Establish a culture where all employees accept responsibility and have freedom to act accordingly.

7. Staff Size—It is my goal to control overall number of employees using appropriate measures. We don't want to expand too fast and end up laying people off. Help people to feel secure in their position by not forcing job turnover.

8. Mentoring—We pair all new sales representatives with a mentor. We want the new hires to feel the support of a team. We want the mentors to know their expertise is valued. A strong mentoring program reduces failure by providing role models for the sales reps to emulate. Mentoring is an art, and it requires both time and energy. Some successful sales representatives may seem too busy to provide explicit counseling. However, sales skills can often be better and more quickly learned, practiced, and mastered under good mentorship. I, and other mentors in our company, love the awe-inspiring ripple effect of passing these skills on to others.

Unstructured Environment

There is another way to look at all this. Remember, it doesn't matter what your field of endeavor is, you'll only find five percent of your competition to be overachievers. Twenty percent have average potential, and the rest probably are playing with less than a 52-card deck. They are the group that followed the great comedian Rodney Dangerfield to the beach, "picked-up their special seashell, held it close to their ear and got a busy signal."

I am saying if you can be in the top 5%, you will easily beat 75% of your competition. Set your business goals to be in the top 5%. Get out ahead quickly and stay at it. Each year, aim to break your own records. Remember to keep your edge.

My Father the Coach

Coach Joe Calabria Sr., my father, gets much of the credit for the outstanding success of a truly great high-school basketball team, Reading Catholic. When Coach Calabria took over the reins at Reading Catholic in 1937, he was still a high school student in his senior year. The school lost the funding for the coach position, and the team voted my father in as coach. He immediately strove to strengthen the players in exact court mechanics, accurate shooting, teamwork, and the will to win. I know this, because when I came along, he was still at it. By the end of the 1938-39 season, he began to see the results of his labor as his team began to win more than lose.

My dad's first championship team

By 1940, the boys proved that my dad was not mistaken in his belief in them, for they showed their mettle. His early years of struggle were at last rewarded, for when the final whistle of the 1940-41 basketball wars blew, his team had won sixteen games and lost but two. They were crowned champions of the Eastern Pennsylvania Catholic League, unconquered in league competition.

Because of his gentle disposition, much like mine, he earned the nickname "Little Caesar." Over the next 20 years, he became more than just the coach to the boys on his teams. He was their friend and adviser. Whenever the team lost, he was more disappointed than anyone. I remember that he used to say that each defeat was his fault, because of some omission in the training. He was always working to improve the drills, plays, and strategies of his teams.

When they won, Little Caesar was the picture of joy, shouting, smiling, laughing, and slapping people on the back. He believed in every player on every team he ever coached. A victory was a tribute to his faith in the individual ability of each player. He tried with word, gesture, and attitude to let every player know they succeeded!

My dad was definitely in the top 5%. I believe that's why when his high school lost its basketball coach, he was the first student ever to take over as head coach. His school had one of the smallest enrollments in its sports league, yet he won championships against schools with enrollments three to four times larger. As I hope you can tell, I'm proud of my dad. Because of his example, I have always strived to be in the top 5%, to have my company in the top 5%, and to assist my employees to rise to their full potential. Thanks, Coach Calabria.

My First Interview

How do you interview for a large corporation? Many people entering college are hypnotized by the prospects of finding a job. In my case, like many others being brought up in an impoverished environment, I was led to believe that employment with a major corporation was the only barometer of true success. Talk about pressure!

Upon arrival at home for the Christmas holidays my senior year in college, I was met by an ad cut out of the paper and strategically placed on our kitchen table. The ad highlighted interview times during the coming week for jobs with a major corporation. My mother had already set up an appointment for me to interview with the local IBM branch manager. Thanks Mom. Way to make my holidays stress free. But hey, my mother back then was fast and efficient, and today at 99 years old, she's still sharp!

When I arrived at the interview, my first impression of the branch manager was positive. I had no way of knowing at that time that he was not wearing proper IBM dress attire. He was not in a suit. I remember thinking, "Who is his tailor?" He wore a sports jacket and gleaming loafers and was chewing a big wad of bubble gum. He took the gum out of his mouth, put his feet up on the desk, and stuck the gum behind his right ear. So this was what it was like to interview with a prestigious, major corporation.

About ten minutes into the interview, he asked me two important questions. I could tell the success of the interview hinged on these questions. The first question was, "What are your qualifications that will lead you to a successful career in computer sales?"

I answered that I had a very successful summer career selling cookware, that, in fact, I was the national sales champ.

I don't know why, maybe it was the gum behind his ear, but I added that while selling cookware, it wasn't unusual for me to ask my potential customer, if she was a good-looking single gal, to go on a date with me, as well as to buy some of my goods. I explained that my potential customers often chose both. I told him I had led the country in the cookware sales that summer with a 45% close rate. He seemed impressed.

He then asked his second question, the really important question. He asked, "Do you now have a steady girlfriend, and if so, do you have a picture of her?"

Yep, that is how the major boys rolled back then. Unbelievable, isn't it?

I answered, "No, I don't have a steady girlfriend."

He then requested a review of the girls I was dating. He wanted to see pictures. Back then, political correctness wasn't in play. I pulled out my wallet and showed him a few pictures, including my favorite, which was the picture of the beautiful girl who would eventually become my wife. He smiled when he saw that one, and handed the photos back to me.

"Why do you want to see the pictures of the girls I am dating?"

He answered, "All IBM salespeople marry good looking women."

My future wife's photo helped me to pass my first test with a major corporation. It was a good thing I had a college education or she might not have ever dated me. Then I wouldn't have gotten the job. This was Memorable Moment #30—enter the corporate workplace.

As an aside, I guess the political correctness police would go nuts if such an interview were to be reported today. In general, I think political correctness has gone too far, but I have to admit in this instance things have changed for the better, at least in the corporate interview world!

My First Quota Sales Territory— Memorable Moment #33

During my second year at IBM, I spent six months of active duty as a new member of the Army Reserve Unit in my hometown. After an extensive training period, I was given my first sales territory. I was both elated and intimidated. This sales territory centered on Pottstown, PA. It didn't take long to realize I needed to exert an absolute sphere of influence over each and every competitor I found doing business in my sales territory. I was thrust into this mentality. I needed to be fast and efficient or close up shop.

On my first day, I got a call from a law firm looking to purchase dictation equipment. While I was waiting with some apprehension in the law firm's lobby, the owner of a competing office equipment company came over to me. His name was Jim, and he asked if I was the new IBM sales representative. I guess my white shirt, tie, and three-piece suit gave him all the essential clues he needed.

Jim articulated in a loud voice that he had past success with this law firm and in this town. He told me that he intended to tar and feather me on my way to a painful, agonizing eviction from selling in "his" town.

That was an uncomfortable moment sitting in the lobby together. I didn't say anything to him, but I vowed silently that he would fail in his efforts to run me out of town.

Jim was called in first to see the law office manager. A few minutes later he came out boasting that he had the sale, and that my demise had already begun. He was going to go pluck the feathers off a plump chicken to plaster all over my face.

"Nice to meet you, as well," I said. Then it was my turn to talk with the office manager. I soon learned Jim had secured an order for office supplies, but I was the one who got the order for the dictation equipment, which was a far bigger sale.

Feeling a bit of confidence as I left that office, I calmly took an oath that I would never lose to that competitor. It wouldn't be easy, but I could do it. I certainly had better products, but at an admittedly much higher price. I was further handicapped without any options for price discounts, trade-in allowances, free supplies, or extended warranties. But let's face it; Jim was an unlikeable man. I was young and friendly and would get to know every one of my customers personally. I would listen to them and work to get exactly what they wanted.

Five years later, I had replaced all the typewriters in that lawyer's office and never lost a head-to-head proposal to Jim. One of my favorite memories was selling a typewriter to the local YWCA. I knew my machine was twice as expensive as Jim's typewriter. He really wanted the sale. I visited the YWCA every day for 30 workdays straight. Each day I stopped by with a smile, and I always had a slightly different selling point to share with the staff. I talked about resale value, the speed of the machine, reliability, energy efficiency, durability, versatility, and the list went on and on. I got the sale.

When I was promoted to our headquarters, I heard Jim thanked the world that IBM was moving me out of "his" town. That was as good as winning an Emmy! Jim thought he needed to pluck a chicken to tar and feather me, but what he really needed to do was to eat crow.

Seriously, we don't succeed by bragging, threatening, or intimidating others. It is a waste of time, and it's impossible to be efficient when you waste time.

Recruiting Philosophy

In my own business, I have come to realize job recruiting is inherently a relationship-driven endeavor. I remember one time having difficulty in convincing a highly successful sales rep to leave a competitor and join our organization. It takes time to build relationships. After months of calls to win him over, I decided to take a different approach. I would sell our advantages to his wife and ask her to persuade her husband over the hump and to join our organization. At this point, it seemed to be the most efficient way.

I gave her a call and explained who I was. We chatted for a while, and then I gave her some selling points. For starters, her standard of living would go up if her husband accepted the job with us, because his income would go up. I explained that our company was not solely about making money. Corporate values were also very important to us. We even had a rule (it's my 12th law) that we would honor service over gold. I continued by telling her that her husband would be able to work from a remote office near their home if desired. We would be highly flexible with his work schedule. Finally, we were a company on the move and would want her husband to be involved in the strategic planning to help us forge our future together. We talked about all these things. She asked questions, and I responded honestly.

The next day her husband accepted my offer to join our company. He went on to sell more than 250 million dollars in computer products for us.

I only want high-level talent in my company. It may take longer to get these people, and it may require some creative methods to help them to decide to sign on with us, but in the end, it's by far the most efficient route. I have found it's critically important to win over anyone your prospective employee respects. Invest the time in relationships to achieve the positive results you seek.

Be Prepared for Your Interview

Many people would like to become flight attendants. The glamor of traveling by jet around the country, and even around the world, is a strong pull for many of us. I want to share an interesting story about that hiring process. For me, the story is about finding the fast and efficient way to get your dream job.

Several years ago, a major U.S. airline was set to resume its hiring practice of yesteryears by hiring young, beautiful flight attendants. At that time, I was on a connecting flight out of Atlanta when the announcement was made that three trainees, hoping to graduate in one week, were assisting the assigned flight attendants. As the attendant in charge walked past me, she remarked how pretty the trainees on board were. I asked her if she knew about the director of personnel in charge of hiring 50 years ago, or his son who carried on in his footsteps. I had heard that they both sat in a rocking chair while they conducted their interviews.

That attendant laughed and remarked she actually interviewed with the son 26 years ago, and yes, he sat on his father's rocking chair. She asked me how I knew about their hiring practices.

I shared what I had learned from a flight attendant on a commercial flight from NY to LA 45 years ago. At that time, a flight attendant was referred to as a stewardess, but I will stay with the phrase "flight attendant." She told me she and all the other flight attendants were interviewed in the director of personnel's office and he sat in a rocking chair. This story and the enthusiasm with which she told it, was interesting to me, because this particular fight attendant didn't seem to fit the mold. She was outgoing and bold. At the time, that was unusual.

I asked her how she made it through the interview. She paused, laughed, and said it took two interviews. I asked, "Well, what happened the first time?"

"He asked about my hobbies and what I did in my spare time, and how I spent most weekends. I told him that I loved being outdoors, hiking, and water sports. In fact, I loved all sporting events."

She said that after her application was rejected, she realized he didn't think she would be happy in the job. She began to wonder if he thought that her personality couldn't handle a closed-in, tight work environment with the primary responsibility to ensure safety and control of passengers. But she really wanted the job.

"Six months later," she continued, "I reapplied for the job. I was again interviewed in the same office, same interviewer, and same rocking chair. I was very nervous that he would remember me and immediately tried to cancel my interview. But to my surprise the secretary told me it was too late to cancel or ask for a rescheduled interview."

That flight attendant smiled at me and came a little closer. She said this next part a little more quietly, "On that second interview, I crossed my fingers and spoke about how I enjoyed knitting, cleaning my apartment, reading, and experimenting with cooking new recipes. I was hired on the spot."

She moved back away from me, but added, "I got my dream job, and I didn't have to lie. I just needed to talk about the things the boss wanted to hear."

On this current flight out of Atlanta, the head attendant laughed with me. "That was just how my interview went," she said. "They were the same questions, and the same rocking chair."

If you want to get your dream job, take the time to find out what the company is looking for in its candidates. Talk to other people if at all possible. It takes longer, but believe me, it's the fastest way to get the job. I like the advice of motivational speaker Denis Waitley: "Why me? Commit to saying, Try Me!"

Never Too Young to Recruit

I want to share a personal story about what I look for in a good salesperson, the type that will be fast and efficient. There are some innate qualities that people possess at a young age that allow them to be natural salespeople. The best future salespeople may not currently be salespeople at all.

Take a lesson from the college coaches going to 8th grade games scouting for talent. Sometimes these coaches are already asking for verbal commitments. We need to do the same in business, and I think the most critical position is sales. I firmly believe that without sales success you won't ever succeed in a corporate headquarters. Even if you don't sell products, you have to sell ideas, systems, and strategies.

The youngest sale representative I've ever recruited was 12 years old. At that time, I was enjoying dinner with my family, when my 12-year-old grandson challenged my wife and his father to a game of Palindrome, a game in which you must come up with words that are pronounced the same forwards and backwards. After a fast start, the competition stalled, and my grandson excused himself and skipped away to the bathroom. It was awhile before he returned; we all started wondering if he was OK. He finally returned, and they resumed play. To our grandparents' pride, our grandson played the next few rounds quite well, coming up with some great words. My wife was impressed, called him a genius, and playfully teased his dad, as he was now in last place. When my wife asked our seemingly brilliant grandson how he thought of the palindrome "kayak," he provided a quite logical rationale. He calmly stated that "kayak" came to mind because his father had promised to take him whitewater rafting.

However, as smart as I thought my grandson was, I soon learned that my daughter was even smarter. Being his mother, she knew instinctively that "Mr. Brilliant" had most likely spent his time in the bathroom on his phone researching palindromes. What a sneaky yet smart young boy. It is the kind of trait I look for in a great salesperson. When an answer is unknown, knowing where and how to find it is a great quality to possess. Heck, he has the potential to be a successful sales manager! Just like a college coach scouting future star players, I'm working on getting a verbal commitment from him to become my lead salesperson.

Application for Employment—Answers

Since in this chapter we are talking about getting noticed, I want to share some fun employment applications that definitely caught my attention. Over the years, I have received many eye-opening applications. Here's a flashback to unusual application answers I have received.

Q: Desired position? A: Reclining.
Q: Special skills? A: Yes, but they're better suited to a more intimate environment.
Q: Do you have a car? A: I think the more appropriate question here would be "Do you have a car that runs?"
Q: Personal interest? A: Donating blood, expect time off with pay.
Q: Do you smoke? A: Only when set on fire.
Q: Experience? A: Starbucks, quit because it was always the same old grind.
Q: Education? A: Finished 190 out of 200 in my high school class.

Q: Comments? A: Although my resume lists fifteen jobs in ten years, please don't misconstrue this as "job hopping." I have never quit a job.

A bit of humor is actually a great way to get noticed. People listen immediately after a good laugh, so make sure you plan what you're going to say after your joke. It seems a Rodney Dangerfield quote would go nicely here: "When I was born, the doctor took one look at my face, turned me over, and said, 'Look, twins.'"

The Board Meeting Debacle— Memorable Moment #39

Quite a few years ago, I had a scheduled presentation in Armonk, NY, before IBM division VPs and corporate officers. I worked most of the night on my presentation and dropped a draft copy on my secretary's desk before finally heading home. I left her a note asking her to finalize my material when she arrived at 7 a.m. After just a few hours of sleep, I was back in the office by 8:15 a.m. I picked up my work from my secretary, heavy-footed my car's accelerator, and arrived at IBM's corporate headquarters for my 9 a.m. presentation. Whew, I arrived with one minute to spare.

But one minute later I'm standing in front of everyone without having had the time to review my finished work, which was a series of overhead-projector slides. For those of you who don't remember what that was, it was the precursor to PowerPoint. I wasn't two minutes into explaining my first slide, when a corporate officer in the crowd raised his hand to say, "Five lines down, three words over, there's a misspelling."

My eyes traveled down five lines. They ticked three words over. They widened. Oh, crap! There for all to see was a misspelling. I am not a great speller, but I can usually tell when a word is misspelled. I just need to look up the correct spelling. As I viewed the misspelled word I was mortified, flustered, rattled, and shaking in my shoes. In those days, corporate bigwigs at IBM didn't tolerate less than perfect briefing graphics.

In their eyes, a mistake reflected the preparer's inattention to detail. I was instructed to get my things and "come back when you're really ready."

Like a puppy who just had an accident, my tail between my legs, I collected my materials and waddled back to my office. I had to tell my boss that I had been thrown out of the meeting by his boss due to a typing error. I didn't tell him that the typing error was one my secretary made. It wasn't her responsibility to ensure my slides were perfect; that was my responsibility.

The lesson I learned that day was to get my work done early. I needed to be faster and more efficient. Only then would I have the time to carefully proofread my slides. Of course, the lesson isn't just about proofreading slides. Anything done at the last minute puts my work at risk. Ultimately I have to take responsibility for whatever I do. It's the same for you. We need to remember that good preparation takes time, so get started early if you want to get noticed in the best way, not the humiliating way in front of corporate officers.

I would like to add that it does help to surround yourself with high quality people. Now, when interviewing for administrative support positions, I find it's a worthwhile practice to provide a draft document to prospective new hires and ask them to proofread it and comment on grammar and clarity. This little exercise saves heartache later on. After all, I don't want to get thrown out of any more board meetings. My tail likes to wag, not to hang down in shame.

CHAPTER ELEVEN

Calabria's Law Number 8

Excellence is…

…Our ultimate goal

L ET'S BE CLEAR, A JOB DONE WELL IS A JOB DONE RIGHT. THINGS that are done half way are usually not acceptable. I say do it all the way, or not at all. There is something very gratifying about doing a job to the best of your ability. Many of us have ideas on how to improve our efforts, but don't have the energy to implement them, or the time, or the money. When everything comes together, it is a great day. That's where I am aiming, right towards greatness. Excellence is our ultimate goal.

There is nothing sweeter than an excellent day, excellent job, and excellent life.

Employee Shower

A big part of my life is trying to inspire others toward excellence. I have found that one great way is to make our environment an excellent place to work. As our company grew, we added a spacious workout room for employees to use before work or on their break. We also encouraged our workers to take walks outside when weather permitted. Exercise and fresh air are definitely two of the healthy ingredients for cooking up an excellent pie, or rather, enabling your logistics team to make up excellent pie charts.

It is only appropriate to have an area to freshen up after a good work-out, especially when heading back to work. We had a shower installed in the bathroom near the workout area. A lot of employees liked the shower, however, as often happens, someone will abuse a privilege and ruin it for everyone else.

One new employee moved from another state to join our company. He lived in a RV, and we allowed him to plug his vehicle into our outside electrical outlet, store his food in our refrigerator, and use the shower before work. Our new employee's messy habits had our old employees refusing to shower and forced us to take a strong position, eventually terminating his employment. Excellence often precipitates difficult decisions. Make those decisions, or suffer the smelly consequences of your inaction.

As the long-lived comedian George Burns said, "If you're old enough to know better, you're too old to do it."

Half of a Schilling-Penny

We started our business without the asset of accumulated savings, so we looked at what we could do to control or reduce costs. Reducing business costs became my Memorable Moment #36.

"A penny saved is a penny earned" is never more true than when you own your own business. We took to it with gusto and excellence in mind. Whatever savings we made, we reinvested into our business. Here are a few examples of being pennywise:

- Purchased a low-end soda machine, purchased sodas and snacks from SAM's Club, and sold the products to our employees at a reduced price.

- Profits from sodas allowed us to offer free coffee to our employees.

- Established credit with multiple credit-card companies and used the cards to purchase the IT products which we resold. The reward miles generated using these credit cards offset air travel costs.

- Maintained company profits in our company banking account versus distribution of profits to our stockholders. Over time, we eliminated bank borrowing and thus saved any interest-payment costs due for using a line of credit.

- Used a direct-sales approach to increase sales. The Market Development Funds were converted to pay for our office equipment. We doubled the pot by buying manufacturers' demo equipment at a reduced cost.

- Extended our sales commission plan to our administrative staff by offering bonuses for timely collection of receivables, and cost savings by the purchasing department because of additional negotiations prior to purchases.

- Capped the number of new hires to less than 5%, but increased overall productivity by more than 10%.

- We avoided recruiting commissions, by doing our own recruiting.

- When a client delayed payment, we charged late fees. These covered any interest fees on the credit card payments. We simultaneously paid our vendors, and in effect, increased our available credit.

Be Careful How You Present Your Offer

It is great when you discover an excellent candidate. I once interviewed a college graduate who showed real upside potential. She responded to an ad we placed, "Urgent—Computers are coming after your jobs. PLEASE only humans need apply." Near the conclusion of this interview, I gave her a verbal offer, "We will start you at $10 per hour, and in 3 months you will receive a raise, which will bring your new wage to $15 per hour." After enough time to comprehend my offer, I asked, "When would you like to start?"

She answered, "In three months!" I had been outplayed. She got the job!

Action/Take One

Back at IBM, one of the first sales management experiences I had took place in 1978. This was the era of "equal opportunity." Businesses were on notice to look for opportunities to promote minorities (women included). I was promoted in June of that year to field sales manager in Bridgeport, CT.

On my first day, a salesman named Will (minority) came into my office complaining he was being mistreated. His sales quota was too high, and his territory lacked opportunity compared with other assigned territories in the office.

Being new, I hadn't received much background information on the personnel in my office, but I was aware Will had sold less than 50% of his quota year to date. I told him I would review his situation and get back with him in the morning. The following day, I told Will he had a fair quota and plenty of opportunity within his assigned territory, and he needed to get back to work and make it happen.

He asked me if I really thought it was fair. I told him I really thought that it was. I had managed the quota and manpower-planning department in our division headquarters at IBM. I knew what I was talking about. I told him that he just needed to believe in himself. He was selling a great product at a great price, and he was a great salesman. Nothing more was needed. I told him he didn't need an adjustment in his territory. He needed an adjustment in his confidence. I told him, "I am your manager and I can tell that you've got this. Just get out there and make your calls, ask for the sale, and watch what happens."

He did just that. Will's numbers got better each and every week. By December his sales totaled his annual quota. I was excited to announce he was to be recognized with a 100% club trip, a special perk for those who hit their numbers. He had exceeded his sales quota for the year.

I called Will into my office to congratulate him and remind him that

I had to report to my district manager, and I needed to brag about the outstanding job I did with him. After all, good sales management is the art of getting someone who's underachieving to do superior work. I asked him, "So what did you do to turn your sales around?"

Will said he didn't know. He asked for the sale just like before, but now he was receiving positive customer responses. I chalk it up to the Law of Attraction. Will's clients were now looking into his eyes and believing what Will was saying, because he believed it. You better believe that makes a difference! It's huge. Everyone who has ever achieved excellent results believed in him or herself. This is a critical concept that has huge implications for sales, recruiting, and fundraising, basically all of life!

When society labels you as a minority, it can be hard to believe in yourself. I know a little bit about this, because Italians were not always enthusiastically welcomed into America. Society tries to tell you what to think. But what matters most is what YOU think. Start with believing in yourself and excellent things will follow. It should always be your ultimate goal. Believing in yourself gives you the edge, which is like the difference between cutting a raw piece of meat into slices with a sharp knife, verses trying to cut it with a dull spoon. Everyone who wants to cut his or her way through the competition needs to remember this.

SWOT Matrix— Memorable Moment #70

My wife and I started our small business on our own. I was the only employee and she was the Chick in Charge. We obviously grew our business, and we take a lot of pride in providing dozens of jobs while making payroll every week, all self-financed. As owners, we feel a responsibility to our employees. We work to maintain a long-term health in the business. There are a lot of challenges that come with increasingly aggressive competition and ever-changing market conditions.

We conduct semi-annual, strategic-planning meetings with our staff. This practice has allowed us to protect our profit margins. SWOT analysis—strengths, weaknesses, opportunities, and threats—takes information from both internal and external sources and helps us to stay on track with our goal of achieving excellence. We take the analysis seriously and use a trained facilitator to guide the process.

The truth is that without such planning meetings, and reality checks, any manager can get twisted. We can get so caught up in the day-to-day of our business that we sometimes lose track of reality, or at least the big picture. We need a break now and then to regroup, refocus, and reenergize. One of the things that emerges is a list of our top initiatives for any given period.

Having top initiatives is no guarantee that desired results will be achieved. Rather, the champions of these initiatives must be provided with the necessary resources, support, and training to accomplish them. The key is innovation. The initiative must be within the ability and capacity of the manager, and that manager needs the ambition to make it happen. Here are some points to remember. These can help anyone who wants to get something done, both personally and professionally.

1. Develop a strategy to get to the future; a strategic vision is a must.

2. Develop yourself or train your leadership team to embrace the risk and controversies it takes to get to your goal.

3. Protect and build your resources; build on your assets.

4. Work with smart, ethical people.

5. Be savvy, flexible, and resilient.

6. Focus on opportunities, not problems.

7. And finally, after you figure it out, don't take a nap. Get to work!

Be aware that action items will expand to fill the hours of the day; don't let them! PLAN your work; then WORK your plan.

This disciplined approach is how the top initiatives will be achieved. Jump in and watch the magic happen.

Mike Ditka, professional football coach, tells it like it is. One of his famous quotes is, "Success isn't permanent, and failure isn't fatal."

Forecasting

In my day, most sales careers at IBM followed a straight line within the sales division. The norm would be to start as a salesman, then become a sales-school instructor, followed by sales manager, staff-sales position, and then finally a promotion to branch manager. My strategy was to one day own my own business, and I decided on a well-rounded route with my professional activity split between sales, financial, and marketing positions.

This unorthodox series of promotions gave me varied experiences to parts of the business beyond sales. No doubt, this has helped me tremendously in my own business. This non-traditional path also helped educate me in the finer, sometimes subtle, distinctions required in problem solving. I needed these skills if I was to strive for excellence. These challenges related to the integration of various aspects of a successful business. This was my training ground for later in life when I had to address the many interrelated complexities of running a start-up business. So let me tell you about a couple of those challenges.

After six straight years of exceeding my sales quotas, I was promoted to a staff position in the forecasting department. IBM's business plan included a two-year operating plan, current year plus one, followed by a five-year strategic plan. Each plan's updates followed in six-month increments. First we updated the operating plan, then the strategic plan. At the conclusion of each year, the plan was revisited and adjusted accordingly.

Forecasting included both announced products (currently being sold) for the operating plan and unannounced products (not yet available) included in the strategic plan. After one year, I was promoted to manager of the department. I enjoyed this work and showed strong understanding in the business-planning process. That promotion was Memorable Moment #64.

My job, along with my staff, was to predict sales. Now one of the members of my staff had his PhD in economics. I already told you I wasn't exactly an honor student. In fact, I just barely graduated. Here's the thing, though: I could always tell what really mattered. I might not have been the smartest guy in the room, but often I was the one most aware of what really was at play. In my opinion, my PhD friend didn't have a clue. He drank his coffee and read the Wall Street Journal without any guilt for not contributing to our department's mission.

He also hadn't had a raise in years. He was stagnating, and as his new boss, it was my job to energize him and help him to use his intellect to support our mission. Well, I got him engaged, and I got him a raise. It took discipline on my part and a suspension of judgment, but together we produced some excellent work.

IBM was a sophisticated company, and I realized that its corporate economists had a great deal of influence in our forecasting and operating plan. But we found their analysis was based on lagging indicators, such as gross domestic products, consumer price index, and balance of trade. These measurable economic factors change only after the economy has begun to follow a particular pattern.

I decided to find a lead indicator, one that was a future indicator of sales. Well, we found that typewriter sales measured by market segment was such an indicator. Office equipment sales results followed changes in the commercial typewriter sales sectors. In other words, we found in certain sectors that when typewriter sales were increasing or decreasing, it was a sign that other larger equipment would soon follow.

I then convinced my PhD worker to examine past economic conditions that could be matched with our current sales environment. He did the research and came up with a series of charts that displayed certain past economic conditions and what happened in their next years. We were headed into a depression and matching percentage changes above or below a base line, we found one period's recession matched perfectly to our current environment for our forecasting model. We used it as our lead indicator to create our plan to calculate our sales predictions. It was essential that we had the research, because if you can't justify your sales predictions, you won't believe them. And if you don't believe them, you won't be able to convince your president to go against your corporate economists' recommendations. My PhD worker got the numbers crunched correctly.

However, the senior corporate economists disagreed with our estimations. In fine IBM style, we placed a wager on the numbers and the winner would be treated to champagne. We made our prediction and convinced our division's senior management to reduce the sales forecast for the upcoming year. As we predicted, there was a large sale reduction, and our numbers were amazingly accurate.

We then matched the uptick and projected a total recovery the following year. Wow! We were right on the mark. Our corporate economists lost the argument on our plan. They also lost champagne since my department predicted the plan recovery within 1% of actuals.

Another time, my department worked on phase three of an unannounced copier product. This is somewhat complicated, but I thought some readers might enjoy, or even benefit from, reading how a major company phases in a product. Phase four would be the actual new product introduction to its markets. Each phase of the product development has a decision to continue forward or discontinue from the program and measure its financial expectation.

We created an algorithm to make our new product sales prediction. Based off market research, we took many variables into account. This research measured end-user attitudes of copier attributes. Each attribute was then weighted by usage and price elasticity for industry sales. For example, copy quality was more important if usage was 5,000 copies per month, but not as important as speed if usage was more than 100,000. We forecasted sales within each usage cell. After completing the forecast, we tested our method by back casting the prior product announcement. Our method predicted within two percentage points its actual sales history. We had developed a new reliable forecasting tool! All we needed to do now was get upper management's approval.

I reported to the director in charge of the division's planning department. His recommendation would have a major impact on our ability to move forward with our future-operating plan. To better understand the atmosphere of this meeting, imagine a well-educated, but inexperienced, first-generation Italian immigrant at the knee of his neighborhood's godfather trying to explain to him how to better service his neighborhood. It was a very delicate situation. If I angered him in the least, my horse could lose its head! No, wait; what I really mean is that our forecasting tool could end up in the trashcan.

I presented an in-depth analysis of the research and convincing methodology proving our forecasting predictions. At the conclusion, "the Don" congratulated me on my work, and I returned to my office overly pleased, with the swagger of a winner. Then the phone rang. Apparently the Don had just realized my proposal saw a forecast increase three fold, and was howling that he'd been had and that our forecast was unrealistically optimistic. After an ominous, intimidating warning that I was about to be terminated, he agreed to rehear my presentation. I went back to his office, this time with a lot less swagger. Luckily for me, he embraced the new methodology. The Don was even apologetic. I was vindicated.

These varied experiences included management promotions in quota sales, manpower planning, and worldwide new-product announcements. They allowed me to skip through the sales-planning positions and get directly promoted to branch manager. That's right. I became Joe Calabria Branch Manager, Memorable Moment #63. I got there without ever becoming a sales school instructor or taking a staff sales position.

If you want to know how to be excellent at what you do, follow through on your instincts and observations, and don't let the Don, or the PhD, intimidate you. Believe in yourself.

CHAPTER TWELVE

Calabria's Law Number 9

Time is my most precious commodity…
…*Don't waste it*

T IME IS A FUNNY THING. YOU CAN'T BUY IT. YOU CAN'T HOLD IT. You can't see it. But, everybody knows it's important, and wise people know it is precious. To give away your time is a true gift. I am more than willing to share my time with people, but please, don't look a gift horse in the mouth. Do not waste my time. Honor it! I'll do the same for you.

One of the best lines that President George H. W. Bush ever said was, "I think the process of aging could be slowed down if it had to go through Congress."

The Sales Peddler

As a sales trainee at IBM in 1965, my manager wanted me to work with the #1 sales producer in our office. Herb was anything but modest. He possessed influence of importance in the office and was nicknamed the "Senator" by the office sales force. The Senator was upset that he was asked to babysit a new rep. He said to anyone listening, "If I have to babysit, couldn't I have at least gotten a cute baby?"

My skin was thick enough to take his ribbing, but he set out with an attitude of coldness toward me. That troubled me. Nonetheless, I wanted to learn everything I could from him. The Senator had just gotten hold of a newly announced demo product. I knew he was excited to see how well it would sell.

His first call was to a lawyer's office. He didn't talk to me as we waited in the reception area to speak with the office manager. Basically, as far as he was concerned, I wasn't even there. But, when he got the nod to come into the office, I dutifully followed. We sat down. He took the product out of its case and explained and demonstrated. It was a portable dictation machine. You could take it anywhere! He was animated, smiling and laughing. He was given a purchase order on the spot for the new machine. As we left, a ravishingly beautiful secretary handed him a note with a time and place for an after-hours drink.

By noon that day, he had secured three separate sales orders and two notes from stunningly beautiful women. Over lunch, I asked Herb if this was a normal day. Herb answered, "My boy, this was an average or slightly below average morning for me. You have to have high expectations."

Before we left the restaurant, Herb told me to come closer, and he would tell me the secret of his success. I leaned in from across the lunch table. He cracked a joke about having a different woman for every need a man could have. That was as deep as he got.

Our afternoon went about the same as our morning calls. That is until the Senator challenged me to give a demo of our new dictation machine. Of course, I accepted his challenge and was anxious to outperform his pitch. He pulled his car over and led me into a building. He opened a door and coaxed me in. "You go in there by yourself," he told me, "and don't come out without a sale. There is a group of people in this room that will act like they aren't interested, but at least two of them are excellent customers. Now, go get 'em kid." He slapped me on my rump and in I went.

The place was a smoke-filled room with people sipping coffee, reading, and sleeping. I asked for their attention, "Good afternoon gentlemen. My name is Joe Calabria and I have something stunning to share with you today. This product can change the way you do business. It will save you money and our most important commodity—time itself."

It was at least five minutes into my presentation when I realized I was in a Yellow Cab lounge filled with cab drivers. Nobody in that room was a customer. This was a joke on me being played by the Senator. "Well, thanks for your time, everyone." I packed up my product and left the room.

Embarrassed and red faced, I walked back to the car. I took a deep breath before I got in. When I opened the door, he took one look at me and burst out laughing. This was absolutely hilarious to him. I thought he might bust a rib, he was laughing so hard. At first, I didn't think it was funny at all. But, when he kept laughing, it was contagious, and I had a good laugh, too. I started to enjoy myself.

The Senator never taught me anything directly. I had to figure it out for myself. You have probably heard that experience is the best teacher. I think it is the most efficient teacher, as well. This guy was the most successful salesman in our office. He taught me in no uncertain terms if you want to be good, you better have fun at what you are doing. It is the fastest way to a sale.

Of course, when making a sale, the basics need to be covered, but when people make our day more enjoyable, we appreciate them. People we appreciate are the ones we want to buy from, work with, and get close to. That little nugget of wisdom is worth its weight in gold. Thank you Senator.

Baseball, Football, and Banking

My banker once asked me the secret to starting a successful business. Instead of a simple answer, I gave him two sports analogies and a little bit of his own banker's wisdom. My answer startled him, especially my conclusion.

I told him, "Let's start with baseball. Did you know that the Japanese love baseball and incorporate strategies from the game into their business practices?" I stated that after Pearl Harbor was bombed, we eventually defeated Japan. Unlike so many times in the past, we felt remorse and set up a far-reaching plan to rebuild Japan. In that process, baseball was introduced into the Japanese culture.

In the years that followed, the Japanese incorporated their love for our national pastime of baseball into their new strategy of becoming a global business powerhouse. They set a goal of beating the Americans, and every other country, on an industrial level. Textiles and automobiles were two product categories that emerged as business targets for the Japanese people.

Their business strategy was to always play a nine-inning game, incorporating strategy changes during the game. They implemented baseball jargon into the business environment with only one objective: to win the game by the bottom of the ninth. They began using terms such as, "advance a runner, bunt, change up, double play, home run, pinch hitter, sacrifice bunt, relief picture, and grand slam."

Today, the Japanese are revered for their outstanding textiles, and their automobiles are the most popular in the whole world. My banker wanted to know the point of the story. It's simple. If you don't want to waste your time in business, take a lesson from baseball. Keep your eye on the end game. Use your resources from the dugout and the bullpen. Stay flexible till you get the last out!

I continued my analogy by interjecting some wisdom through the great game of American football, which is played in four quarters. Having recently turned 70 years old, I realize it's more important than ever for me and the Chick in Charge to support and donate to worthy causes. In my view, the game of life is similar to the game of football. Like football, life consists of four quarters, if you're lucky! Halftime occurs around age 44, or later. At 66 years old, you're only starting the fourth quarter, again if you're lucky. Always remember, though, the clock is ticking. Time management is essential.

As in a lot of games, many of the significant points, or donations, are scored late in the fourth quarter. Some football jargon can be inspiring and instructive. Try applying the following terms to your business and your life. Great concepts to consider include, "huddle, goal line, man-in-motion, forced fumble, first down, interception, unnecessary roughness, Hail-Mary pass, touchdown, field goal, two-point conversion, overtime, and sudden death." Again, watch the clock. Time is your most precious commodity. Don't waste it!

My summary to the banker of what it all meant was to work hard from the opening kickoff to the closing whistle, but always keep your eye on that goal line. That said, also realize that as the game is coming to an end, and you are lucky enough to be way ahead, put some of your second stringers in the game to help them become better players. Spend a little time to wave your helmet to your fans who helped you get across that goal line in style. Share the excitement of your win! Be a role model for your community, not a sensationally tragic story in the newspaper. Bring your best game into the stadium of life and business everyday you enter it.

After I got my point across with the sports metaphors, I turned to a subject that I knew my banker loved. The subject was "interest on a loan." I believe interest is the bank's equivalent to a contractor's "change orders." In my business, anytime a client asks for an adjustment after the contract has been written, we add in a price increase to compensate our company for that effort. A key to business is to make sure to reinvest back into your company, increasing the company's cash reserves. When you have money in the bank, your banker pays you interest on your cash reserves.

With a smile, I told my banker solemnly, "Don't let your banker increase your line of credit and lure you into borrowing more money. He'll write you a check and simultaneously raise your interest rate. That is no way to be successful, unless you are a banker. So a successful businessperson takes the time to learn from what the banks do."

I told him that the formula was actually fairly simple. "Reinvest after-tax dividends. Lower your need to use your bank line of credit. Increase your cash on hand. Have the banks pay you for the money you have worked so hard to earn."

I finished my explanation to my banker with the following conclusion. "Remember, football and baseball are played everyday with games on TV, even on holidays. It's hard for a business owner to get the time off during the workweek to see them in person. However, banks have time off so that bankers can attend these games, plus they get special lunches, golf, and social meetings. And let's not forget, a banker is never late for dinner. In my next life, I want to return as a banker, because I love those bankers' hours!"

As a side note, if I do get another life, I also wouldn't mind coming back as my wife's cat! "Res ipsa loquitur," which means, "The thing speaks for itself."

The First Call

In business, time is money. I am not a fan of "busy work," those things that we do when we don't have anything else to do, or even worse, those things that we do when we are avoiding what really needs to be done. Business is full of difficulties and difficult people. It is natural to try to avoid some of those challenges, and the people behind them. Unfortunately, we can't, and we waste time trying.

One of the most helpful practices I have found to energize my day is to take on the hardest call of the day first. If there is conflict in the air, a difficult person I need to contact, or a tough sales call I have to make, I don't avoid it. I take care of it. I tell my employees to do the same. The benefits to this difficult-things-first approach are numerous. And, yes, I know there are exceptions to this rule. Be smart and use common sense.

Here is my case. First off, this no-avoidance approach gets your heart beating. It is a natural stimulant, in some ways better than coffee. It jumps starts your day. Second, it's already on your mind and will hang over you until you finally address it. That means you are not focused on what you are currently doing. Third, there is a sense of accomplishment in being brave enough to take on the things that other people avoid. That jolt of affirmation can carry over into the rest of your day, giving you the confidence that makes you fast and efficient. Give it a try some morning and see how it works for you.

Superpowers of the Company Gang

It saves time when you know the strengths, weaknesses, and personality quirks of your staff. If you think everyone is the same, you're wrong. I am a fan of keeping short-summary appraisals of each person. I don't necessarily write them down. I keep them simple enough to remember them in my head. These appraisals help me to know how to delegate responsibility. To focus on strengths, I sometimes think of this as my superhero log. I assign each person's strength into a superpower!

You can use this same technique for the people at your work. The people on your list don't have to be your employees. They could just as easily be your boss and his or her superiors. Or, if you're a student, they could be your friends, teachers, coaches, or professors. Here is a fun example of names and their superpower strengths from a fictitious company.

The Superpowers of XYZ Incorporated

- Alex—The Barometer. As office pressure increases so does his beard length. He expresses himself well, especially in harried situations.

- Cindy—The Happiness Machine. Work is her priority, flower in hair, slip-on shoes, and a never-ending smile.

- Dan—The Problem Sniffer. If there is a difficulty up ahead, Dan is sure to get wind of it first.

- Frank—The Charmer. He is able to get people's attention and make them feel comfortable.

- Kathy—The Word Generator. She is never at a loss for words, always has something interesting to offer.

- Dean—The Humor Doctor. He is a comedic great and brings fun to every situation.

- Al—The Boulder. He is a stable force and keeps the rest of us from blowing this way or that way with the latest trends.

- Paul—The Sheriff. He follows the rules diligently and makes sure that others do as well.

- Monica—The Sales-Closing Beast. She can close any deal.

- Ernie—The Brave Soldier. No situation or person is too difficult for him to tackle.

- Chris—The Energizer. Naturally very animated, he's an authentic cheerleader.

- Jarrod—The Showstopper. His great presentation skills get every audience applauding.

- Dave—The Baker. He understands the ingredients of business and is great at cooking up tasty pie charts.

- Tom—Lone Wolf. He works best by himself, but is capable of devouring any project.

- Jane—The Camera. With a near photographic memory for detail, she can recall every situation.

- Irene—Bulletproof Smile. Even the nastiest person can't upset her.

- Hannah—Attack Dog. She's bold, brash, and in your face, perfect for past-due collections.

If you try a technique like this, keep one more thing in mind. Always be looking for surprises. Look for the people on your list to grow, mature, learn, and become better human beings. When we focus on strengths, people tend to increase their superpowers. You might not think it is possible, but hey, you read it in a book, so it must be true!

Things to Do Today

I incorporated a $25,000 idea to revolutionize my employee-training model. Let me tell you about how it got its price tag. This method helped my wife and I build a $260,000,000 per-year company without any outside funding. We built our company from scratch. That means we built it from nothing. Nobody gave us anything at the start. What is waiting for you? What's does Divine Providence have in store for you? Whatever it is, here is a way to start.

From a variety of online sources I have put this story together. One day in 1918 an efficiency expert named Ivy Lee got a chance to solicit Charles Schwab, president of Bethlehem Steel Company, and one of the richest men in America. Lee explained his organization's methods for management efficiency to Schwab, and ended by saying something like, "As you can see, with our service, you'll know how to manage your people better than ever."

Now let's just imagine how the conversation went from there. Nobody knows for sure, but the gist of it was probably like this: "Hell," said Schwab, "I already know how to manage better than I do. What we need is not more knowing, but more doing, not knowledge, but action! I need you to light a fire under my behind. If you can give us something to pep us up to do the things we already know we ought to do, I'll gladly listen to you!"

"Agreed," answered Lee, "In the next 20 minutes I'll teach you something that will step up your action at least 50%."

"Now you're talking," said Schwab. "Let's have it. If you're long winded I'm going to miss my train."

Lee handed Schwab a piece of paper and said, "Write down the six most important things you have to do tomorrow." Swab scratched his chin, looked at the paper, and began to write.

A few minutes later, Lee said, "Now, rank them in order of their importance one to six." Schwab tapped the paper with his pencil. He narrowed his eyes. He picked out his most important task and wrote #1. He continued until he had them all ranked.

Lee folded up the paper and said, "Put this in your coat pocket and when you come in tomorrow morning look at the list and start working on item one. Don't stop until it is completed. After that, work on number two; and then three, and so on. Do this until quitting time. Don't worry if you don't finish the whole list, because you will be working on the most important ones. Anything else can wait. If you don't get your work done using this method, another method won't help, and chances are without taking the time to do this method you wouldn't be clear which tasks to do first."

Lee continued, "Do this every working day. At the end of the day, make your list for the next day. After you've decided if this works for yourself, have the people who work for you give it a try. Take as long as you need to decide if it is valuable for your company, and then write me a check for whatever you think it is worth."

The whole interview between Schwab and Lee reportedly took less than a half hour. About a month later, Schwab mailed a check for $25,000 (about $400,000 in today's money) to Lee with a note explaining the method was more effective than anything else he had ever learned! In five years, this plan was largely responsible for turning the unknown Bethlehem Steel Company into one of the biggest steel producers in the world! And it helped make Charles Schwab more than a hundred million dollars and perhaps the best-known steel man in the world. Not a bad return for $25,000.

Perhaps this method could help you to make your dreams come true, like it did for me. Don't waste time. Get started today. And when you are ready, send me a check for what this advice is worth to you. I promise to put it to good use, or perhaps a nice bottle of Grey Goose.

Thanks to Wikipedia, Rick Roberge, and James Clear for their versions of this story on the web. Look up "The Ivy Lee Method" for more information and other people's ideas about this story.

Unemployment Benefits

I'll tell you what really gets my goat. It's people who waste my time and expect me to pay them for their disservice. Unemployment benefits are a very good thing, but unfortunately people who abuse the system make it almost impossible to stay positive about these benefits. These abusers give heartache to a job creator such as myself, and all the other hard-working staff who have no intention of free loading. Here is one story of what we are up against.

Several years ago, I had a seemingly terrific receptionist who one day started complaining she was getting sick while working at her desk. She would complain about people wearing too much perfume or scented lotion. She also claimed it was the chemicals the cleaning lady used to disinfect the office. I took action, and first reminded all employees that our employee handbook made reference not to use perfumes or scented lotions in the office. Second, I instructed the cleaning company to switch to "green" disinfectants, which had no harmful odors. I hoped this would resolve the issue, but no such luck.

My receptionist then suggested that if I moved her office just a few feet from where she regularly sat, that might prevent her from being sick. I thought it was unrealistic to have my receptionist move to this new hidden space. After all, she was supposed to be our first point of contact to greet people. So I made more efforts to find the source of her ailments by covering the cost of a series of allergy tests for her, all of which came back negative. Additionally, I had the heating and air-conditioning duct system cleaned, the entire office carpet shampooed, and I even replaced her floor pad. I drew the line when she suggested we clean the office with vinegar.

Despite all my actions, she ended up quitting. OK, that's fair, but then she filed for unemployment. Now that is a kicker, and a giant waste of my time. I did everything I could to keep her, and she quit. Then she wanted me to pay her while she was at home. I didn't think that was fair, and certainly not healthy for her. She hadn't cleaned her entire house with vinegar! It wasn't long before I found out she was working at another company, who used the same cleaning company as us. Are you kidding me?

We appealed her unemployment claim and won. She appealed the decision and her benefits were re-instated. We took the final appeal option to the industrial claim office, but shockingly lost. I know we have to look out for the worker, but come on people. Not every business is out to hurt people. The great majority are out to help people, but it is mighty hard when the clearest cases of abuse are not dealt with in an equitable fashion.

In the midst of these legal battles, the state ran out of funds for unemployment payments. We then had to pay interest on the unemployment payments, because the state had to borrow the money to pay for these claims. By the way, this one example is multiplied by a large number in every state in our country, because dishonest workers are expecting unemployment benefits when the company is not at fault. The net result is that the companies, and all the hard-working honest people in them, have to pay increased fees to keep the unemployment fund solvent. The harder we work, the more they take. This previously healthy claimant and all who feel like they don't have to work for a living should not be entitled to get anything. The rest of us are paying increased workman's compensation rates because they want to get compensation for staying at home. Let's work together to spot this fraud in our midst. When people rant about living in an age of "entitlement," please keep this story in mind.

Did You Ever Wonder Why?

When it comes to government and taxes, I have to take a stand. It is not just that this affects me personally, but this is a problem on the national scale. It affects all of us. Wasted money is wasted time. Of course, our government does lots of things right. I have my challenges with the system, but I am successful working within it. But please, let's strive to be better and smarter. If I operated my business like the federal government operates, I would be out of business.

Here is one example of an incredible waste of time and money. The United States government spends tens of millions of dollars through the Office of the Surgeon General to warn Americans about the dangers of smoking. That is a good thing, right? Well, yes, except at the same time, through loan guarantees and direct grants from the Department of Agriculture, our government spends tens of millions of dollars to subsidize tobacco farmers. Your money and my money, which we spent our precious time to earn, goes to such self-defeating causes as this.

Ever wonder how we pay for it, besides borrowing from China, that is? Consider this comparison to paint an accurate, albeit very unpleasant picture. Not too long ago, while fighting the so-called Axis of Evil, we had 98,000 US troops in Iraq. On that same date, Feb. 28, 2010, the United States Internal Revenue Service had 101,054 employees.

What this Country needs are more unemployed politicians. I think all of our lives would be better with much simpler tax laws. If we could do that, we wouldn't need over 100,000 IRS employees. Let's be clear, I am not talking about big tax breaks for the rich. I am talking about working smarter as a nation, everybody pitching in to do their fair share, and eliminating wasteful spending that would never be tolerated in a business environment.

The Company Tax Rate

How can you manage the stress that comes from high tax rates? I'll share my answer in just a moment, but first a word or two about the tension of taxes! Soon after we formed our company, Congress enacted the tax reform act in 1986. At that time, marginal tax rate fell to 28% or lower. That was good news. But, since 1986, multiple additional taxes, coupled with increased rates for existing taxes, have put pressure on our company to be able to maintain profit as a certain percent of revenue. That is the heart of our business plan and it is in jeopardy.

As an example, I paid a recent Florida Power and Light bill for one of my properties with the electric service amount due being $6,094. Adding up the storm charge, gross receipt tax amount, franchise charge, the utility tax, plus the sales tax, my total bill was $7,643. Are you following here? That is more than $1,500 in tax-related expense for one bill! As I mentioned earlier, my company is all about lowering costs, but with tax charges like that, I start to wonder if I can afford to keep the power on 24 hours a day. Questions like that make it very hard to embrace starting a new business. To be clear, taxes are a huge barrier for job creation.

People like me have to find a healthy way to cope with our tax burden. My advice is to search, hunt, grope, rummage, ferret or relieve tension somehow when the conversation is about taxes due! One method that has worked to calm me down was to envision a three-tiered pond with live fish and then bring it into reality. Staring into the rippling waters of this cascading pond is the perfect fix for tension.

Creating the structure was a labor of love for me, and some of my staff. We were awarded with lots of opportunities to exercise patience. One challenge was that we needed to ensure that the pond would drain properly. If it didn't have the right drain, it would have to be emptied by hand, bucket by bucket. That certainly wouldn't be a fun job. We applied for a permit to drain the pond into our waste system. Don't make our mistake and ask the city to approve the pond's drain plan. If you do, expect to be told not to drain this little pond into the city sewer line through your internal plumbing system. The city's total sales and use tax rate only included taxes for non-profit human-service agencies, open space, jail improvement, and flood recovery, but nothing for a fishpond draining system.

This was one of those difficult moments where time seems to stand still. Was I in reality, or caught in some land of endless taxation, but no water drainage allowed? This little pond calmed my nerves, but getting it hooked up was causing me heart problems. Eventually we came up with a simple solution. We did what we needed to do to fix the problem. Our system now drains through a pipe under the floor until it finds an opening outside into the parking lot and follows lower elevations to the city street. From there, it finds easy access to the street drains. Problem solved. No permit needed, but the water is still going into the city's system. At least that knowledge releases some of my tension.

A tranquil pond

After we had the drain issue solved, we created a ring of light to add to the tranquil atmosphere of our bubbling, three-tiered fishpond. This beautiful, stress-free, no-taxes-allowed environment resulted in our employees taking ownership of the space. They even named the fish in the pond, although there were such strong opinions about fish names that this did cause some brief periods of tension. But the calming waters soothed the debate. We added to the scene by hanging colorful birds and butterflies above the pond. Finally, we installed a grade-A filtering and oxygen system so the fish would also have a tension-free home!

We are all challenged, but who wants to waste time worrying? We have to find what calms us down so that we can let go of our worries and be our best. We often call that "being in the moment." If we don't get there, we are just wasting our time. This fishpond has been a great help to me. Find what will help you. And do it before taxes increase!

Free Tax Calculator

OK, this is a refrain for me, but please consider the following. We are taxed on what we build, what we buy, what we sell, what we use at work, what we drink, when we travel, and when we die. Sometimes people don't see this whole picture. So, I have created a little tax reminder to keep us all better informed. It shows you how much every one of the candidates is going to tax your family. That is right; whomever you vote for, you will still be taxed until you bleed green as every last dollar is squeezed from your income. Enough is enough. By listing all the taxes we incur, we can analyze our true-taxed percentage of income and life. This should be a mandatory exercise for every high school senior. They should be asked to do a case study by methodically examining their family taxes over a 30-day period. It's an eye opener into adulthood.

It's surreal when you remember we left British rule to avoid taxes! I bring this up in this chapter, because I believe there is much waste in government. My money is my time, and the government keeps taking it from me. Of course, as I write this, there are lots of proposals to change tax laws, but I predict taxes will remain high.

Sometimes it seems that love of nation has been translated as taxes of nation. Here is a little reminder of all the ways we get to show the love.

How Do I Tax Thee, Let Me Count the Ways

1. Federal tax. Everybody's favorite! Note: increasing up to 39.5% of your taxable income.

2. Social Security and Medicare tax. Everybody gets in on this one for at least 7.5%. Small Business owners pay to the tune of 15.3%. That'll keep you whistling.

3. Sales tax. Pay your favorite state up to 7.25% more than your purchase price.

4. Water tax. That's right; you don't just pay your bill, you pay taxes on your bill. Plus, if you add employees to your business, you win an increased rate since each usage amount has a higher tax rate.

5. Death tax. Also known as the estate tax. It currently doesn't affect you unless you are worth at least $5.4 million. But, if you have made it to that milestone, 40% of your estate goes to the government when you die. Consider that, next time you hear that the rich don't pay taxes. The death tax takes money out of circulation forever, which reduces future taxes from future profits, while the government spends it all in the first year.

6. Life Insurance tax. If you are lucky enough to have your employer provide a high-value life-insurance policy, surprise, you'll pay taxes on that benefit, because it becomes part of your income!

7. Travel tax. There are lots of ways to pay! For every gallon of gas, the federal government gets 18.4¢, and if it is diesel, 24.4¢. Truckers particularly like that deal. Purchase a car and pay a registration fee up to $500. Drive over a bridge, or down a nice stretch of road, and get to pay a toll of 50¢ to $30. Boy oh boy, that adds up if it's part or your route to work, and you can double dip by taking the same route home. Makes you want to run away and stay at a hotel, surprise! Hotel taxes make travel more

fun. Welcome to St. Louis, where it costs up to 17.7% just to book the room.

8. Property tax. You get to pay to keep your house and land! If you don't pay, the government takes it all. This is especially comforting when you are retired and on a fixed income.

9. Utility tax. Pull out your magnifying glass and you'll find hidden taxes in your phone bill, cable bill, gas and electric bill. The fun never ends.

10. Federal Real Estate tax. It is at 3.8% for the profit on a high-value property transaction. You have to make more than $250,000 on the sale before you incur this tax. Don't worry; it is just for the rich. Think of it as a possible reward tax for your dream house. Oh you're rich? Well, rumor has it that you don't pay taxes, and anyway, this isn't even 4% of the deal.

11. Local Income tax. Take pride in your town and give 2-4% of all your earnings to city hall. If you work in more than one municipality, you often get to pay multiple places every year!

12. Grocery Bag tax. A boring 7¢ in Chicago, but an exciting 10¢ each in Boulder.

13. State Income tax. You almost forgot, didn't you? The percentage varies by state, but this is your chance to pay up to 13% of your income to the state of California!

14. Health Insurance tax. This one is built into the high cost of purchasing insurance premiums. It's best described as a method of making money for unscrupulous attorneys. Think of it as a "killer cost for business." Health insurance is so expensive it is literally closing companies. You get to see the source of this tax every time you see an ad on TV, or a billboard, suggesting litigation!

15. Marriage License tax. You'll love this one for the rest of your

life. Turns out the vow of unending love is really a metaphor for taxes!

16. Liquor tax. After looking at all the ways we are taxed, who doesn't need a drink? You have to admit, that's just good planning on the government's part.

Permission Granted to Copy Your Friends

Join me on a deep dive looking at the practices of a company designed to save other companies time and money. If knowledge is power, I am about to share some powerful information that can make or break a company. Once again, this is not just about my situation; it's about every business in the United States, and even beyond. I am speaking about Dun & Bradstreet (D&B), which advertises itself as the world's leading source for commercial information and insight on businesses. It grosses billions of dollars ever year. Dealing with this company has been a huge waste of my time and money.

After many years of D&B inaccurately depicting our business' financial strength, I decided to take some action to protect my company's reputation. My goal was to eliminate lost business from the distribution of erroneous and outright false information. I consider D&B's actions an example of "business terrorism" against our business and other small businesses unable to protect themselves without paying "bribery" monies to D&B. We sent a letter to our valued business partners.

In our letter, we explained that D&B generates unsubstantiated reports and uses algorithms that have never been verified. They refuse to share how they arrive at their conclusions. Our business CPI is healthy financially, but you wouldn't know it by looking at the D&B reports. CPI has audited financials, strong bank and trade references, and recommendations from our largest suppliers.

Why should I have to fight to prove that we are a legitimate and healthy company? It is obvious that we are, but D&B continues to put out reports to the contrary, and I have been cold-called, shaken-down, and extorted to purchase one of D&B's

packages with the promise to clean up my firm's profile in their database. After the letter to our clients went out, some of our partners informed us that they, the federal government for example, are mandated to pay for D&B reports as part of their supplier-vetting process. This causes additional work for CPI, to prove the D&B reports as false, to ensure we are awarded these specific contracts. It is not just my company that suffers the expense. These D&B reports purchased by our government are very costly.

Their end objective as told to me by one of their senior officers is to replace the social security numbering system with a worldwide D&B numbering system. Have you read anything in 2017 about the Equifax debacle over social security numbers? Yeah, I don't think we want D&B handling the numbering system for the world! Actually, I don't want them doing anything.

As a taxpayer, I think the amount of tax dollars invested in D&B's reports is a huge waste of resources. Per the Federal Procurement Database, awards with a total contract value of $798,512,685 were issued to D&B for these reports and use of D&B's numbering systems since 1978. That's the equivalent of an annual investment of $15,147,246. Over the last 20 years, it would require approximately 5,000 unlucky taxpayers to pay $10, 594 per year to fund these expenditures. In recent years, our government has spent tens of millions of dollars more on D&B products.

Talk about a headache and a waste of time.

Hey! I'm the guy who built the racehorse algorithm in college to pay off his tuition. I'm the guy who built the algorithm at IBM to predict our district office sales revenue. I know a thing or two about this, and D&B's system is faulty.

Basically, they want you to pay them to insure your reports are positive.

Revenge of the Nerds— Memorable Moment #38

I am not done with D&B yet, but don't worry, the chapter is almost over. Forced to endure the endless attack by D&B's publication of chicanery reports, sold to both federal government agencies and commercial businesses, I was left with being bullied and treated as an outcast and misfit. I was forced to either play ball or challenge extortion, but I found another way. I saw the movie, "Revenge of the Nerds." Lewis Skolnick, Betty Childs, and Dudley "Booger" Dawson were attending school and being bullied and treated as outcasts and misfits. They mustered their strength and resolved to fight back for their peace of mind and self-respect. I decided to do the same.

On July 31, 2000, I bought one share of Dun & Bradstreet stock. This got me their annual report, one vote for new board members, and as I recall, a quarterly dividend of about 19¢. In 2005 they asked me to sell my share. Why would I give up this commanding position? I smiled every time I imagined what it cost to process the dividend check every quarter.

I have two advantages in receiving the cash versus a partial stock reinvestment. 1) They had to process 37¢ (growing dividend) and also pay for postage, and 2) I never need to worry that I forgot to get my wife a present when I could always put this dividend check in my wife's card. Eventually my long position of one share got me a second share with their stock split. My last distribution was 74¢.

The annual report gets me easy access to board member names, compensation, and other strategic information. I also take voting for new board members with a thoughtful, determined, and sincere responsibility. That's why my first write-in vote was Charles Ponzi. I often wondered if anyone counting the votes knows he lived from March 3, 1882, to January 18, 1949, so even if I got him elected, he would have to stay underground. Another favorite write-in candidate I voted for was Bernie Madoff. I also think Pewee Herman would be a nice addition to the board.

In 2017 I requested a paper proxy for the annual meeting. Forty days after my second request, and five days after the annual meeting, I received my proxy card. They are slime. I sent my vote in late with a written complaint, but received no answer.

On a serious note, watch out for Paydex, SER, or other D&B products because they do actually remind me of a Ponzi scheme. A red flag goes up for me when I see a fraud disguised as a legitimate information report, and that is D&B's specialty.

OK, we'll waste no more time on this, but knowing what I have shared could potentially save you lots of time and money makes me feel good.

Business Travel

Travel has been a necessary evil in my life. I feel like I have wasted way too much time getting from here to there. Let me share some thoughts about these memorable times. Much of it involves airplane, or jet travel, which of course we do to save time, but it comes at a cost.

Narrower seats, more rows—my company's CPI Journal reported that frequent flyer Jeff Botkins fidgeted nervously as the man seated next to him coughed continuously. Botkins remarked, "Putting you closer to your neighbor does increase the threat of germs if the person does have a cold." Yeah, I'd have to agree with that little pearl of wisdom. Save time and get sick is not the trade we want to make.

There's no way around it; there will always be an excuse to travel. Here are some moments for the young to look forward to, and the old to fondly recall. On every airplane ride there is always something that makes us appreciate time. Usually, it is that moment when you think, "I can't wait for this to be done." Here are some of my favorite airplane people and situations:

- The Uncontainable—requires all of his seat and one-third of your seat. Learn how to set reasonable limits of time on your space.

- The Talker—dominates a conversation with their blatant self-image and family history and opinions about the state of the country and their recent experience at a Chinese restaurant and their new socks and haircut.

- The Knee Defender—when you try to recline, they'll knee your seat until you're upright.

- The Animal Lover—believes you should share your space with their cute little "Mr. Friskers," and learn about his recent loose bowel experience after eating a dirty diaper.

- The Wiggle Room Index—the distance between the edge of your khaki pants, or dress, and the edge of the overalls sitting next to you.

- The Flirt—says I am so glad I've gotten to sit next to you, because you are the best listener and your eyes shine like the moon, and you smell really good, and yes, I would like another drink if you're buying.

- The Food Choice—would you like dinner? What are my choices? Final response please, yes or no?

- The Business Card Exchange—never leave the plane without accepting the business card of all those sitting near you, and the guy three rows back, and a big thank you to whoever invented recycling bins.

- The Sneeze—when your pale white companion coats your face with sneeze mist, expect 21-days of quarantine before returning to work. In the meantime, try not to breathe oxygen into your lungs, but if you do, expel it as soon as you can.

- Your Flight is Delayed—this is airline speak for your departure time of 1:05 p.m. will be incrementally added to in 30-minute segments until you actually depart at 8:35 p.m. Please stay near the gate and don't even think about getting something to eat.

- The Last Flight Today—sorry your flight has been canceled.

TSA—Touch, Squeeze, Arrest

After spending the night away from your comfy bed, and getting up at dawn to try and catch your flight, you realize you're going through security one more time. This airport doesn't recognize that your last pat down was so thorough, that you only need it repeated once every five years. If the passenger ahead of you is wearing an unusually decorative shirt, such as one monogrammed like this, "I can't see London, and I can't see France, unless TSA sees my underpants," move to another line to avoid further delays.

My Registry Hotel Room

Hotel staffs are usually very attentive, concerned, and mindful of your needs. Here's an example. On a recent stay, I returned to my room after dinner and found this note, "I am sorry I could not turn your bed down because your clothes and luggage were on the bed. Good Night!" Confucius said, "The one who is afraid to touch suitcase, must not touch pillow."

Trade Shows

In my Company's first years, to save money I shared a booth with a business acquaintance at the annual Comdex show in Las Vegas. The first year I learned that even if you had no discretionary funding, the unions were not interested in cutting you any slack. From the moment we first tried to enter the convention hall with a few boxes, we were at odds with the union.

A union representative advised against us trying to deliver our boxes to our booth and demanded we pay him a small ransom, and he would deliver our packages the 20 or so feet to our booth. Not knowing what to do in the face of what we thought was clearly extortion, we immediately came up with a 3-part plan. It worked like a charm. Feel free to use it.

1. Wait 30 minutes.

2. Tell the union supervisor we wanted a worn rug replaced in our booth. Pray that would keep the staff busy and distracted.

3. Move quickly to get our boxes and other gear to our booth.

During this show, Vegas hotel rooms were at a premium, but I got rooms in various hotels through barter. As mentioned earlier, barter deals were my bridge to becoming an entrepreneur. Through a contact, I had met a man I will call "Hubbub." He was a regular on the strip in Vegas. He got comped rooms, meals, and shows. In those days, that was standard practice without lengthy time requirements for play at the tables, as long as you exceeded the average wager. Hubbub made the rounds to various hotels and was comped at each one. He traded us those rooms with the only requirement being that he had to sign in and get the room key, and we weren't allowed any room changes. I saved thousands of dollars in hotels and expenses for our week at Comdex. We traded Hubbub some of our product for the rooms, and he converted the product into cash.

The first year it was easy to get volunteers to work the show. "Free trip to Vegas" and I had more volunteers than I needed. The second year was a harder sell since word got out I worked my staff the full 10-hour day while the trade show was open. A featured Vegas "show" was the only fringe benefit, unless you include the valuable lessons learned from losing money at the tables and slots. The Vegas trade shows were a good move for my new company. I was able to promote my business and was one of the few vendors who left Vegas with a profit. We sold right off the floor and made sure all the products we displayed were sold with pick-up on the last day of the show. This also solved the union problem; we were able to leave without their involvement. Time is precious and those were good times to build our business.

As we grew, we started attending other business shows. On one occasion, I sent a sales team to meet prospects at a local business trade show. Our neighbor in the next booth was trying to get attention by using a strip tease theme. They had a double booth with two women giving unusual promotional objects. One was a sample bottle of White Lightning, whiskey, and the other looked like a matchbook, but it didn't have matches in it. It was personal protection in case you got the itch to get lucky that night.

I pulled our team; this was a no-win situation for us. The strip-tease double-wide booth was overshadowing us. It was a total embarrassment for our employees as well as most visitors attending the show. Afterwards, I sent a letter to the show's sponsor complaining of their lack of discretion and our neighbor's inappropriate display. I demanded a full refund.

The show's management offered a 50% credit against next year's booth rental cost. What kind of customer relations is that? We will never again attend that trade show. I sent copies of my letter to every vendor we knew who also displayed at that show. We had our time wasted at that show. I wanted to make sure others didn't suffer the same fate. As you know, I like the Scottish proverb, "A good tale never tires in the telling."

The Little RMA (Return Material Authorization) Refund That Wouldn't Close

I want to finish this chapter with a couple of brief stories about working with the vendors that we buy our product from. This first story is a reminder that if someone burns you once, cut ties with them before they burn you twice. Otherwise you are just letting them waste your time.

After months of working with a challenging customer, we were finally able to close vendor books on a 9-month return/replacement process problem. To complete our transaction with our customer, we needed a total of 5 vendors to remit their paperwork; all but one vendor closed their returns promptly.

The last vendor was digging in and refusing to respond to requests for a $396 refund. In April of 2014, we began emailing the vendor's president as well as accounting staff requesting a refund. It was not until June that the vendor replied stating a refund was not due. Keep in mind this response only came after a threat to remove the vendor from our approved vendor list and take them to small claims court (for the $396).

We promptly provided evidence of our payment for both the original product that was returned and the replacement product that was shipped out. At this time, the general manager of their firm stepped in, and after completing a full account reconciliation, he found the refund was due. Ten days later, a check was issued to us, after which we removed the vendor from our approved vendor's list. The last thing we needed was to keep working with these guys that had just wasted hours and hours of our time over $396.

Two days later the vendor asked if they could take our New Mexico team out to lunch. Wow, really? I bet that would cost about $396! And I know it takes months and months to get something like that approved. I politely advised that of course they could take the sales team out for lunch, but the sales team would no longer be able to purchase from them. I encouraged their general manager to always to be aware of Allison Raul's quote, "Into every life a little rain must fall, but I think someone's mistaken me for Noah." NO COMMUNICATION SINCE.

The second story is working with vendors who understand business and help my firm to make the best use of our time. As new products come out, the manufacturer reps want to show my sales staff the new products. This is an on-going process and can be rather time consuming. And frankly, not everything they show is going to fit into our lineup.

I came up with the idea of "Lunch and Learn." We gather our staff together during their lunch break. The manufacturer's sales rep comes to us and provides lunch. This helps our people to want to be there for the next sales pitch, because they are getting a free lunch out of it without leaving the office. The sales reps are happy because they have a captive audience. Everyone wins.

Time is precious. Let's not waste it.

CHAPTER THIRTEEN

Does Not Exist.

We removed it after several readers of the rough draft were lost in the intensity of the pages!

OK, here is a riddle.

Q: What do you call the deathly fear of the number 13?

A: Triskaidekaphobia. (Unfortunately those who have it usually can't pronounce it!)

We now take the elevator to the 14th floor; I mean, 14th chapter.

CHAPTER FOURTEEN

Calabria's Law Number 10

When a reasonable offer to buy is refused…

…Lower it

I N BUSINESS THERE ARE CONSEQUENCES. IT IS KIND OF LIKE PHYS-ics. Remember, I have a degree in physics. We all know Newton's third law, or at least we could look it up on the Internet. "To every action there is an equal and opposite reaction." This is all about force. Things happen in pairs. When one object hits another, the size of the force of the first object equals the size of the force of the second object.

From a business perspective, when people treat you right, you treat them right. If people treat you poorly, it doesn't mean you have to react inappropriately, but you do need to react with equal force, for instance, cutting ties with them very quickly.

Now in my business, we have to buy a lot of products. If we make a reasonable offer to purchase some product, and the vendor refuses to sell us the product at that price, there are consequences from that situation. So if later that same vendor wants to sell to us, we will lower the amount we are willing to pay for it. If we don't, there is no leverage, no incentive for the future to accept our first bid.

In good business, there always has to be a reaction after an action. If you are sitting under a tree and getting hit by apples, you had better move, even if you are smart enough to know that gravity is at work.

Gold at the End of Rainbows Over America

In 1984 I met Philip Hwang, a Utah State University graduate born in North Korea. He had run a business producing cathode-ray-tube monitors for arcade games since 1975. Philip told me his story of leaving North Korea on a riverboat when he was very young. He landed in South Korea and became a house worker for a US military captain stationed there. Through this contact, he eventually ended up in the Midwest of the United States.

He was a hard worker and excellent student. After graduation from college, he moved to Silicon Valley and started his business, TeleVideo. He was soon producing personal computers, based on the Z80 processor. The rapidly changing technology quickly made his unit obsolete, so he started an effort to build a MS DOS compatible personal computer with an Intel© chip.

Out of funds, he tried to get the money from venture capital investors to continue the work on his new product, but he was unsuccessful. He offered the majority position of his stock to the investors, but they turned him down. Desperate, he went back to South Korea without even enough money for cab fare. He felt he had to continue his journey to raise the funds so that he could continue his product development. He found an investor and returned to the US. As he closed in on his second-generation product announcement, he again ran out of funds. This time he was two weeks behind on payroll. Philip told me he mortgaged his home to pay his employees. Finally, he weathered all the developmental hardships and announced his new product. It was a huge success and the rest is history. His company sold millions of computers and video terminals.

An interesting story followed. One of the venture-capital investors came back to Philip and asked to invest in his TeleVideo company. Philip smiled at me and explained what he said to the investor. Whereas during the tough times he had been willing to give the investor 90% of his company, now for that same amount he offered the investor only one-tenth of one percent of his company. That is how it goes in business.

Out of curiosity and because he had been so forthcoming with me, I asked Philip how much he was worth. After all, in my business of selling computers, I was in the presence of a superstar. I couldn't help but wonder how much the guy who couldn't afford cab fare was now worth. He refused my request, but said that he had many, many millions in savings and no longer needed to work. He could live off his interest earnings. Memorable Moment #18 for me would be able to live solely off dividend income.

I left our lunch enthusiastic that one could still get rich in America. Tell your friends and relatives to work hard and put in the effort. To every action there is an equal and opposite reaction. That effort breaks down barriers and opens up new possibilities. Know what you are trying to do and go after it. Remember what author Susan Ertz once said, "Millions long for immortality who do not know what to do with themselves on a rainy Sunday afternoon."

The Start

Since I have written about Philip Hwang's business beginnings, let me spend some more time on my humble story. My start as an entrepreneur began in 1985 when I lost my job with Otrona and found myself desperate in the unemployment line. I wasn't sure we could pay our mortgage, and I felt humiliated buying food for my family with my unemployment check. All this happened just before Christmas. The only immediate job possibility was fifteen hundred miles to the east and that was too far for my family. My only hope seemed to be to get a little consulting work and bridge the gap to my next job. Our family had just moved west a little more than a year earlier, and no one in my family was willing to uproot again so soon. Christmas that year was a little like the poor Cratchit family in the Dickens tale. Our families sent what they could to help carry us over.

Maybe Barter

I wasn't going to take a job 1,500 miles away and commute back and forth on weekends, and I really didn't like the idea of becoming a consultant. I needed something that was a better deal. One day I had the thought, "Maybe I could make some money by barter. I could trade goods for more goods, and string together a series of deals that would eventually make my family some money."

I had almost no interest in being a consultant. But "barter" got my heart pumping in a good way. I would get people what they wanted, and help my family at the same time. My thoughts that day jumpstarted my dream to become an entrepreneur—Memorable Moment #56.

For centuries, countries would trade each other their surplus goods. While thinking about bartering as a way to survive, I came up with an idea. Admittedly, it seemed like a crazy idea, but I thought it just might work. I imagined buying a large number of computers and trading them to Boeing for a plane and some cash. Yup, you heard me right; I was going to trade computers for a plane! I would then take the plane and trade it to an airline for tickets and some cash. Yup, again you heard me right; I was going to trade that plane for some airline tickets! By the way, this answers the age-old question, "Which came first, the airplane or the airline ticket?"

Making any sense yet?

No, I didn't think so.

Then finally I was going to use those tickets to get computers, plus some extra, much-needed cash. Seriously, in my entrepreneurial innocence, I really thought I could pull this off. As my excitement grew, I imagined this as a done deal. I expanded my plan to add another high-value product that I could easily trade, but it had to be available at a steep discount.

That additional product would be advertising. If I could pre-purchase full-page flight magazine ads for a substantial discount, I could leverage surplus product buys with the advertising credits. Finally, I thought distressed or end-of-life products could be resold below published list pricing for cash and that would complete my business plan.

I started searching for a trade partner. Roger Arnold, business and economics writer and lecturer, describes barter as a double coincidence of wants between a buyer and a seller. My first step was to identify available surplus products and become a buyer. Step two, become a seller of my product to someone else as the buyer. I had an action plan.

HP Printers

About this same time, HP had just announced a second-generation ink jet printer. This left a short-term demand for its first-generation ink jet. Seizing on this opportunity while looking for surplus buying opportunities, I identified that my former employer, Olivetti, had an excess supply of these first-generation printers with their label pasted over the HP name. In the industry, that's sometimes referred to as "private labeling." It's the practice of selling someone else's product as your product. I purchased the 300 printers I found in Olivetti's warehouse at liquidated pricing and moved them in less than 30 days for a quick profit.

Imagine my customer's dumbfounded look as I pealed the Olivetti labels off to show these were original HP printers. I paid cash for the printers and I sold the printers for cash. It proved that I could make money with my business plan of buying and selling distressed product. My next plan was to try different options to purchase surplus products.

My second transaction was a little more complicated. I found a company trying to get out of the printer business. Their books had a $78 per unit cost per printer with a listed sale value of $98 per unit. Their remaining inventory of 5,000 units would hurt their bottom line if they agreed to my offer of $39 per unit. I found an advertising agency in New York City who pre-bought airline magazine ads at $45,000 per page. The retail price tag was $60,000 for one page. The company trying to get out of the printer business had an advertising budget for the next year and hadn't used airline ad pages in the past, so they qualified for credits. It was a perfect match.

Through a deal mixing cash and advertising credits, I was able to move the printers for this company. This allowed their books to show a breakeven transaction and they were able to reduce their book credits with discounts applied against the listed advertising cost in one year. They were thrilled. I netted about $35,000 in this transaction (sold each printers for $51). My plan to use advertising in the deal proved successful.

Alas, I never got my hands on a plane, but after this second deal, my plans went sky high.

There's always an opportunity to make a profit. So says the old Polish Proverb: "When opportunity knocks, some people are in the backyard looking for four-leaf clovers." My opportunity got me off the unemployment line—Memorable Moment #54. What a great day that was! I accomplished two achievements simultaneously as I became a full-fledged entrepreneur and got off the unemployment line. That was better than finding a four-leaf clover.

Barter Broker Kingpin Talks!

Joe Calabria of J. C. Market Consulting in Boulder has endeavored once again to explain to us what a barter broker transaction is...other than the chief way Joe makes a living.

It seems that a vendor finds himself overstocked with a certain item. He sells it to Calabria's firm, which then sells it in a way that doesn't disrupt the vendor's existing distribution channels—and prices.

Thus, a thousand printers may find their way into the hands of a Fortune 500 company through direct sales, at a fraction of the going retail price.

In these days of computer-industry oversupply, Calabria's firm is making deals you wouldn't believe, and we can't talk about. But Joe will, if you call him at 530-

An article about my work

As my business was being launched, a write-up appeared in the Value Added Reseller Magazine describing my work. This fulfilled a dream of mine of being publicly recognized— Memorable Moment #90. This was a great time of meeting some of my long sought-after goals.

Dual Marketing

Also in 1986 another deal appeared on my horizon. I came in contact with a software company utilizing a dual marketing technique. It was selling its retail-packaged products for one price, and at the same time selling a discounted white-box version for system integrators for bundling purposes. In both versions, the higher the number of authorized users, the greater the price.

Upgrades were possible with the return of the original registration disk in either version. Every upgraded package was sent out in original retail packaging. The cost of the upgrade plus the white box version was less than 50% of the new retail-package cost, if purchased as a first-time buyer. The opportunity to make a quick profit would be upgrading the white-box version from a user license for 5 users to a new license for 50 users. The upgraded product and its license came in brand new retail packaging, but at half the price of buying the retail-packaged product.

My contact had sources available to get the white-box version and upgrade it from the manufacturer. He quickly became a millionaire selling me the retailupgraded packages, which I was able to market directly to the largest authorized distributor for this product. That distributor used its price advantage to increase its market share by selling at a price below its competitors.

Everyone made money in the deal including me. OK, here is little lesson in business. Those who excel may not be the most intelligent overall. The ones who excel may not be the ones that study the hardest, or the ones that graduated with the highest GPA. We all know that I didn't, and it is pretty clear that I am not a genius. Here is what I do know: the people who excel are ones who learn how to think and execute on a few important and basic principles. These people apply these basic business principles to a variety of different situations and this often results in success.

We could summarize my story here with six important elements of business. These basics principles include:

- A product to sell

- Method to sell it

- Profit to make from it

- Buyer for it

- Know when to raise your price

- Know when to lower your price

Put those basics together and you've got a deal. Even though I wasn't a genius, my business quickly grew, because I was good at the basics.

My Flight to Dallas

Now let's continue this business lesson. When you have a good thing going, you look to replicate it, or better yet, magnify it.

A large corporation had purchased thousands of software upgrades and didn't need all of them. They must have miscalculated the final number of licensed software products they owned. The software vendor refused their request to return the extra upgrades. As it turned out, that software company had sent the upgrades not as upgrade-only packages, but instead as new product in retail packages with new unregistered serial numbers. Now the corporation that had bought these upgrades had purchased so many of them that they were given a steep discount on the price compared to buying a single unit.

Stay with me here. The basics were all falling into place. The upgrades were all in retail packaging. Unable to return the unused units, the corporation went looking for a broker to help move the excess. The broker found me. So I had the product, the seller, and the potential for profit all set. I got on the phone to find a buyer. Within a week, I had buyers for the whole shipment.

I went ahead with the deal. This was a major purchase for me and I wanted to make sure everything went smoothly. I flew to Dallas where the exchange of goods was to take place. Once in the city, I arrived at the corporation with three large freight trucks and a certified check for the broker who found the deal. My plan was to first inspect the product, then second to pay the broker for the product, and third to ship the product around the country. I had already pre-sold the inventory because of the potential financial risk.

While I was on location at the corporation headquarters, the broker I was partnering with received a call from the software manufacturer threatening legal action. I immediately recognized this transaction was at risk. It was a good thing I was there or the whole deal could have easily gone south.

I suggested to the corporation that the solution would be to eliminate the broker from the sales transaction. The corporation held title to the product and was able to sell it to me as an unrestricted sale. The selling corporation didn't want the broker shut out of his profit. I agreed, and said I was able to pay a finder's fee to the broker. I guaranteed I would wire the money at the original agreed-to price and that I would pay the broker the difference between his agreed-to purchase cost and my agreed-to purchase price as a finder fee. The corporation agreed and gave me a bill of sale. I wired the broker his money. We got the product loaded on the trucks, and we were on the road within two hours. This deal, and so many like it, was not the product of genius at work. It was the product of business basics, and paying attention to simple details, and staying abreast of changing situations. In the end everyone made money.

As it turned out, though, the broker made two times the profit I made on this transaction. Some people might have gone through the roof when they found that out, not me, though. My philosophy was, and still is, symbolized by the "equal sign." This is my Memorable Moment #28. The way I see it, if I am satisfied with my side of the equation, the other side doesn't matter to me. A deal is a deal. I have my criteria for profit, and when I get those criteria met, I'm happy. Let me add that this isn't just about business. This is a formula for happiness in life!

This is why when I make a reasonable offer to purchase and it is refused, I lower my offer. I pay attention to my side of the equal sign. Keep this philosophy and you will stay happy based on your criteria, not by what everyone else is getting or expecting. Trust in yourself. It is a basic principle of business and life. You don't have to be a genius to see that it is the sure bet.

CHAPTER FIFTEEN

Calabria's Law Number 11

Soar as rapidly as possible…

…To achieve a longer glide pattern

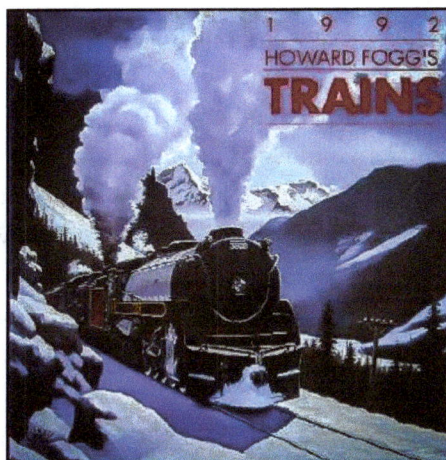

I T IS SAID THAT TIMING IS EVERYTHING. IN OUR LIVES, SOMETIMES we only get one chance. When the time is at hand, we need to seize the opportunity. There is a temptation in our lives and our careers to say to ourselves that there is plenty of time to succeed. We don't have to rush things along. While there can be wisdom in that sentiment, I believe there is no time like the present.

When opportunity knocks, answer the door. Even more than that, seek out opportunity. Don't wait for tomorrow. Make your dreams come true as rapidly as possible. Climb as high as you can so that you can glide through the heights.

When you achieve your dreams, you are not done. New dreams come to you. There is always new hope for tomorrow.

Train of Life—
Memorable Moment #27

As I think about my life and my career, certain times stand out. One such time was when my wife and I left Reading, PA. We had lived there since I graduated from college. It was where we had started a family, and where I had had some success as a salesman with IBM. It takes effort and guts to leave. Many people stay in one place their whole life. They don't stay because they are happy. They stay because it is all they know. We left, because I thought it was time to climb the corporate ladder. My life's train was leaving its first station.

Often I think too many people ride the train of life with a feeling like the Kingston Trio song about Tom Dooley. "Hang down your head Tom Dooley. Hang down your head and cry."

These people only see miles of life rolling by, never looking either forward at the engine that is pulling them, or past the caboose at what they are leaving behind. They might curse their life for what it was, just a blur passing by too quickly.

I want to see the train from above. I want to fly high and see what is going on below. I want to have a clear picture of what is up ahead on the tracks.

The immense power of a coal train is a strong metaphor for life. I talked about this earlier and how it became a theme of our offices. I sometimes think of my life as the energy from burning coal. The wheels race along the track. The wind, rushing at the engine, sometimes frees particles of coal before they are consumed by flames. I think of these coal particles as opportunities. They are in the air, and at any given time you can get a burst of power from one to push you to your next destination. I try to take each opportunity that comes to me, because I never know which one will be the best or even the last. The worst-case scenario for me is just watching life go by. Don't let that happen to you.

Why not look forward to the experiences life holds? On the November page of the 1992 Trains calendar by Howard Fogg, there is a picture titled, "Teamwork on Black Fork Grande." This picture shows seven huge H-9-class engines attacking the 3 percent eastward grade in Blackwater Canyon toward the summit at Thomas, West Virginia. These heavy coal trains required one engine per ten cars. This train certainly generated many particles of coal (opportunities) on its hard climb to the summit.

Putting this metaphor aside. Great things are being done all the time. As great people do great things, little particles of opportunity are all around us. Don't look down at your feet. Look from above. Look forward. Find something in your path and climb as fast as you can. My wife and I left Reading on the train of our life. You don't have to leave where you live, but you do have the opportunity to live where you dream. The tracks will show you where to climb. You can do it with endurance, passion, and enthusiasm. I'm bringing yesterday's memories and tomorrow's vision into my first book.

As Paul Harvey, the great radio commentator, once stated, "I have never seen a monument erected to a pessimist."

Completed My Military Obligation ASAP— Memorable Moment #23

I served in the Army Reserves from 1967-1972. By 1969, at the peak of the U.S. involvement in Vietnam, more than 500,000 U.S. military personnel were involved in this conflict. More than 3 million people, including 58,000 Americans, were killed during the war. The U.S. sprayed more than 19 million gallons of Agent Orange, the most commonly used defoliant mixture, to clear selected jungle areas. This mixture caused serious health issues to U.S. servicemen, and the people of Vietnam.

My unit was on stand-by alert for the full length of my service commitment. Somehow we never got deployed. We trained two weekends and two Thursdays every month. We also trained with two-week encampments under improvised shelter, or no shelter at all, in mountain regions loaded with snakes and poison ivy. Although I realize these hardships were nothing compared to those of our men and women in Vietnam, they did provide for some interesting stories and life-lessons. And hey, I wanted them to be over as fast as possible so I could soar in another direction.

Being the Catholic soldier that I was, one Sunday morning during one of our two-week stays, I was awaiting a ride to attend mass. I had gone home the night before and had just arrived back at base. I was hitching a ride on the back of an open truck, which was not luxury transportation. I promised myself to try to remember that whenever given the choice I would always opt for limousines over Army trucks. Do I want to ride in a Jeep now? No, no, no! After I fulfilled my military obligation, I never owned or rode in a Jeep again.

While in the mountains, we didn't have a library, probably because we were supposed to be training instead of reading. Yet, I had a little time so I decided to improve my mind by reading whatever I could get my hands on. Now the only available reading materials in camp were magazines such as Playboy, and I just happened to have one with me. I must admit that I did feel guilty sitting on my duffle bag roadside paging through such a magazine, while waiting for my ride to church. However, the excited heartbeats of my guilty pleasure were quickly replaced by heart-stopping fear as the head of a snake peered above the top of my magazine, seemingly ready to strike. Was this the snake from the Garden of Eden?

I could hear the hair on my head whoosh through the wind as every strand stood straight up and came to full attention. In one swift motion, my right hand snagged my shovel out of my duffle bag and with my left foot forward I lunged away from the snake. I fell on to my backside and rolled over. The snake was lying on the Playboy magazine and flicking its tongue at me. I took another step backwards. It's beady black eyes burned through me. As far as I was concerned that snake could have the magazine, but I needed my duffle bag. I took a step forward and slashed my shovel on the ground. The snake charged toward me and I jumped to the side of the road. The snake slithered on and left me alone. I picked up my duffle bag and tossed the magazine into the ditch. I was sure someone would find it and think it was there lucky day, but not me.

For me that snake was the personification of evil. The Devil was coming after me. What was my life-lesson learned in the mountains of Pennsylvania that day? Don't be looking at Playboy on my way to church!

"To one who has faith, no explanation is necessary; to one without faith, no explanation is possible." –Thomas Aquinas, Philosopher and Theologian.

Sergeant

During basic training our barracks were at the bottom of a hill. Every time it rained, the water and mud would flow into our living quarters and make a mess of everything. It would then be our job to shovel out our entrance area and clean the place up.

After this had happened twice, I had the idea we could avoid a third occurrence if we took the time to inter-stack the sandbags near the bottom of the hill. This method could prevent the sandbags from collapsing and thus divert the runoff and the mud entering our living quarters. I told my sergeant about my great idea. I remember how he responded:

"I didn't ask for your suggestion, but I will respond to your comment. You're now on KP duty."

KP duty was the kitchen patrol, cutting apples, peeling potatoes, and washing dishes. I also got a good look at how the food was prepared and how unsanitary the kitchen staff was. If you had to use the toilet, it was much closer to use the nearby woods, and that didn't mean you needed to wash afterwards. There weren't a lot of spices, and the guys used to joke, "You have to add flavor however you can."

After my stint in KP, I never ate the prepared food again. All I would eat was bread, jam, and milk. The other food was truly disgusting.

Poison Ivy

Halfway through one of our two-week bivouacs, those times when we were in temporary shelter in the wilderness, nearly all the troops ended up with a severe case of poison ivy. Perhaps the reason this happened was the fact that our sergeant had put our camp right in the middle of a poison ivy paradise. The medical team traveled from the main fort to our camp to determine who had a medical emergency and needed to go back to the barracks for isolation and medical care. Depending on the severity, some stayed put in the camp while others were transported to receive more medical attention.

I, of course, was extremely careful around snakes, spiders, and poison ivy and consequently had only two tiny blisters, but I was desperate to get out of this area. I was praying that I could get out of there and an idea came to me. I lathered myself with Calamine lotion and wrapped my hands, wrists, and arms to conceal my silky-smooth, clear skin. I poured water on my wrappings to imitate the pus effect. I next put bandages on my face and rubbed some dirt on my lips.

There was a long line of soldiers waiting for their medical evaluations. I angled to the rear of the line shaking my arms, as if in pain. When they brought me into the tent, I told the nurse that I had it so bad she shouldn't come near me or she would catch it too. Seeing the wet gauze wrapped neatly around my arms and with Calamine lotion and Band-Aids on my face, her eyes widened. She had a look of pity as she gazed at my sorry sight. Then she noticed the inscription I wrote over the gauze wrap, "Transmission Covering Protection."

She immediately sent me back to the barracks. Once I was out of the bivouac, I bluffed my way through the medical attention until the week was over. My reward? No snakes, a hot shower, bread and jam from the mess hall, and most importantly, no more exposure to poison ivy. Whoever said prayer isn't just a Band-Aid? In my case, it sure helped. Always remember to pay attention and listen carefully, then take the opportunity to call for help if you need it. For me this was growing a miracle to get me out of the jungle and into the garden. It's my Memorable Moment #24.

Perhaps you wonder if I feel bad about being so creative? Not in the least. I hated that place. I still can't believe they put us in the middle of a poison ivy patch. There was no chance to suggest obvious corrections or helpful changes. It was a nightmare, and I was itching to work on my dreams, not on blistery skin.

"Things aren't always the way they seem from the outside," author Phil Nolan.

Soar With Wind Horse Power

In one of my upcoming chapters, I am going to explain the significance of some of the amazing and inspirational items I have collected and keep in my man cave office at my house. Here is a little sample of one of those things. We ship surplus computer components around the world. I asked my sales director, who was going on a business trip to China, to find me a replica of the famous Wind Horse.

The Wind Horse is an awesome symbol to soar as rapidly as possible. I am not a Buddhist, but I admire this concept. Here is some paraphrased information from a description I read in Shambhala: The Sacred Path of the Warrior by Chogyam Trungpa.

The Wind Horse is energy. If we let go of what we know, we can begin to sense something more in the world, something that is always available to us, and always self-renewing. No matter the circumstance, this energy is there for our benefit. It is a kind of basic goodness. This energy is called Wind Horse.

Imagine that the wind is your good fortune. It blows into your life every day. This wind brings us basic goodness. It is exuberant and brilliant. This basic goodness can be ridden. This is why it comes to be known as Wind Horse. On it, you can find tremendous power.

One must be totally in the present moment to ride the Wind Horse. It is not just about power. It is also about a feeling of stability. With the Wind Horse, confusion and depression slip away. This is about riding the energy of your life, and it is not only about movement, but also being practical and making good decisions. With the Wind Horse comes stability. After all, you have four legs to stand on! I don't know about you, but I love the idea of riding the wind.

In business, we have to be fast on our feet. We have to sense

The Wind Horse

what trends are in the air. We need mobility and endurance. We need to be stable and reliable. The Wind Horse is a symbol for all these things. For many people it is much more than that. My faith is different than Buddhist beliefs, but I still gain inspiration from the magnificent Wind Horse my sales manager brought back to me.

If you want to soar as rapidly as possible, surround yourself with reminders of the qualities you want to use to reach the heights in your dreams.

This replica of the Wind Horse is on display in my man cave office.

I Majored and Received a BS in Physics— Memorable Moment #4

OK, let me take you back to my college years. In many ways, this sets the stage for my success in life. When you consider my grade point average, it may be hard to believe, but read on and see what you think. On a warm, muggy Sunday afternoon in September 1961, I entered the hallowed confines of Aquinas Hall at Providence College and registered as a member of the Class of '65.

I averaged between 19 and 20 credit hours per semester, in courses such as General Physics II, Atomic Molecule Physics, Nuclear Physics I & II, and Mathematics of Physics and Engineering. After four years of strenuous, backbreaking, and exhausting study I learned:

- Don't LOOK at anything in the physics lab
- Don't TASTE anything in the chemistry lab
- Don't SMELL anything in the biology lab
- Don't TOUCH anything in a medical lab

Most importantly of all, I learned The First Law of Philosophy: For every philosopher, there exists an equal and opposite philosopher. And I learned The Second Law of Philosophy: They're both wrong.

Although I majored in physics, I was also required to take advanced courses in mathematics and chemistry. I never got a bonus question to help my GPA. Consequently, I was an easy target for my daughter to surpass my GPA. Some 28 years after I graduated, she graduated from Providence with a GPA double that of mine. As a student, I always wanted to get bonus questions that might up my test grade and my overall GPA. Could I have shined like the legendary student below who supposedly was given the following bonus question? You can find this story all over the Internet, and its origins go back to a humor piece by a scientist in the 1920s. I share it here, because it is one of my favorites. I have added a few of my own little touches.

Bonus Question: Is Hell exothermic (gives off heat) or endothermic (absorbs heat)?

Most students wrote proofs of their beliefs using Boyle's Law (gas cools when it expands and heats when compressed) or some variation. One student got his GPA boosted by writing the following:

"To answer this question, first, we need to know how the mass of Hell is changing in time. So we need to know the rate at which souls are moving into Hell and the rate at which they are leaving. I doubt many are leaving. I always heard it was a permanent home. I think that we can safely assume that once a soul gets to Hell, it will not leave. Therefore, no souls are leaving. As for how many souls are entering Hell, God only knows, but let's look at the different religions that exist in the world today. Most of these religions state that if you are not a member of their religion, you will go to Hell. Since there is more than one of these religions and since people do not belong to more than one religion, we can conclude that all souls go to Hell. Sorry if that is a disappointment to you, professor. With birth and death rates as they are, we can expect the number of souls in Hell to increase exponentially. Now, we look at the rate of change of volume in Hell because Boyle's Law states that for the temperature and pressure in Hell to stay the same, the volume of Hell has to expand proportionately as souls are added."

"This gives two possibilities:

1. If Hell is expanding at a slower rate than which souls are entering, then the temperature and pressure in Hell will increase until all Hell breaks loose.

2.   If Hell is expanding at a rate faster than the increase of souls, then the temperature and pressure will drop until Hell freezes over."

Pretty good so far, but this student took his thinking a bit further: "If I accept the postulate given to me by Teresa during my freshman year that, 'It will be a cold day in Hell before I sleep with you,' and take into account the fact that I slept with her last night, then number two must be true, and thus I am sure that Hell is exothermic and has already frozen over. The corollary of this theory is that since Hell has frozen over it follows that it is not accepting any more souls and is, therefore, extinct. So only Heaven is left, which indicates the existence of a divine being, which explains why, last night, Teresa kept shouting, 'Oh My GOD.'"

As the story goes, that student received an A+. I have this story in my book, not just because it is funny. It shows great creativity and innovation. Since my days as a college student, I have tried to incorporate these traits into all that I have done. More importantly, I am always looking to work with people and hire people who also demonstrate these qualities. If we are going to soar as rapidly as possible, creativity is a great way to climb.

While I didn't get extra credit while attending college, I did learn the intricate art of playing cards and losing money. As mentioned earlier, I enjoyed going to the horse track and with my winnings I paid off my college tuition debt. However, playing the horses proved easier than playing cards. It appears to me that the demon of bad luck follows a passionate card player. I am nothing, if not passionate.

During my first year at college, I quickly realized I could accomplish anything by midnight that upperclassmen accomplished by one o'clock, if I started my project an hour earlier. Smart, huh? One of the secrets of soaring as fast as you can is to start a little earlier than everyone else!

During that first year, I also started wearing my Fedora black hat. I became kind of a noticeable guy around campus. My friends thought I should run for Student Congress. I think they thought I would get some restrictive campus rules revoked, like no motorcycles in the dorm rooms. With the aid of my winning smile and help from Jim "Flash" Foley, who promoted my campaign by plastering my "Fedora" picture all over campus, I was elected to Student Congress—Memorable Moment #45.

*Yours truly on the famous Harkins Hall balcony
at Providence College: 1963*

One of my favorite accomplishments while a member of the Student Congress was sponsoring a bill to show cartoon films in conjunction with semester exams. Yes, sigh, that was my most memorable accomplishment! In my defense, this cartoon idea quickly became a tradition, which grew over time to be called "Cartoon Scream." The event took place during final exams in December and May. It was intended to be a harmless gathering to let off exam tensions by watching Bugs Bunny or Spiderman's Peter Parker.

The following year I ran as an underdog candidate against a senior-packed slate and was elected treasurer of the Student Congress—Memorable Moment #46. In retrospect, serving in the Student Congress helped get me nominated for the distinctive society of Who's Who Among Students in American Universities and Colleges 1964-1965. That was Memorable Moment #14. In addition to mentioning my student congress membership to feed my enormous ego, I also mention it because it taught me another life lesson: If you want to make things better in your life, get involved, and if possible, get involved as a leader, that way you can make things better for others, as well as for yourself.

My goal was to position myself so that I could create jobs. For me, college was a necessary step to actualize my dream to become a job creator, to own my own successful business, to be a recognized entrepreneur, to create a lifetime of memorable moments. With all the success I have experienced, it helps to keep Star Wars star Carrie Fisher's quote in mind, "You're not really famous until you're a Pez dispenser."

I had plans to run for Student Congress President the next year, but alas, the college had a C+ GPA requirement. I was close, but no dice. But hey, I didn't give up. That was when I perfected my racetrack algorithm. I also minored in math and became proficient in two languages…English and Profanity.

I'm just joking. I have never been proficient with English.

There is one more academic study I would like to pursue. Memorable Moment #88 is to complete the quantitative analysis of actresses with isotopes ranging from 32-24-32 to 36-25-35. My research probably requires me to attend at least one Victoria's Secret fashion show in person (with wife). I am sure it will become Memorable Moment #101.

The Bell Curve

Let me finish out this chapter with some thoughts on the bell curve. This curve represents my law and the importance of soaring as rapidly as possible to achieve a longer glide pattern.

My first experience with the symmetrical bell-shaped curve was when Dr. Robert Barrett graded my first nuclear physics test with a B+. I had scored a 22 out of a possible 200. Obviously, a score like that is absolutely terrible. I should have received an F-. It turned out though, he graded the test on a "curve." The mean (average) score on that test was considerably below 22. He gave the mean score the grade of "C." So my score of 22 out of a possible 200 put me toward the top of the class! I saved and framed the test. After all, you can't brag to your daughter about your grades without hard evidence. Memorable Moment #25 was scoring a B+ on a nuclear physics exam.

As the semester proceeded, more test scores were graded using the infamous bell curve. These were my best grades in all of college! Heck, looking at those grades, I should have been a nuclear physicist! I could have led the team at Three Mile Island, and been forever remembered as causing the greatest nuclear disaster in U.S. history. Upon further reflection, I now agree with Dr. Rick Yount, who wrote, "The bell curve is to education, what the rack is to interrogation. Both produce unreliable measures of truth."

Despite the inappropriate use of the bell curve in grading tests, many companies have allowed the bell curve to migrate into business as the standard for assessing employee performance. Using this method, your bad employees can receive positive evaluations in comparison to your terrible employees. Such a deal. Again, that is not what I think of as appropriate or reliable. Personally, I evaluate employee performance by an individual grading system, not off a company bell curve. This is not only to make sure I know when I have lots of underperforming employees, which by the way, I don't, but also to help me see when I have lots of over achieving employees, which by the way, I do!

The Industry Bell Curve

A bell curve can be helpful in understanding certain concepts. For instance, the bell curve often appears throughout the life cycle of a product. It begins with the product introduction and moves to its highest point when peak revenue is reached. From there, it declines until the product becomes obsolete. That is the bell curve plain and simple. Strategically, think of multiple new products correctly timed to sustain maximum growth. You could look at each product's life-cycle bell curve overlaid to form a family of stable curves. This image creates an industry bell curve.

My math and physics training at Providence actually helped me to use this theory when I worked for a computer start-up company in the mid 1980s. It was supported in an article written by Theodore Levitt, American economist and professor at Harvard Business School. Yup, I am dropping an Ivy League name here as a colleague. One of the things I noticed was that things we learned in school could seem distant and unimportant, but in our work, and in our lives, theories, formulas and models become personally important and useful.

Normal Distribution

The Bell Curve proves you either continue to grow or fall off the map. Businesses experience large numbers of varied events that result in a bell-curve distribution. We don't use symmetries and derivatives in the formula of extending my current company's bell curve. As I explained earlier, we use the strengths, weaknesses, opportunities, and threats (SWOT) planning system. It is advantageous because it's a much simpler and easier-to-implement formula for extending our company's revenue growth. We integrate all functional departments into our strategic plan and overlay the results as if each is its own bell curve.

It is interesting to look at our individual careers as a bell curve. At some point, the end of our career is closer than the beginning. This reminds me of when Tom Withers, sports writer, interviewed basketball great LeBron James, who had just turned 30. LeBron said he doesn't take a single moment for granted. Time is flying, and he said that he is determined to savor every moment.

LeBron is a great example of soaring as fast as possible to achieve a longer glide pattern. We are all on the curve. You can climb by using your creative power, your tenacity of spirit, your sense of humor, your intellect, your ability to relate to people, and by keeping in mind what is most important. However you get there, I suggest you soar as early as possible.

Think about that first thing tomorrow. Then do something about it.

CHAPTER SIXTEEN

Calabria's Law Number 12

Service measured not by gold...
...But by the golden rule

S O WE HAVE COME TO MY LAST LAW. I WANT YOU TO KNOW, though, that it was the first one I wrote down. It is the most important to me. It is a combination of faith and good business.

The golden rule can be found in all religions. It is summed up as, "Do unto others as you would have them do unto you." That is a great business principal. Business boils down to one word: relationships. If you want to build customer loyalty, sure price is important, yes having a quality product is necessary, but if you don't have a trustworthy relationship, your boat is sinking.

Service is built on serving others. If you truly have the best interest of others in mind when you do business with them, it won't take long for them to find out. When they do, when other things are equal, they will always choose you. Even when things aren't equal, sometimes they will choose you as well.

The Gomez Family

Let me go way back to when I was a kid. I got my first real job in 1952 when I was 9 years old. I learned a lot about relationships in that first job. I had an elderly neighbor who lived with her mentally challenged son directly across the street from us in a dilapidated house. It had a dusty appearance and a broken-down back porch and a front door with peeling paint. The house was a wreck, but this was the home of a proud family. Nonetheless, the old woman was feeble and weak, and I couldn't understand her son.

Now there was an older brother, who was an adult, and came by regularly to help out his mother and brother. I'll call him Fester. One day he spotted me in my yard and he called over to me. "Hey Joe. Come here a minute. I got a question for you."

I looked both ways, and then walked across the street to talk to him.

He said, "You're a big boy now aren't you?"

I nodded. That was obvious. Heck, I was about to turn 10. I was as old as you could get and not have double digits in your age.

"We could use some help over here cutting the lawn. What do you say, Joe, you want a job? I'll pay you for your time. It'll be a good deal. Well, do you want the job?"

"Yeah, sure. I'll take the job. I just need to check with my mom first." I ran inside and told my mom, and she thought it was a great idea.

Just like that, the brother hired me to work in the yard cutting the grass. I was employed. I was somebody. I had a real job. I was filled with pride. It would take a lot of work if the lawn was ever to receive any award for dazzling landscape design, but I was the guy to do it.

Fester took me around to the backside of the house. The back porch of their house had a solid trap door to the cellar, not that I was interested in going down there. Beyond the porch was a shed used to house the outdoor tools needed to work in the large yard. This was my business environment. I would call it "creepy."

I was at a very impressionable age, and our trip to the shed was kind of spooky. The door creaked as he opened it. As I stood on the back lawn I kept an eye on the back door to the house. Somehow I imagined someone might come out and pull me inside and never let me see the light of day again. Fester pulled the lawn mower out of the shed. It was a 16-inch hand-push, non-powered, non-electrical, manual reel mower. I would soon begin to wish that I could use a gasoline-powered cutter! But at this moment, I didn't know that. I was excited to get to the job.

I pushed the mower across the lawn and cut my first row.

"Hey wait a minute," said Fester. "You got to cut the rows in straight lines, and you start at the border of the property."

Walking over to the edge of the lawn, I started the job in earnest. Before long I was covered in sweat. It took forever to finish that first job, but I did it.

After that, I certainly didn't let the grass grow too long, because unlike a gas-powered unit, I provided the power to this mower. Every time I used it, before I was half done, I felt like I was out of gas.

At the end of August, Fester stopped by while I was hard at work to inspect the yard. He was seemingly unaware that as I worked in his yard, I was dreaming about becoming rich. This was my ticket to the big bucks. My payday was just around the corner. In fact, I thought, today might be the day.

In any event, he asked me for my summary of hours worked. I told him the cumulative total was 100 hours at 10¢ per hour. He gasped! A moment later, after he inhaled and was able to close his gaping mouth, he said to me, "That'll be fine. You have worked hard and deserve the money, but I have one question for you. Do you want your payment in gold?"

Did I want my payment in gold? Of course, I did. Everybody knew gold was the most valuable money there was. "Yes, I'll take it in gold," I said.

He led me to the back porch. "My mother keeps the gold down here," he said, and opened up the cellar trap door. That was my first experience with the extreme fear-and-greed meter. Have you ever experienced it? Here is how it works: You're scared to death, but you would kill for the money. Now decide what to do. My 9-year-old brain said, "Go for the gold."

The trap door squeaked open as Fester pulled it up from the floor. I reluctantly followed closely behind as we descended down the steps. The cellar was filled with a jumbled collection of odds and ends, broken furniture, old milk jugs, and antique tools. It was all preserved in spider webs. Finally, at the far end of his cellar was a cloth over an old bench.

"The gold is under here," he told me. He pulled the fabric off and revealed the gold. It looked a lot like rusty metal, but Fester assured me that gold had that appearance in the dark. He loaded my gold into a wooden box. I held my new-found fortune in my hands, and I was certain I had hit the jackpot. It was so heavy I could hardly hold it. My lawn mower days were over! I was rich. I had a box full of gold.

He covered the box with a rag and instructed me not to uncover it before I got home. He took the box from me and carried it out of the cellar. It took me at least twenty minutes to get home, struggling with my heavy box of gold all the way, resting every 10 feet.

When I finally came in the house, I yelled for my parents to come see. Of course, my parents were disbelievers but were willing to review the evidence. We were in the kitchen when I removed the rag and found that the "gold" had somehow transformed itself into pipes covered with rust.

"Get this box of junk out of here right now," said my mother.

"You bring that box back to Fester and get your real payment," said my dad.

Now I had the same laborious, time-consuming struggle to return my rusty non-treasure. I found Fester, who was still in his Mother's cellar. I told him I needed real money, not the fake gold. He took the box from me and clicked his tongue. He only had one comment, "It was your fault, Joe! You let the sunlight in when you were taking the gold home."

Then he smiled at me, rubbed my head with his hand. He reached into his pocket and took out his wallet. He removed a crisp $10 bill. He held it up in front of me. "You did a good job, Joe. Here's your money!" He handed me the bill and shook my hand.

I went home a rich man, and as I walked through their yard, I admired my work. Their lawn looked good. It might not have won any awards, but that lawn was smiling at me all the way to the street. I guess I would call that service with a smile.

It occurred to me that gold wasn't all of what I wanted. It seemed the important thing was to get a handshake and a smile, and the money would come with it.

I must admit when my parents sent me out of the kitchen with my box of false treasure, I felt like a failure. All these years later I remember the words I read by an anonymous author, "Failure is a detour, not a dead-end street."

The American Flag—
Memorable Moment #7

Let me share with you my image of the true symbol of service. For me, it really came home during my time in the Army Reserves. The early '70s were a scary time for me, and millions of others. My unit was always on standby alert, and at anytime could be sent to Asia. For whatever reason, we never were deployed.

But 2.7 million other Americans were sent there, and 58,148 of them gave their life for our country in that war, while some 304,000 were wounded. Those numbers are breathtaking to me. I was well aware while I was in the Reserves of the men and women who had it far worse than me.

During my time in the military service, the American flag was always at full mast at the Armory where I went six times a month, and we opened and closed every meeting saluting our flag. This meant a great deal to me. Service to my country was important. I might not have liked everything about it, but I was not going to fail it.

A few years later, my wife and I agreed we would always display the American Flag outside our home and in our office. It is a symbol of living in the land of the free. Every time I see it, I give thanks to the brave men and women who protect our country, and for the ones who gave their lives in service to others. They are the teachers of service. They are the ones who give us the opportunity to pursue the American dream. I get choked up when I see our flag flown over the Capital of the United States. My wife and I see it as a celebration of all the brave Americans who have served and met the challenges of adversity since the Revolutionary War right through to the challenges we face today in the Middle East.

In 2014, I replaced our 29-year-old office flag with a new one, which included this citation, "This is to certify that the accompanying flag was flown over the United States capital on July 24, 2014. At the request of the honorable Jared Polis, member of Congress, this flag was flown for CPI."

I agree with Jamie Paolinetti, the famous American bicycle racer, when he says, "Limitations live only in our minds. But if we use our imaginations, our possibilities become limitless."

That is the hope I have for our country. My hope is grounded in service, the type of service that we would want for ourselves and are willing to give for others. When we make something of ourselves, and our businesses, we improve our nation. Every time that happens, we honor those who have given their lives serving our country so that we might have the freedom to use our imaginations and enter into the limitless possibilities.

That is what our flag of the United States of America means to me.

Londenshire

Most sales reps take a lot of time off for lunch. I never did, because there is a limit to how many sales per labor hour are possible per day. In my IBM days, the lunch hours offered me an opportunity to call on those customers who were less likely to buy. I saved prime-time sales calls for the better sales opportunities.

One lunch-time call was to a Bell Telephone office. I was surprised to learn there were only a manager and a single office employee present. Almost immediately, the manager started to describe his undying love for his recently deceased wife. He pulled a folded note from his wallet, which contained several type-written aspects of his wife's strategy for a happy marriage in the form of a poem. His eyes teared up as he held the paper in his hand and explained its significance to me.

I was moved by his sincere comments and asked him if it would be all right if I had his wife's note printed as a tribute to her, so that others could see her beautiful and inspiring poem. He agreed and allowed me to take the note. A few days later I returned with his printed page and of course the original note.

I suggested he copyright the poem and publish it as a formal tribute to his wife. He declined, but offered me the publishing rights. After considering this opportunity for a few days, I decided to take him up on the deal. I really wanted to do a good job with this. I wanted to treat this project as if my wife had died and I was going to share her poem with the world. I needed advice on how to do this in the best possible way. I proceeded to visit a few clients I was friendly with for advice:

1. Ed, an advertising manager, helped to title the poem, "Twelve Expressions of Love" and chose the ideal typescript.

2. Bernie, a newspaper editor, helped wordsmith the language of the poem into a slightly more romantic version.

3. Sam, a printer, suggested a wood mounting with accent cuts, deco covering, and slightly-burned paper.

4. Dominic, a local shipper, helped order the ideal boxes for shipments.

5. Jack, an attorney, agreed to partner with me and establish a company called "Londenshire" to produce and sell the plaques and take care of the governmental regulations and taxes.

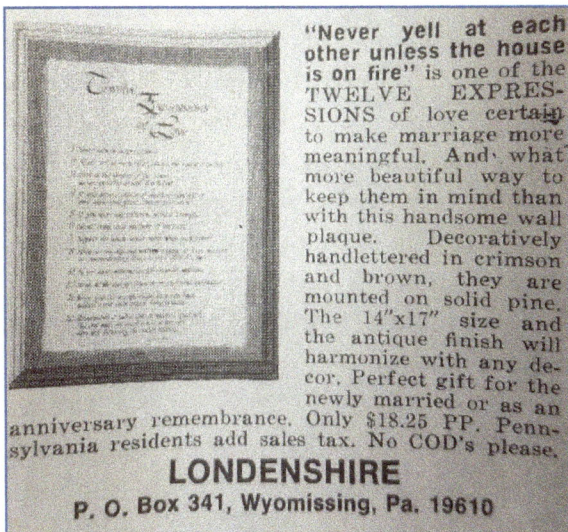

A company to sell plaques

Truthfully, I was honoring this gentleman's wife and her poem, but I was also ready to embark on getting rich. I decided to establish a commercial price point and placed an ad in Yankee Magazine. We sold some but weren't satisfied with the run rate. I decided direct marketing was what was needed and found a couple who had started a candle-selling business modeled along the same strategy as Tupperware home parties. The couple agreed to sell our product and marked our plaques up 100%.

While working with this couple, I began formulating a plan to really expand my participation, and profit, in this effort. I decided to try and purchase the candle selling company. I offered the couple a generous deal and asked them to stay on to run the operation. I was positive this was a perfect franchise opportunity with increased revenues by direct manufacturing of candles. The product was not only disposable, but varied by season, and was important in the lives of women, a perfect product for easy recurring sales. Our plan also would include building a manufacturing plant to produce the candles. A recurring revenue stream is a must for any startup business. I had all the plans in my head. I felt I was being creative and ready to start up my own business, which would have been Memorable Moment #56. Unfortunately, the couple refused our offer, and a month later I was promoted to the division headquarters of IBM.

That business never happened. But two things did happen. I honored that gentleman and the memory of his wife. I treated him just as I would like to have been treated. Secondly, I learned a lot about business, about reaching out to others for advice, about incorporating a small business and paying sales tax, about working with a partner, and about expanding a vision and working toward a dream.

That business never came to fruition, but I gave it my best. My service was by the Golden Rule.

Manufacturer Spiffs

It would be great if everyone who did business followed the Golden Rule. You know that is not the case. Here is an example. Manufacturers like to bypass owners and pay spiffs directly to sales staff. "Spiff" is a funny word. It would be a good one for the jargon game I told you about earlier. A spiff is an immediate bonus paid to a sales rep to entice the rep to sell a specific product, rather than another manufacturer's product. I have always objected to this practice for two reasons.

First, these baseless, one-of-a-kind payments are always reported to the IRS by the manufacturer. The payments are often ignored by our sales reps when they file their tax returns. This can lead to an IRS audit and all the stress that comes with it, including sometimes a fine with interest. Second, the payments help undermine our business plan.

Case in point, the electronics giant NEC went around me and put a $25 spiff on every NEC monitor sold one February. Our monthly sales averaged 300 total monitors per month, before, during, and after the spiffed month. That month we did sell more NEC monitors, but the percent increase to NEC was at the expense of other manufacturers. Only a small percentage change carried through to the next two months. After that, the original split between sold monitors by manufacturer reappeared. So there was no long-term change in preference of manufacturers.

However, that February our sales reps used some of the spiff money to lower the price of the NEC monitors. That is how they got our clients to buy that specific product. After the promotion, the sales reps were unable to increase the selling point back to its pre-promotion level, thus lowering the company's profit and lowering the sales staff's pay. Because of the spiff, we experienced an overall 2% average revenue decrease in the month of February, and that negative change continued for months after the promotion.

In the end, the spiffs and the resulting client discounts didn't generate increased monitor sales, but did lower our revenue, and also that of the other manufacturers we work with. Obviously, this isn't how I want to be treated, and not how I want to treat our clients. This is against the golden rule of business. I hope the manufacturers will read this and get the point!

Perfect Theory for Compensation—Memorable Moment #12

When it comes to making money, I want to give everybody the same chance. I don't want to assume that everyone should get the same amount. In other words, I don't want my employees to all get the same salary, even though I know they are all in need of one. I want to give them the chance to excel and make more than they thought they could.

As I understand it, no employer was required to pay salaries in the ancient city of Atlantis. Ah, the good old days. Everyone agreed to this, because profit sharing was the norm. So here's how it was structured. Everyone had a compensation plan designed around payment as a percentage of gross profit. The harder you worked, the more you made.

Here is something that seems obvious to me. All business functions on ratios. In other words, there is a fixed percentage of profit, which is available for your sales force. Any salary paid to an under-productive sales rep has to come from lower commissions to your most successful sales personnel. If you eliminate salaries as they did in Atlantis, you will pay the maximum amount possible to your most productive personnel. Your "hiring mistakes" wouldn't be subsidized by your best sales reps.

For me, that sounds like the Golden Rule.

Of course, I know there are exceptions. People need time to learn the ropes and need assistance in their first year or two. I also think there are times when a worker, because of personal or family reasons, might also need help. I do want to be kind and generous with my staff, but I don't want them to think that their efforts don't matter.

I recently got a strong endorsement for our hiring approach when I read an article in the Recruiting Daily Advisor entitled "Hiring the Wrong Sales Person is a $2-million Mistake." The author Joseph Dimisa points out that it isn't just a matter of salary and training, it can also mean $2 million in lost sales.

Since my company operates in the highly competitive information technology sector, margins are tight. We have to generate a lot of revenue to make a decent profit. We require a first-year salesperson, after training, to sell $6 million in product revenue.

For one person it is overwhelming, daunting, and seemingly impossible. For another, it is exciting, inspiring, and the chance of a lifetime. Let's face it. There are jobs that are not right for us. I can't see myself as a high school English teacher, or a clown in the circus. I know some people probably think of me that way, but I know that is not the job for me. I want everyone to have a chance at making the money they are motivated to make, because that is what I want for myself. That is the Golden Rule and also the perfect payment plan.

I have talked about this before, but let's frame it in the Golden Rule context. I want everyone in my company who wants to increase his or her salary to be able to do it. This theory isn't just for sales staff. It flows through procurement, the people who buy the products that our sales staff then sell. They share in the savings they negotiate as they haggle with suppliers. When they negotiate a better price, the company makes more money, and they should get a percentage of that profit.

Strong administration managers also join in the opportunity. When they bill collections promptly and collect on past due receivables, this eliminates interest payments charged by banks. That means more money to the company and the Golden Rule says share it with those who earned it.

Our employees are our ambassadors to our clients. We want to be known for our stellar service. We want to be a company that treats others just as we would want to be treated. In the end, that pays off for everyone.

Law Intro

As I finish this chapter, and this section of my book, let me say a little bit about the laws I have been sharing with you. Laws have existed since the beginning of time. Corporations live by different sets of laws. Individuals often create their own laws by the daily actions they establish for themselves. So, I first set out to write my company's laws in such a way that my personal business ethics would be reflected in my employees' conduct at work.

I put the laws together as I experienced the wild frontier of business over many wonderful years. I hope sharing my "laws," which helped me to navigate obstacles, will also help to guide you. Perhaps they will even help you to formulate your business standards.

It is necessary to have laws because they are your guideposts through your career. You could even think of them as weapons to use in overcoming those business threats that will arise almost every day.

I must admit, that law number 10 is my favorite. Remember that one? "When a reasonable offer is refused…Lower it."

Law number 11 is my best advice for my children and my grandkids. I know we just finished that chapter, but I'll mention it again since kids have such short attention spans. "Soar as rapidly as possible…to achieve a longer glide pattern."

Many years ago, when the time came for me to work on developing the company logo, the laws were on my mind. Since I always had respect for tradition and a desire for truth, I trademarked a knight with a message engraved on his shield, "Service Measured Not by Gold, but the Golden Rule." As you know since you are reading this chapter, not only is this part of my company logo, but it is my 12th and final law. It is the one that best describes my beliefs. I hope you also find it helpful.

Before finishing up the book, I have more stories to share. These next chapters are about things and people near and dear to me. So hold on to your seat belt, we're about to speed into the final chapters.

SECTION 3

WHAT MAKES
ME TICK

CHAPTER SEVENTEEN

Family Joy

A s I MOVE TOWARD FINISHING UP MY BOOK, IN THIS FINAL SEC-tion I want to share some thoughts about things I really enjoy in life. I am a people person. I like people. Sometimes I like them to be quiet. Sometimes I like them to be in the next room. Sometimes I like them to be in another state, but I do like people!

And it could be because I'm Italian, but I especially like my people, my family, blood of my blood, flesh of my flesh, Visa holders of my Visa account.

The Guessing Game

Our daughter's college in Providence was 1,958.2 miles from our home in Boulder, CO. Nonetheless, she graduated from Providence College, class of 1993. I often remind my daughter that she had twice as much fun in college as I did. She likes to reply, and rather hurtfully I think, that she had twice the grade point average too. When she first went away to school, we weren't getting much correspondence from her. When we asked her to stay in touch with us more, she replied that she was always studying. Her course load made it next to impossible to send off any-thing more than an abbreviated letter.

As an example, I once received a letter from her, neatly printed and spaced on a standard sheet of paper, containing just five lines, which read: "Hello, busy studying, test tomorrow, send money. Love Sharon."

She must have forgotten that I had gone to college too. I knew there was a lot more going on than studying. My response to her was written on a check stub; no check, mind you, just the stub. Subtle, huh? The stub was about an inch wide. On it I wrote eleven lines utilizing both sides, and neatly printed as follows: "Dear Sharon, if you, write, on one inch, paper, over, you could, send me, a two-sided, letter. Love Dad." I'm sure she would have better appreciated the check, rather than the check stub, but I think she got the point.

I enjoyed sending our daughter care packages while she was away at college. Sometimes before I sent a package, I would send her clues as to what was in it. She would try to guess its contents before it arrived. It was a little game we played to heighten her expectation of the coming package. It also helped me stay in contact with the little girl I missed, by playing games with the grown-up woman she was becoming.

I filled the packages mostly with treats, games, and snacks. Sometimes I would put in something unusual, such as a homegrown special tomato. I sent the packages and played these games, because I remembered that my own college experience of cramming numbers, writing papers, and memorizing facts didn't leave me much time for snack shopping.

Additionally, to add to the fun, and to help her financially, I added a little "carrot" to the game. If she guessed the contents before the package arrived, I would send her a Franklin C-note. That's $100! Sharon made new friends and roommates and convinced them to get in on the action, so our little father-daughter game soon became a dorm game. The good news/bad news results were four years without her and her gang ever guessing the correct contents of any package. Here is an example of how our little game was played. My clue: "Sharon, we spent the weekend in Las Vegas for my birthday. I'm sending you something special from the past. Remember our last summer vacation at Atlantic City. You have ten guesses."

Her answer:

Dad,

Hi! Here are my 10 guesses…

    1. Poker Chips from Vegas

    2. Matches

    3. A deck of cards

    4. Dice

    5. The notepaper from the hotel to write letters

    6. More computer bag stuff (headphones, mouse pad, etc.)

    7. Towels from the hotel

    8. Suntan lotion

    9. Ticket stubs from a show

    10. A fake ID in case I lose my real one

Tell mom hi.

Love,
Sharon

Package arrived with Salt Water Taffy! I kept my C-note for my next trip to Vegas! We all know money can't buy you love, but at least you can have some fun with it.

Our Son

My father was proud to tell everyone he had a son to carry-on, not only the family name and traditions, but especially his name and his traditions. That's why he made me his namesake, Joseph Calabria, Jr. That's right. That's me! My wife and I decided to pass along this badge of honor by naming our son the "III." We also agreed there were many reasons to follow this tradition, which would help set him apart, grow, and mature.

1. Honor your Father (and grandfather)—sharing the same name is the ultimate family bond. It creates a special interest in the namesake.

2. Confidence—there's little chance that he'll ever have an inferiority complex. Having his father's name, or grandfather, or great grandfather's name, will provide a kind of psychological defense mechanism with seemingly magical properties. This title instills in him an innate belief that he has the ability to succeed.

3. Peace of Mind—comes from the birthing identification, which opens doors whether going to an Ivy League school, community college, or local racetrack. Having the number "III" after your name allows you to fit in anywhere.

4. Un-squandered Inheritance—in 2012 a researcher at Ohio State University found that Americans who receive a substantial inheritance save about half of what they get. They spend, donate, or manage to lose the rest. If your inheritance is the namesake title of III, IV, or V, you can never squander it. That title is better than money and stays with you forever. My father did not have money to pass on to his children, but he passed on to me his life lessons and his name. That is the most valuable inheritance I could ever have.

5. Good Looks—especially true with "juniors," namesakes are better looking than other people.

6. Arm Wrestling Champions—Because of the extra endurance and strength it takes to write out these lengthy names, those people with namesake legacy are champion arm wrestlers.

I've shared this list of benefits to many "juniors," and I'm happy to report almost 100% have followed the namesake tradition. Our son named one of his sons the "IV." His fancy name gives him automatic cache.

Our son was a talented golfer and twice qualified for the Colorado State High School Championship. After he graduated from H.S., he declined any opportunity to continue with golf. His son decided to try golf, and liked it well enough to teach himself the game. He set up a chipping area in his home and has progressed to the point he's very competitive in his county. I'm proud he is strong-minded and dead set on becoming a professional golfer.

My Granddaughter the President

After returning from a trip one day later than planned, I found a note from my 9-year-old granddaughter. She had had the previous day off from school, and her mother had no option but to allow her to spend time at my company. Upon their arrival, she immediately told her mother she needed an office to work in and asked for the key to my office. During the day, she bugged my office receptionist and inquired if she had time for a meeting. Since it was a busy day, my receptionist and other office personnel were pleasant with her, but didn't have time to play with her. So she went about inspecting the office. When I arrived in the office that next morning, I found a note written on a yellow pad entitled, "Talk to Joe." The note read:

1. The water in the fish pond is cold

2. Hiring people—there are too many open desks

3. Healthier snacks for the snack machine

4. Clean the walls by the stairs, $150 to $200 should cover it

Upon reading the note, I walked into her mother's office with a Grand-Canyon smile on my face. I handed her the note and said, "While I was away the temporary owner did an assessment of the facility. I think she makes some great observations. Please follow through on her suggestions."

We had a good laugh. And we did clean up the hallway, put out a new employment ad, warmed up the fish water, and got some healthy snacks!

All my ladies add spice to my life. My wife loves to announce for the amusement and entertainment of anyone who makes an effort to pay attention, that when I attended Providence College it had been an all-male school. Years later, the alumni were asked for input on the idea of the college going coed. I voted against the change to tradition, but how lucky am I that my vote didn't sway the results? I have great pride that my daughter followed in my footsteps and is part of the Friar alumni community. I was the first to congratulate our daughter after she received her diploma and I mentioned the famous words of comedian Jon Stewart, "The unfortunate, yet truly exciting thing about life, is that there is no core curriculum. The entire place is an elective."

After more than 20 years of hard work at our company, my daughter was recently named the CEO. My wife remains the Chick in Charge. A few months later, the new CEO buzzed on the intercom and asked if my granddaughter was in my office. I answered in the affirmative, and she told me to send the little lady, who was now 10 years old, to her office to do some filing. My granddaughter was seated at my conference table with chips and a drink, overheard the instructions, and replied, "I'm still on break!"

That didn't sit well with the CEO, who firmly responded, "Now!"

My granddaughter blatantly replied, "When I'm done with the break." At 10, the human adventure was just beginning.

One thing is for sure. My granddaughter does not have a chance to double her mother's GPA, even if she is an overachiever. Statistically it is not possible. In a way, though, I wish she could, because the fact that my daughter has done it to me is one of my greatest achievements!

There are a million reasons to live this life.

Happy birthday to my awesome Pop pop!!!

A nice message

I think we can sum up happiness and why it is so great to live a full life in one word: Family. I'm not saying that it is easy. I don't know any family that doesn't have problems, and not just little ones, but big problems. Yet, we work through them. We do our best to get along, to forgive, to have a good day every day. It doesn't always work, but we keep trying.

I strive everyday to be grateful for my life. My gratitude list starts with my wife, my children, my grandchildren. From there, it is a very long list, but I will never forget where it starts. Everyday, I thank God for my family.

My Memorable Moment #17 is to celebrate each day with the millions of reasons to live this life.

Since one picture is worth a thousand words, our 5th grandchild, sums up my point nicely. He also understands at a very young age the road to a big inheritance.

The Sunsets of Aruba

IT TOOK ME A LITTLE WHILE TO RECOGNIZE IT, BUT SUGAR AND I have found our favorite vacation destination. Those of you who have seen my golf game know that I love the beach; I spend a good amount of time in the sand every course I play. And we love our beach home in Florida, so it is probably no surprise that my top pick is in the sand. Sugar and I have finally decided that Aruba is our favorite place to *get away from it all.*

This island destination in the Southern Caribbean Sea is spectacular. Nestled off the coast of Venezuela, it is actually part of the Kingdom of the Netherlands. The taxes are low. The crime rate is low. And the food is delicious. The weather is spectacular all year round. Because of its southern location, hurricanes very rarely affect it. Visitors can expect sunshine, a slight breeze, warm temperatures, low humidity, beautiful beaches, and crystal-clear water. Yes, I know, I am quite a salesman, and once you go to this place, it is a winning bet that you will want to return.

We went for five days and decided it wasn't enough. We extended our trip before we left. The next year we returned for another five days. What were we thinking? Didn't we learn anything from the previous year? We had to extend our vacation again. Since then, we have traveled there four more times, and we always try to stay for 10 days.

So maybe I am easy to please, but here is what I like to do. We stay at the Hyatt, and there is a casino right there on the premises and golf courses nearby. That adds to the flavor, but most days, we rent an umbrella and beach chairs then soothe our souls while watching the waves tumble onto the shore. Sometimes we get a water mattress, and I push Sugar across the pearly seas. After that, I agree to a beverage or two from the strolling waitresses. I love to watch the people walk the beach. Some seem to be whales that have become stranded on the shore and have learned to walk. Others, shall we say, have very fit fins that glisten in the sun.

There is great food there, too. Being next to Venezuela, the beef is outstanding. And the seafood couldn't be fresher. There are lots of interesting choices for other food within walking distance. You can eat at the seaside by candlelight with your feet in the sand. That much romance I can only handle once per trip. We often stop in the tiki bar for nourishment. Sometimes that visit turns into a big lunch, and then in the evening we have hors d'oeuvres and drinks at happy hour and call it a night. Sugar is happy to join me in that routine.

My marriage partner and I have never tired of seeing the sunset. The sun seems to go down more dramatically in Aruba than in other places. It sits for a moment on top of the water like a gleaming jewel and then just drops down into the Caribbean Sea. The colors blaze out from the horizon. There is a bandshell near where we stay. The island music can fill the air. When my head hits the pillow at night, I rest well knowing I have once again achieved my Memorable Moment #66—Watched A Sunset in Aruba.

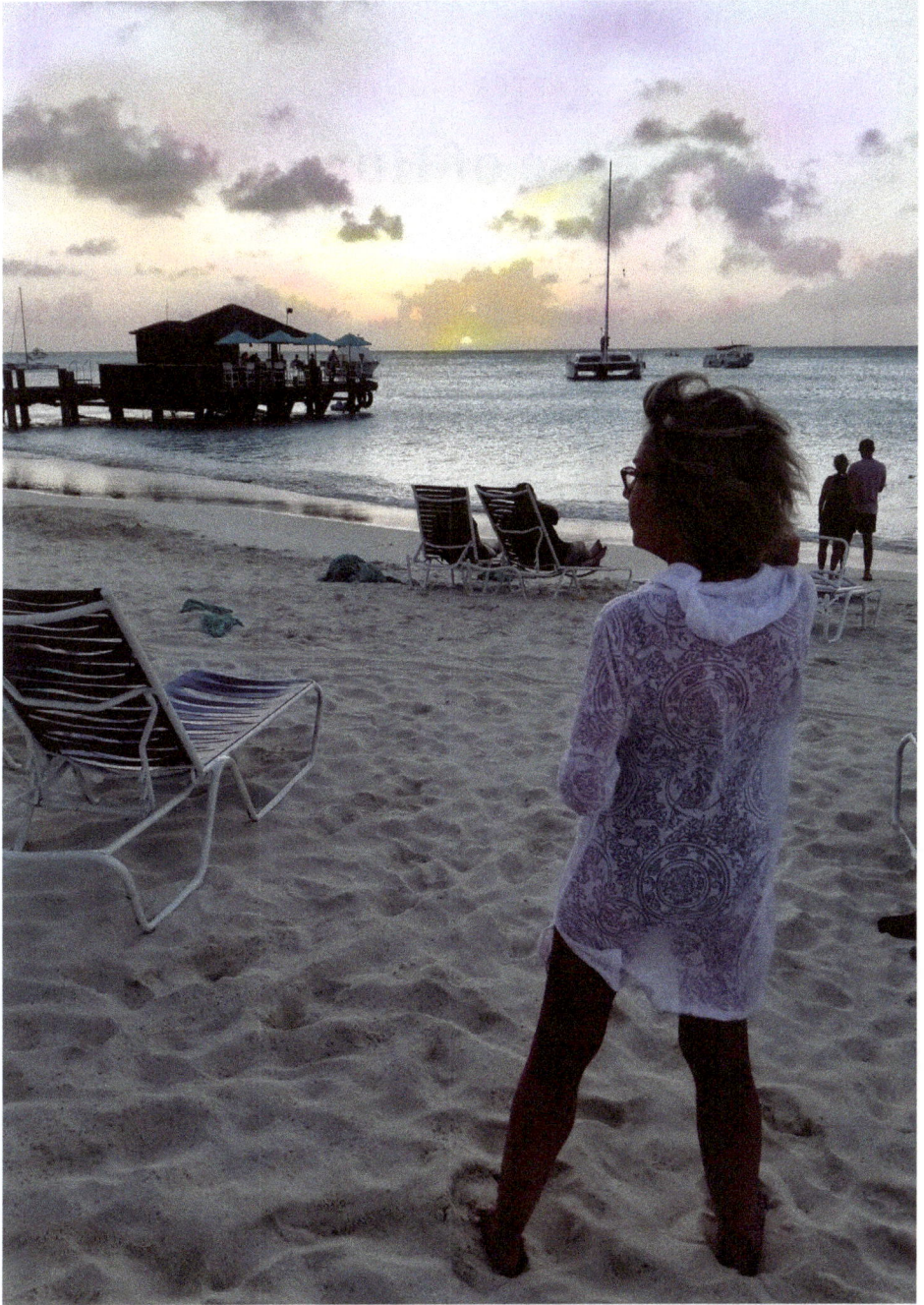

CHAPTER EIGHTEEN

Sense of Humor

L IFE WOULD NOT BE THE SAME WITHOUT LAUGHTER. MANY OF the happiest moments of our life are surrounded by, sandwiched in, right smack in the middle of uncontrollable laughter. If you want to experience one of the most holy and beautiful moments of life, watch a toddler and an old person have a good laugh together. Someday when I get old, I hope to experience that, but I have quite a long time to wait. Humor bonds people together, makes a dull day a fun day, and a tragic day bearable.

Hey, that reminds me, what's got four legs, sharp teeth, and is known for being naked?

The bear!

What is the toughest bear to eat?

The gristly bear!

What bear fits in at the golf course?

The polo bear!

Recognition

When I worked at IBM, the pressure was always there to make your estab-lished quota for the year. If successful, your achievement was awarded corporate recognition and a trip to an enviable vacation site like Miami Beach or San Francisco.

I started my book by sharing that on the first such trip I won, I remember walking through the lobby of the Fontainebleau Hotel and seeing the VP of sales shaking hands and saying, "Hello, How Are You? I want to welcome you to my event. Have a great time." It felt as if my recognition was on his dime. When in fact, his trip was because of my efforts, and the efforts of my hard working colleagues.

Later in life, when it became my honor to shake the hands of successful people who worked for me, I always remembered to say, "Thank you, you are here because you did a great job for our company. I am here because I want to personally say thanks for all your hard work! Now take this time and really enjoy yourself!"

I also realized on the first trip that the presentation of awards was too blah, blah, and really blah. I said to myself that if I ever had the opportunity to run one of these recognition holidays, it would be a fun event, one with a proven dynamic speaker. I would ensure the presentations of awards were intermixed with humor, stories, or captivating business experiences. These exciting evenings would include specialty foods, premium beverages, and dancing girls. No wait, I mean, dancing with girls, or guys, or crowds of people just having fun together on the dance floor.

I also thought if I were in charge of a sale recognition event, I would use a catch phrase like, "Hello, thanks for coming. You're Awesome!" I'd put it in plain sight, impossible to miss, like on the back of my shirt! Plus, this would allow me to welcome twice as many people with my friendly message, because I would also have it tattooed on my forehead.

Over the years, I have tried to fulfill those early expectations. I tried to bring humor into each event. In this chapter I am going to share a few stories I have told to help our employees enjoy "Humor Beyond Imagination" at our annual recognition dinner. Before I tell some of the stories I've used, I'd like to share some I actually experienced. Here is one more from Miami Beach, the first IBM conference that I earned the right to attend.

Pork Chop's Elevator Ride

After official opening remarks that first year, a group of us proceeded to one of Miami's favorite watering holes. The bartender at that establishment had a gaze I will never forget. You see, he had a glass eye. At first I didn't notice anything unusual about him, but then he said to me, and my buddies, who were seated in the bar stools facing him, "Excuse me while I clean this off."

He picked up a rag, and I thought he was going to clean off the bar, but instead he put his finger into his left eye socket and popped out his glass eye. "It gets itchy, you know," he said as he rubbed it down with the rag. Then he stared at the eye in his hand for a moment, and placed it carefully back into his eye socket. At just that instant, he made a popping sound with his mouth, which gave the impression that the eye was popping back into position.

As if that wasn't enough, which it certainly should have been, I now saw that he had something in his eye. I was trying to figure out what it was when he came a little closer to me and said, "Can I get you something else?" My eyes focused on his glass eye, and I saw a beautiful blonde lady, stark naked, looking back at me. I looked away and then looked back at him and his provocative eye, and yes indeed, I was seeing a naked lady. He had a naked lady painted onto his eye.

He rushed off to serve another customer at the other end of the bar. A little while later, I saw him take out his eye once again. He cleaned it off and popped it back into the socket. When he came close again, I said, "I am ready for another."

He poured my drink, looked right at me and said, "I think I've got just what you'll like."

I stared into his glass eye and this time I saw a naked brunette!

It wasn't long before a redhead came onto the scene! Every now and then, he would take out his glass eye and a different naked woman would appear. One could say that this bartender maintained excellent eye contact. Sales school #1 always preaches the importance of maintaining eye contact. This bartender was clearly a master of his trade.

Hours later, we returned to the Fontainebleau after a night of acting like what one of my Aussie friends would call, "a bunch of pork chops." As you might guess, that means silly people. We decided to hit the hay since we had awards in the morning. On the elevator ride up, one of our friends passed out. We decided since we had seen those naked women all night, that it was time for a naked guy. We stripped our buddy down to his underwear, stopped at a floor and grabbed a hallway chair, and tied him to it. We pushed all the buttons on the elevator and left him to impress as many people as possible.

As we later learned, hours ticked by and he finally woke up, got untied and stood, staring at the elevator-floor buttons. He couldn't remember what room he was in.

He made his way down to the lobby and asked what room he was in. It was quite a stir, and he was given a large towel. However, because we had his clothes, he had no ID and no way of proving who he was. He begged the front desk for 45-minutes to give him his key. Finally, they told him that he was supposed to be roomed with L. Reed and told him which room it was; however, they wouldn't give him a key. So at 4:30 a.m. he made his way up to his room, and started banging on the door so that this L. Reed character would wake up and let him in to get some sleep. The door finally opened, and L. Reed stood in the doorway, looking far beyond aggravated, and she demanded that he explain himself immediately; that's right, it turns out the L. stood for Linda.

Even though he had no idea who this Linda was, he pleaded with her to just let him in; he didn't want to sleep with her; he just wanted to sleep somewhere before the awards ceremony in the morning. After refusing several times, she finally let him into her room, but only to sleep on the floor.

The rest of the night passed far too quickly, and the sun came streaming through the window. Our good ole' buddy came to his senses and remembered his room number. He left the room of Linda Reed and was soon knocking on the door of Larry Reed, his roommate. Larry opened the door, and our friend got cleaned up, and made his way down to breakfast.

We had rehearsed our straight faces so that upon his arrival we could pretend as though we hadn't been a part of anything, but the look on his face was priceless, and we all burst out laughing. He didn't say a word to us for the whole meal. We made our way to the award ceremony after breakfast. Not everyone receives an award at these things, but our ole' buddy got called up. He was to receive national recognition and when he reached the stage the VP of sales remarked, "Hello Pork Chop, I met you last night in the elevator."

Our friend rather sheepishly replied, "Thank you for my award." He looked rather good on the stage, considering all that he had been through.

In my eyes, though, when I look at him, I'll always see the image of him tied up in the elevator! I wish I could swap it for one I had seen in the eye of the bartender.

The Nest

Sad but true, not every planned vacation goes as planned, but that doesn't mean you can't still have fun, especially at someone else's expense. My wife and I were planning to join two other couples on a trip to Palm Springs. At the last minute, my best friend Jack and his wife had to beg off. But my friend Doc and his wife went as planned.

On the second night of the trip, we decided to get a traditional Italian meal. My selection was linguine with seafood, which included a blend of clams, shrimp, squid, lobster, and scallops. My linguine and fish entrée was served in a large round Italian bread bowl. Everyone's meal was huge, and we all had something with fish.

The conversation shifted to our absent friends, Jack and Mary, and their disappointment at having to remain home. We were relaxing in Palm Springs and learned there was a forecast of heavy snow on the way to where Jack and Mary lived. This gave me an idea; they needed to be cheered up! I took my almost empty bread bowl, gathered the other leftovers of fish, garlic, pasta, tomato sauce, etc., and put them all in my bread bowl. This concoction now looked like a full nest of food to feed our friends back home.

After dinner, we went looking for a box to send the nest to our snow-bird friends. Once back in our rented vacation home, we froze the meal. It had already started to smell. The next day we packaged the frozen nest in the box and sent it by FedEx to Jack's office. No doubt the first thing that package did was to sit in a hot truck under the constant Palm Springs sun.

Two days later, the delivery driver must have been careful in handling the box marked fragile. No doubt its odor molecules forced him to hold his noise. By this time the two-day-old meal had grown wings. Perhaps the driver was overwhelmed with curiosity. What was being delivered to this prestigious fourth floor law office?

By the time the package was on Jack's desk, a small crowd of office-mates had gathered to get in on this spectacle. Jack opened the parcel and set the full aroma free!

Unfortunately, common rules of decency prevent me from printing here the response that Jack immediately faxed back to me. Geez, sometimes even your best friends don't understand your concern for their happiness.

Later I explained to Jack and Mary, a fine sense of humor is aged like a fine wine. They pointed out, seafood linguine doesn't improve with age in quite the same way.

The Plane to Miami International Airport

Here is another funny story with my buddy Jack. I hope you have friends that make you laugh. It is an important part of life. I savor the stories of these good times, and I look forward to creating more of them. So this story happened after my fourth sales recognition trip to Miami. Before going home, I took a three-day extension, and was joined by Jack and a couple other friends.

We were a foursome ready for some recreational championship golf. Of course, the four of us wanted to play the Blue Monster at Doral. The Blue Monster is one of the most challenging and famous golf courses of all time. The Pro Golfers' Association had hosted a tournament on this course just a few weeks earlier. We decided to challenge the tournament-winning score. That's right, our foursome would take on the best in the world, and have a great time in the process. After we teed off on the first hole, it was clear we were the underdogs! And we remained that way, even with our inflated handicaps.

After our first round, Ben and I decided to play a second time while Jack and Chris stayed at the bar. About four hours later, the guys left the bar and backtracked from the last hole looking for us. Spying us coming down the sixteenth fairway, Jack climbed a tree next to the 17th tee box.

This plane had a low approach pattern.

Ben and I finished the 16th and moved to the 17th hole. Unbeknownst to us, Jack was in the tree, and Chris was hiding behind it. Ben put down his ball and took a practice swing. Just as he was getting ready for his drive, a Boeing 747 jet roared over us on its approach to Miami International Airport. I doubt it was more than 500 feet above us and certainly sounded like a volcano erupting. I put my hands over my ears. At the instant, Ben was in his back swing, and the plane was directly over-head, Jack leapt out of the coconut tree screaming for his life and landing with an earth-shaking thud just 5 feet from Ben.

It looked to Ben like a passenger had fallen out of the plane. He immediately dropped to his knees and let out a piercing cry of alarm. He pounded his chest to get air and to keep his heart beating. I did a double take and saw that it was Jack lying on the ground.

A coconut tree doesn't have bananas.

"I jumped from the tree," shouted Jack. Chris came out from behind the tree and then everyone burst out laughing. Jack was rolling on the ground practically dying from laughter. I clapped my hands together. This was a good one, and fortunately the ground was soft for Jack's landing. After about five minutes of uncontrollable laughter, we decided that was enough excitement on the course for the day!

Lots of us are stressed and overworked. Some say drink a couple glasses of wine and eat a box of chocolates. Have a nice lunch. That is not bad advice, but nothing beats a good laugh. Take some time off and have some fun. But try not to fall out of an airplane or from a coconut tree. As I think about this story, it might have made more sense if Jack had jumped out of a banana tree. He sure acted like a monkey.

Miami Dogs Pay for Dinner

After dodging falling bodies on the Blue Monster, we decided gambling might ease the tension Ben had just experienced. It was still too early for dinner. The thoroughbreds weren't racing, but there was a greyhound track within a 30-minute cab ride. Off we went to seek our riches. Now you know I considered myself an expert when it came to horseracing. Well, I had no doubt this would carry over to the dogs.

After six races, we had 24 losses (4 players X 6 races). Race #7 was no different for three of us. But Jack's luck changed. He was holding five $20 tickets with the betting board odds listed on his dog at twelve to one. Jack's dog won. Our coconut jumper had won $1200. Jack danced his way up the grandstand steps, "Yeah man, I'm the best!" He was so cocky, stopping every few feet to strike a winning pose on his way to the cashier.

My curiosity forced me to ask him how he was scientifically able to pick this long shot from the crowd of contenders. From my eyes, they all looked pretty much the same. Jack said, "To the untrained eye, they look alike. However, I was able to ascertain an important difference in the winner, a certain quality I did not see any other dog exhibit."

I asked, "Well, what was the winning clue?"

Jack pointed to the end of the track and mentioned he watched the dogs with their handlers as they approached the starting gate. One of the dogs squatted and took a dump the size of a small mountain. Jack said, "When I saw that, I figured that dog was 10 pounds lighter and thus would run faster than any other." He closed his scientific analysis with a bold generous invitation, "Dinner's on me."

This whole story reminds me of a quote from author Robert Anton Wilson, "We all see only that which we are trained to see." Of course, Jack is an attorney, and in that business you have to keep a careful eye on what came out of the winning dog's butt!

The Unpublished Law

Here is yet another great laugh with Jack and my friends. Jack's daughter had just gotten married. We were at the wedding reception. After attending church, dancing with my wife, and displaying all of my good manners, I adjourned to the back of the hall with my childhood friends: Greeks, Italians, Irish, and one blood line unknown. After lighting our cigars, having a sip of our Cognac (V.S.O.P.), here came the wives.

"Why are you guys back here?" they all barked at once.

My Greek buddy leaned over and whispered in my ear, "You're the salesman Joe, tell them something."

Clearing my throat, I said, "Ladies, we were just discussing how much we love our wives. So I am afraid you'll have to leave us alone, because this topic takes a long time to cover."

A good laugh and the ladies scattered, and the fellas had some much needed time together. Every wedding should be celebrated with extended laughter! It's the most fun law in a happy marriage.

The Tie

Earlier in the book I mentioned that the men in my office are required to wear ties. That doesn't mean we can't have fun in the office. Here is a string of emails to support my point. As a matter of fact, one year at our annual recognition party, we shared this sequence for the amusement of all our guests. The story started when my VP of sales emailed a couple of us this note.

From: Joe B
To: Joe C; Dean
Subject: My Tie

While I am vehemently against wearing ties and am in complete disagreement with their usefulness, my tie-less neck today is not a demonstration of protest, but is a result of the wind. I had it draped around my neck when I went to fill my car up with gas this morning, and the wind blew it right off. I did not even know I had lost it until I got into the office this morning. Sorry about that. I will have one on tomorrow.

From: Dean
To: Joe B; Joe C
Subject: RE: My Tie

In my travels today, I will keep a diligent watch for the errant tie blowing about. If I can capture it, is there a reward offered for its safe return?

From: Joe C
To: Dean; Joe B; Sharon, and others
Subject: RE: My Tie

Sharon, give a one-time exception allowing Joe to be reimbursed for a new tie.

From: Dan
To: Joe B; Joe C
Subject: RE: My Tie

I'll take that deal; ties cost a fortune. Plus, Joe's already overpaid.

From: Rodney
To: Joe B; Joe C
Subject: RE: My Tie

Why doesn't he take a few minutes and go across the street to the thrift shop?

From: Sharon
To: Joe B; Joe C
Subject: RE: My Tie
Can't we muster one up from the lost and found over at McDonald's?

From: Chris S
To: EVERYONE
Subject: Halloween
Steve could dress as Joe B, and Joe B can dress as Steve.

From: Joe B
To: EVERYONE
Subject: RE: Halloween
Right. I am not falling for that one. I will be here IN MY TIE, and that is it!

At the recognition event that we shared this email thread, I gave Joe B some well-deserved credit by announcing that his exploits led to an historic race. Did you hear about the two silkworms that got into a race? They ended in a tie!

Jean's Million-Dollar Order

We used that same technique of sharing a humorous email thread another year during the recognition event. This one was between our VP of sales, Joe B., and one of our awesome sales staff named Jean.

Jean: Hello, sir. You are just the greatest.
Joe B: Oh Jean, you are making me blush. Any good I do is just trying to support your amazing efforts.

Jean: Well, life is stinking right now. I wanted to break $1m this month, but that is not going to happen. Best I can hope for is $700k.

Joe B: Oh c'mon, Jean. You are going to hit your target. You've got the arrow in your bow. Take your best shot!

Jean: No, sir, I am going to quit and grow tulips. It has been a lifelong passion.

Joe B: Stay persistent and reward yourself with a trip to the Amsterdam Tulip Festival. Your good deeds and hard work will surely flower into beautiful sales.

Jean: Do you know of any Hare Krishna chapters in the Virginia area? Or perhaps any good deals on a hara-kiri blade?

Joe B: Jean, you are a rock star. I bet you break $2m this month.

Jean: Sir, no way. I am worm poop right now.

Joe B: Did you know worm poop is the best part of the soil in the garden? You are clearly about to grow something big!

One week later

Jean: I got to my million dollar sales mark for the month—LOL. I took your advice and looked at the soil I'd been tilling, took careful aim, and closed the deal. Now I want to get to $2m—the sweet smell of success has charged my battery.

Joe B: Listen to you! I hear nothing but the seeds of growth coming from your two lips!

The Birthday Card

Five hours before one of our Christmas recognition parties, I was bewildered in my search for a theme for my speech. As my birthday is near the Christmas holidays, I got an idea! I went to the grocery store and bought the kind of birthday card one gives to an old guy. Of course, I had never even seen one of these cards before. I planned my party speech to be reading out loud the card and its comments my employees supposedly sent to me. Since I would be the author, and the reader, and the butt of the comments I would write on the card, I decided it would be even more fun if I got all my employees to guess who wrote each of the comments.

I figured this would be great fun, even if some of the employees would probably feel bad knowing they had not signed the card. Well, if they had cared more about me they would have signed it! Now, this was a big card measuring about 8 X 20 inches. So, there was room for lots of comments. I had written about 20 of them.

To start the speech, I thanked everyone for thinking of me and writing such kind remarks. As I began to read "their" comments, some of the smiling faces out there turned into ones with mouths agape. The more I read, the more dumbfounded the expressions became. It was difficult, but I was able to maintain a perfect poker face, the kind I wish I could produce in an actual poker game. Although I was laughing on the inside, I was still maintaining a serious look on the outside. The comments went like this:

> "Glad to see you are staying healthy. Blowing out candles is good exercise for someone your age."

> "How can you tell that you're getting old? You go to an antique auction, and three people bid on you!"

> "What goes up and never comes down? Your age!"

The looks went from person to person wondering who wrote these remarks. Inside I was having a belly laugh. At this point, people were catching on and starting to laugh. I read a few more of the comments:

> "You're not old until you pick up the remote and hold it up to your ear for a dial tone. I bet you've been getting a lot of calls lately!"

> "Sorry to hear you and your teeth don't sleep together anymore!"

"You have survived the humiliation of middle age, so now you should be strong enough to accept the ridicule of old age!"

"Another year, another wrinkle."

"The last thing on your bucket list is to give it a good kick. You better get to it while you can still stand on one leg!"

When I was done, I said, "These comments really mean a lot to me. They are so funny and supportive that I feel 10 years younger. Of course, since none of you actually signed your name to the card, I can assume the sentiment is from all of you."

I expressed my love for my workers, that we were a family and that we look out for each other. I finished my speech by saying, "Your comments were perfect. They couldn't have been better if I had written them myself, which by the way, I DID!"

This brought an explosion of laughter. All the tension was instantly gone. Somebody shouted out, "I knew those comments weren't from us, because they were too nice!"

My wife remarked that she was unaware my employees had given me a birthday card. If she had known about it, she would have stopped it. There was a little lesson she needed to teach me.

Message to all my readers, "The most effective way to remember your wife's birthday is to forget it once." She has been teaching me that lesson ever since.

My Retirement Announcement

In 2014, I announced my retirement at our annual Christmas party. I began my speech expressing how proud I was of our company, but I explained after many years of working, it was time for me to retire. The audience was in complete silence. My employees were staring at me with that deer-in-the-headlights look. No one, not even my wife, had any notion this was a set-up. I then added, I wanted to thank my wife for giving me two magazine subscriptions as an early retirement gift. One subscription was to the National Geographic and the other was to Playboy.

I told everybody, in the card she had written, "Now you can view all the places you no longer have the chance to visit."

Well, heck, I am not a big fan of crying at work, but let me tell you, my employees had tears of laughter rolling down their cheeks. I actually did get the magazines, but I put them in the closet and went back to work. I hope to never retire, and I'll write more about that in one of my last chapters.

The point I hope you will remember here, even with all my corny jokes, is that laughter is a powerful tool to bring people together, to lighten our stress load, and to make life worth living!

CHAPTER NINETEEN

Man Cave

This Month's Password to My Man Cave Is: HEROES

I have always tried to keep a place for myself in my house to be surrounded by things that inspire me. Over the years, my man cave has expanded into a 250 square foot addition in my home office. It is impeccably put together, because it was done under the close supervision of my wife, the Chick in Charge. Since she was involved, there were Do's and some Don'ts.

On the "Do" list was sports memorabilia, fireplace, sauna, treadmill, TV, stereo, and replicas of historical collectibles, statues or treasures from around the world. Below the ceiling, on the walls hang bag tags from golf courses around the world, most of which I've played. And this is where I house my real pirate treasure map, which I mentioned earlier in this book.

On the "Don't" list are projects that will never see the light of day, such as no stripper pole installed with a backdrop mirror; no jumbo beer keg with refrigeration unit under my desk; and no holographic projection unit that responds to my wife with the message, "Yes dear, good idea! I'll get right on it."

The things that I do have in the man cave are things that give me inspiration. It is my belief that by surrounding myself with greatness, some of it will rub off on me. That's the environment I want to create for myself. Building my man cave office was Memorable Moment #19. In this chapter I am going to show you around the man cave and explain some of the significance to many of the treasured items. Really, though, we are just scratching the surface. I could write a whole book about my man cave and all of its amazing contents. This is just a brief tour. My purpose here is not to brag, but to get you thinking about what you would like to include in the environment that inspires you. Who are your heroes? What are your treasures? What are you working towards?

I have lots of sports items. I love sports, and I like to be surrounded by items that represent great players and moments. I am also a person of faith, and I feel Divine Providence, God's plan for my life, is guiding me. So I want to start my description of what is in the man cave with a couple of my sacred treasures.

Our Lady of Fatima Statue

On my man-cave wall, I have a photo of a beautiful statue of Our Lady of Fatima. There is a fascinating story around this statue and the sculptor who made it, but first let me say a few things about the Shrine of Fatima itself.

More than one hundred years ago, May 13, 1917, three young children experienced a vision of Mother Mary. They lived in Fatima, Portugal. When Lucia age 10, Francisco age 9, and Jacinta age 7 saw Our Lady, she gave them a message asking for prayers and specifically to pray the Holy Rosary every day. She warned of future disaster by war, the rise of Russia as a sinister power, the destruction of many nations, and widespread famines. But she promised prayer would bring peace to the world.

Fatima has become known in the Catholic world as a place of pilgrimage for peace and healing. In the original vision, the children were asked to return to the site on the thirteenth of each month until October of that year. They did this, and people have been returning ever since. Today it is one of the most visited holy sites in the world.

My photo of the statue of Our Lady of Fatima is a reminder to seek that peace that can only come through prayer, a reminder that God reaches out to people, a reminder to strive to be my best and offer my life in service to others. These are Dominican values, and the Dominican religious order founded Providence College.

One of those Dominicans, Fr. Thomas McGlynn, was a sculptor and teacher of speech and philosophy at the college, as well as the first professor of sculpture for the college's summer arts program in Italy. In 1946 he sculpted a small figure of Our Lady of the Rosary. Fr. McGlynn was proud of his work on the statue and wanted to see if it was an accurate representation of Our Lady, according to those who actually saw the apparitions. He received permission to travel to Portugal and work with Sr. Lucia, who was now a nun. Sister examined it and had a number of corrections that would make the statue more accurate.

Here I am at The Thomas McGlynn Collection at Providence College, Providence, RI.

The hands were not quite right, the garments were too smooth, her feet needed to be on the leaves of a tree, there needed to be a star on her tunic, and the light which came from her needed to be better represented. Together Fr. McGlynn and Sr. Lucia worked in a space at her convent to create a new accurately portrayed statue of Our Lady. They worked on it each day over the course of one week, and finally both were satisfied.

In 1956 Fr. McGlynn began to work on a 15'6" tall marble version of the statue that was eventually placed in the niche of the bell tower of the new Basilica of Our Lady of the Rosary at Fatima. That is where it rests today. It is seen by millions of visitors every year.

My photo rests on the wall in my man cave, but it fills me with a desire to do honest work, to be prayerful, to collaborate with others, and to remember the good people who helped educate me. When I look at the photo of the statue, I thank Fr. McGlynn and all the Friars of Providence College.

I have not yet been to the Shrine at Fatima, but it will be #71 on my list of Memorable Moments.

The Black Madonna

The Black Madonna of Poland is an ancient painting with an amazing past. I have a statue of it. She's black, according to a Dominican scholar of the sixteenth century, because a dark complexion was simply thought appropriate for a Jewish woman of that time, or as others believe, because the painting has darkened over the years from candle-burning soot. I don't have the answer, but I love the painting and my statue either way!

In 2016, I received my replica of the Black Madonna of Poland from a priest who traveled to Poland for World Youth Day. My wife and I had sponsored some deserving youth and the priest to go on that pilgrimage to Poland. When he returned, he had the statue of the Black Madonna of Poland for us. We greatly appreciated his thoughtfulness, although we had no expectations of receiving anything in return for our gift. The Black Madonna has become one of the most prized possessions in my man cave. Let me tell you a little bit about it.

The original is a painting of Mother Mary and the Christ Child. The legend is that St. Luke the Evangelist painted Mary's portrait on a cedar tabletop, rather than a canvas. And, that tabletop had been built by none other than Jesus himself, following in Joseph's trade of carpentry. As the story goes, while Luke was painting Mary, she personally told him about the life of Jesus that he eventually wrote in his gospel.

This same legend states that St. Helen came into possession of the painting and gave it to her son Constantine in 326 AD. He built a shrine to house it. In a fierce battle with the Saracens, the painting was put on the city walls of Constantinople to give the soldiers strength. Constantine's army was overwhelmingly triumphant. Through the display of the painting, Mother Mary and Her Son had saved the city.

The legend continues that later Charlemagne presented the painting to Prince Leo of Ruthenia, Hungary. It stayed at that royal palace for centuries. In the eleventh century there was an invasion. The king prayed to Our Lady to aid his small army. A kind of darkness fell on the enemy, and they became panicked and confused. They attacked their own troops. Ruthenia was saved. Mother Mary and Her Son had again come through for the holder of this painting.

In the fourteenth century, the painting was transferred to the Mount of Light in Poland. Over the centuries the stories of miraculous power and healing continue to come forth.

I believe there is a power greater than anyone can imagine. I don't claim to know how it all works, but I do believe that prayer works. I am honored to have the statue of the Black Madonna in my man cave. Artwork, such as this, gives me strength and hope. I don't have to figure everything out for myself. There is a power greater than me that comes to the aid of all those who earnestly ask for it. I want to remember that every day of my life.

Two Friar Championship Rings— *MORE RINGS WANTED*

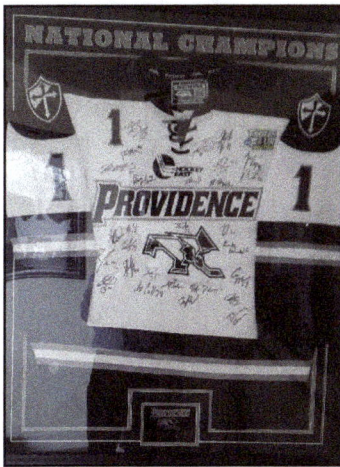

Signed Team Jersey

Let me give you a little tour of some of the sports pieces I have in the man cave. Let's start with two of my most prized possessions that hang on my wall. I'm eternally thankful and honored to have two Providence College Friar player jerseys. Both of these were given to me by the college. The first is an authentic hockey jersey with my name embossed on the back and the number 1 on it. The second is a basketball jersey with my name and the number 65, which is my graduation year. I am glad they have different numbers because it helps me remember which one goes with which sport.

These jerseys represent relationships to me. Over the years, my wife and I have done a lot for the college, and we have received a lot more in return. But it's not that exchange that matters. It is something deeper. If I had to describe it in three words, since I have three jerseys (I'll tell you about the third in a moment), I'd call it gratitude, recognition, and spirit. That is what these jerseys mean to me. They are great symbols to have in my man cave office. Receiving these jerseys was Memorable Moment #48. They remind me to be grateful, recognize others who have impacted my life in a positive way, and to do it enthusiastically with spirit. And the story continues.

Saturday, April 11, 2015, at the TD Garden in Boston, my wife and I attended the Frozen Four NCAA Hockey Championship with the Providence College athletic director and his wife. The final score of the game was Providence 4, Boston University 3. Friars won their first hockey title. Wow!! Talk about exciting! To witness a Friar championship game was Memorable Moment #94. I can still remember the announcement at the end of the game as it echoed through the stadium, "The Friars win."

Sugar and I were ecstatic to see Providence win.

A few months later my wife and I were on the Providence campus and Nate Leaman, head coach of the champion men's ice hockey team, invited us to the team locker room. It's a horseshoe-shaped room with lockers on the exterior portions of the walls. Nate asked the co-captain to come forward. I noticed the athletic director, his wife and other department staff were gathered in the far corner. That young co-captain stepped forward and presented me with a championship ring. My heart about stopped, in the good way.

Nate asked if I wanted to say a few words. I looked over at my wife, and she gave me the go-ahead nod. I held my ring high and said, "I want to thank each and every one of you for helping me to keep the promise I made to my wife 48 years ago."

I paused to let those words sink in, and then I continued, "You see, 48 years ago I promised the woman I loved that if she'd marry me, she would be sleeping with a champion. And now I've got the ring to prove it!"

After we returned home to Boulder, we were surprised to find a third framed jersey signed by all the members of our first hockey national championship team. All three of these jerseys are up on the wall of my man cave. When I look at them, it does something to me. It fills me with that desire to be a winner and to care about the places and people that have helped me to become successful, helped me to take pride in striving to overachieve.

Another inspirational ring I was given was from the 2014 Providence College basketball team. That team won the Big East championship. Providence has the smallest enrollment in the Big East, yet that year came out on top. That was a great achievement, but what I really want is a ring from winning the NCAA Final Four Championship game! Keep those rings coming. I display them in a prestigious case in my man cave.

You may wonder why I have received these jerseys and rings, and why my wife and I are invited to championship games. The reason is we love Providence College. We are life-long fans, and have tried to support the sports program at the college. One of the major efforts that we have helped fund is a Providence College basketball hall of fame. This collection has more than 3,000 elements in it. The official name is the "Joe Calabria Hallway of Legends." I want the Friars who have achieved greatness to be recognized and remembered for future generations. My man cave has a little bit of the hall of fame in it, because I want to surround myself with greatness. A big thank you goes out to my Friar family for decorating my man cave with awesome achievements!

Earned Faithful Friar Award— Memorable Moment #47

The Providence College National Alumni Association presented me with its 2015 National Alumni Association Faithful Friar Award, May 29,

2015. It is a great honor to be given this distinction. The sign acknowledging this award hangs on my wall reminding me to always strive to help others.

Invited to Join College Board of Trustees— Memorable Moment #79

On the board of trustees

I do love sports, but my interest in Providence College goes beyond athletics. On February 27, 2017, I was in the lounge at the Charlotte airport when the president of Providence College called me and invited me to join the College Board of Trustees.

I accepted the offer, and I am proud to serve on the board today. After that phone call, I told my wife I accepted this opportunity. She smiled, sat upright in her seat, and said, "Now I finally have something of interest to write about in your future obituary!" Translation: "I am proud of you honey. You're the best thing that has ever happened to me."

When I look at the various Providence College items in my man cave, I am thrilled to be an active and dedicated member of the Friar family, and want to continue to try to make a difference in the lives of the students who pass through those hallowed halls.

Celebrating Sugar's and my 50th wedding anniversary at Providence College with the athletic director, head basketball coach, head ice hockey coach, and spouses—we love the Friars because everyone believes we are one family with one objective working together to achieve our common goal.

Meeting Terry Bradshaw— Memorable Moment #61

My one-of-a-kind Terry Bradshaw collection

I wasn't always a fan of the brash, legendary Pittsburgh Steelers quarterback, but over the years, he has won me over. I saw him at a meeting I attended in which he was a motivational speaker. The gentleman in front of me was from Pittsburgh and somewhat reserved, but got up the courage to ask Bradshaw if he was still recording records. He knew Bradshaw loved to sing.

"That's a great question," said Bradshaw. They became instant buddies. That is until the four-time

Super Bowl champion asked, "Tell me, which of my records do you own, or which one is your favorite?"

Silence may be golden, but that was not what Bradshaw wanted to hear. The instant friendship was over. The Blonde Bomber, as he was known, was left no alternative but to unleash a stinging series of good-natured insults to my fellow attendee. Let this be a lesson to all of us. The right question can get you in the door, but know what you're going to say once you're in, or you may soon wish you never got to enter.

Afterwards, I had an idea come into my head. Maybe I could get some of Bradshaw's records and perhaps a signed copy of one of the articles that featured him. I got to work on that after I got home. With the help of a friend in Pittsburgh, I got four original records from thrift stores, and I framed them with a signed copy of the 1979 official NFL magazine, which had Bradshaw on the cover.

This one-of-a-kind, Terry Bradshaw collection, I proudly display on the wall of my man cave. If you haven't heard his records, they include gems like:

- Take These Chains from My Heart
- Here Comes My Baby Back Again
- The Last Word in Lonesome is Me
- Less and Less

Here is why I want Terry Bradshaw's likeness up on my wall. The guy has an authentic personality, and he is OK if you make fun of him. Talk show host Jay Leno had Bradshaw on his show 50 times and forever needled him. Leno would tell Bradshaw, "You know you can't sing, right?" But Bradshaw kept coming back.

I admired that he was one of the greats on the football field, but after he retired, he has continued to make news, have fun, and work hard. One of my favorite Terry Bradshaw moments was when he was helping to announce the Super Bowl and at half time Paul McCartney of the Beatles stopped by the announcing booth. Terry says "You know I'm a singer too." Paul doesn't take the bait, so Terry starts singing "Hard Days Night" and before you know it, Paul joins him for a duet! The guy has guts, perseverance, and more than one kind of a record to his name.

Received Arnold Palmer's Signature—
Memorable Moment #62

My man cave would never be complete without something signed and addressed to me from Arnold Palmer. To me, Arnold was synonymous with "old school" character and decency. I will always consider him the most popular player in golf history, inspiring a loyal fan base dubbed "Arnie's Army."

In his prime, he was the best golfer in the world, winning four Masters, two British Opens, a US Open, and more than 90 professional tournaments. I remember during my last college year, 1965, seeing an image of Arnie hunched over a putt. As I watched him work his magic I remember thinking, "Now there's a man who is not afraid of challenging a golf hole with a lag putt." He won 29 events between 1960 and 1963 and was named athlete of the decade for the 1960s.

I sent Arnold Palmer 5 Upper Deck trading cards of himself and asked him to sign these cards, one for each of my four grandkids and one for me. The family has grown since then, but he returned the cards with only two signed. He added a surprise to the package, though. He included a signed picture addressed to me, and he wrote me a personal note. He explained that he didn't sign all cards, because he was concerned they might end up on eBay. One day these items will go to my grandkids, many of whom already love golf. For now, though, they are featured items in my man cave. I love being surrounded by the old world excellence of Arnold Palmer.

The Babe

At the top of most anyone's sports keepsakes would be a signed Upper Deck baseball card of Babe Ruth. I have one! It's my Memorable Moment #65. In my mind, the Babe was not only the greatest baseball player ever, but he was also one of the great personalities of the 20th Century. There was a restaurant in NY City with a famous wall that featured many signatures from outstanding personalities of the 20th Century, and the Babe's signature was prominent. Mama Leone's 1965 menu duplicated these signatures of amazing people. I have one of the menus framed and hung in my man cave, along with my coveted trading card.

"Never let the fear of striking out get in your way," said Babe Ruth. Now that's wisdom I want to follow everyday.

Yogi Berra Signed Picture— Memorable Moment #65

I have a picture of Yogi with the Babe, and it's signed by Yogi. It's another great picture for my man cave. I have quoted Yogi a couple times earlier in this book, and I want to share another quote. This one is about the Yogi Berra Statue at the Yogi Berra Museum & Learning Center. It represents the down-to-earth humility I love about this hero of baseball. "It is a great honor to have a statue. I like it; they did a nice job. It fits perfectly in front of our museum, close to the ground. I hope the birds leave it alone." –Yogi Berra

Joe DiMaggio Signature— Memorable Moment #67

Joe DiMaggio was nicknamed "Joltin Joe" and the "Yankee Clipper." He set a record with his 56 game hitting streak, two years before I was born, and won nine World Series titles with the New York Yankees. That is the kind of excellence I want to be surrounded by, and of course, he's Italian. Like Joe, my father was the son of Italian immigrants. My dad agreed with and often repeated what New York City Mayor Ed Koch said of DiMaggio, "He represented the best in America." In a way, I brought my father and Joltin Joe together when I arranged for my dad to play golf in a charity event with Joe DiMaggio in attendance in 1989.

I also have a DiMaggio Brothers menu from their restaurant, Italian Chophouse, on the Wharf in San Francisco. It's signed by both Joe and Dom DiMaggio. The menu could be folded in half twice with the back section available to be addressed and sent anywhere in the US with just a

3¢ stamp. Of course, that was back in 1967! My signed menu is framed and hanging in my man cave. Every time I look at it, I get hungry for success, or maybe a nice Chianti and some lasagna.

Golf Opens Doors

On the course with Bill Raftery

Another of my treasurers is a signed picture of Bill Raftery, the famous TV sports announcer. In the picture Bill and I are sitting in a golf cart at the Newport Country Club in Rhode Island. This flamboyant announcer was there not only to play in a charity tournament, but also to be the guest speaker at the post-tournament dinner. Raftery has a certain perspective and exuberance that I admire.

There is a moment that we were together that stands out for me. Of course the Newport Country Club was an exclusive place. In the early days, no outsiders were allowed on the course. On the day I was there with Bill, we were part of a diverse foursome. While waiting for our second shot on the fifth fairway, Bill looked to the sky and asked, "What do you think the members from back in 1955 are thinking as they look down and see two Italians, one Irish man, and one black guy playing golf on their course?"

He let that thought hang in the air for a moment. Then he answered his own question and said, "Oh no! Look at them! And not a one of them is carrying a bag."

Bill remains popular with young and old viewers because of his signature swagger. He also peppers his basketball commentary "with a kiss" if a player's shot includes backboard, and the ever-popular "onions" for a clutch play.

I got to know him a little bit that day, because I accompanied him throughout the event from his arrival to departure. It was a non-stop display of his wit and personality. I am reminded of that great day each time I enter my man cave and see the photo of us together.

Own a Home on a Golf Course Fairway— Memorable Moment #20

When we moved to Boulder in 1983, we purchased our home on the eighth fairway of the club we joined. In some ways, our home, and certainly my man cave, is a constant reminder of the game I love. I purchased my most expensive toy, an all black golf cart with Friar logo on the front hood. It has over-sized wheels and wind-resistant covers that allow me to drive at warp speeds. That's important when I am trying to get to the practice range. Over the years, I have spent considerable time at the driving range and the practice putting green. Three shots have emerged as my strengths. My best shots are the practice swing, the gimme putt, and the mother-in-law shot.

I am sure you all know what the practice swing is. That is when you try not to hit the ball. I am nearly perfect at this. I am so good at this shot that I do it sometimes when I am actually trying to hit the ball.

The gimme putt is the putt you don't have to hit in the cup because it is so close to the hole no one would miss the shot. Yet, I have found that it is best to always pick the ball up when you have a gimme putt. Occasionally I have taken the time to hit it in the cup, just to get that satisfying plunk when it drops into the hole. Surprisingly, I have found that a gimme can take two to five shots to achieve that sweet plunk.

Now the mother-in-law shot is the drive that looks good when it leaves the tee box. And you can guess the rest! Certainly, my wish is that it gets even better after that.

If the day comes when I get frustrated playing golf, I'll give it up. But I don't see that day coming. It is a great way for me to blast frustration off at the range. You know what happens after a bad shot, right? I have a chance to take a breath, concentrate, and hit another bad shot! But heck, there is a lesson for life there somewhere, probably on the eighth hole. That is why my man cave exists, for me to figure out the lessons of life.

When I was in my formative golf years, I would enjoy demo day at the driving range. That is when the golf manufacturers let you try out their new clubs and equipment. It did require considerable effort not to replace last year's golf clubs with this year's upgraded version. Recently the club added additional products for fellas and gals my age, which are displayed at the far end of the range to extend our golfing days. These specialty products include instant inflatable porta potties, oxygen tanks with the scent of fresh-cut grass, and electric scooters with golf-bag racks.

Golf is a numbers game, so I like the adage said by math teacher David Pleacher, "Old math teachers never die; they just tend to infinity."

Displayed My Golf-Bag Tags— Memorable Moment #55

The walls of my man cave are painted pale gray and blend with the ultra-pure white ceiling. The separation is now accented with rows of golf-bag tags from around the world. You can get a custom bag tag at almost any course. It can serve as a souvenir, but when you put your name on it and attach it to your bag, it also serves to identify your clubs from those of other people.

Although I had collected them for more than 25 years, my wife was not in favor of me decorating my man cave with bag tags. Finally, she agreed to my plan and left for a shopping visit to the local mall. I sprang into action. I figured I needed two hours minimum to finish one wall with two rows of tags. I had to have it done before she returned. There was always the risk she might change her mind. I know this is somewhat strange, since it is MY man cave, but it is in HER house, and she is the Chick In Charge. Someone once told me that "the older you get, the better you get, unless you are a banana." I may be mighty "appealing," but I knew my wife thought my idea was kind of crazy.

I did more trips up and down my ladder in those two hours then I had done in twenty years. Almost all of my bag tags are hung without the buckle strap. But I got the job done, and she actually liked it.

I have hundreds of custom golf-bag tags. They are all different with pictures or logos, made from metal, plastic, coralline, leather, or wood. Although often eye-catching, they also have a practical use, as clubs use these tags to quickly identify members and guests. I've played many of these courses. Some of my golfing friends also send me their bag tags to add to my collection in hopes I'll offer to send them a free, signed copy of my book! My goal is to collect golf tags from the 100 highest-rated courses in the world. I am well on my way to that goal.

Golf bag tags on my wall of fame

Shot a Hole in One—
Memorable Moment #21

WESTPORT NEWS, Wednesday, September 30, 1981

Man hits eagle, ace

It ain't fair—but just four weeks after hitting his first eagle, Westporter Joe Calabria aced the eighth hole at Longshore. Calabria has been playing golf for 15 years.

"I never thought it was possible," he said.

Calabria used an 8-iron for his hole-in-one on the 126-yard eighth hole—the same club he had used in eagling the first a month earlier.

"I'm gonna save that 8-iron," he said. "Frame it and only pull it out for tournaments."

Curiously, though he usually shoots in the High 80's (Calabria is a 16-handicapper), he shot a 101 for the round that included his ace. The next time he played—without any such fireworks—he shot an 83.

'I guess that the ace was to make me come back the next day, to play another round," he said.

Calabria's oner was witnessed by Jim Awad, Ev Eckberg, and Wade Meirs, who played with him in a foursome. Although custom decrees that the golfer who hits a hole-in-one buy a round of drinks for everyone in the 19th hole, because they were playing early in the morning, Calabria couldn't: the bar was closed. Instead, he bought coffee and donuts for the other members of his quartet.

"It was a cheap hole-in-one," he said.

Daily Camera

SATURDAY
July 5, 1997 ★

HOLE-IN-ONE

Joe Calabria of Boulder aced the 142-yard 15th hole at Boulder Country Club Friday, using an 8-iron.

*Some newspaper clippings
of my golfing success*

At one time, I had more holes in one than heart procedures. Somehow that gave me comfort. I remember that dark day when I had my sixth heart procedure. I lay on the operating table, half asleep, and all I could think of was that my six procedures were now more than my five holes in one. There is a plaque for each of my holes in one up in my man cave.

Unfortunately that disparity between holes in one and heart procedures continues to widen. My advice to those looking for their first hole in one is simple. It starts with a famous, yet anonymous quote, "Golf can best be defined as an endless series of tragedies obscured by the occasional miracle."

I suggest to get that miraculous hole in one, you must allow your spiritual self to guide your club to its heavenly reward. When it all comes together, it's like being suspended in an anti-gravity sphere on the tee box. Remember, you have to take a swing if you're going to hit the ball. Just swing the big club to whack the little ball. Let the wings of angels do the rest. Timing is key. Hopefully there are some angels in the vicinity. It seems lately, my angels have to spend most of their time at the operating table guiding my heart doctors.

One consideration when contemplating a hole in one is that you have to make sure the people golfing ahead of you have gotten off the green. If you are afraid of hitting them, you have two options. You can immediately shank a lay-up, or you can wait until the green is clear and swing away, which for me, usually results in topping the ball and hitting it a few feet past the tee.

My most memorable hole in one came at a course in Boca Raton on the eighth hole. Everything felt right. There was this sense of the club separating from the ball on the back swing and then a perfectly guided reconnection. As I felt the separation-reconnection cycle, there was that beautiful, sweet ping of ball and club coming together. The ball flew straight and true. I watched it almost in slow motion as it alighted onto the green and rolled into the cup. That was my third hole in one, a breath-taking moment for me.

Actually getting a hole in one reminded me of an aphorism I learned during my time in the Army Reserves. The unit captain often quoted what he considered to be one of our mottos, "The difficult we do immediately. The impossible takes a little longer."

A hole in one is an impossibly sweet moment that can't be rushed. Spend time at the game of golf and the angels may take one of your golf balls straight into the cup. It is a great lesson of life. Everyday we have a chance for a hole in one. Savor it when it happens, but make sure you still enjoy the game even when you get a double bogie, or triple bogie, or you take so many swings that you stop counting. That is the wisdom that my man cave offers.

A Survival Kit for the Father of the Bride

One of the most important events in my life was my daughter's wedding. One of my friends sent me a survival kit to get me through the wedding and all its preparations. I keep it in my man cave. As it turns out, it can help for more than just weddings.

For a short while, it looked like there would be very few preparations needed. This was because I told my daughter the total amount for the wedding budget. Then I added, "Anything you spend beyond that amount is your expense, but anything less than that amount you get to keep."

My daughter studied me. "What if we just elope? Then do we still get to keep what we don't spend?"

"Yes, anything under the budgeted amount goes to you."

"Great, then we are eloping."

My daughter told my wife that she was now planning to elope, but my wife begged her not to do that. She said, "It would break your father's heart. Don't you know that he has always dreamed of walking his only daughter down the wedding aisle?"

Let me tell you, they did not elope. The weeks leading up to the event were fraught with tension and intrigue. My credit cards, bank accounts, and seemingly the federal reserves, were maxed out overnight. My wife and daughter appeared to be engaged in a mysterious feminine rite of passage that required me to keep away from them at all times. They were completely capable of making their own decisions. They didn't want the slightest bit of my helpful advice. I learned to lay low and surface only when needed—in other words, to sign checks.

Occasionally, I sought solace from buddies who had weathered such blessed events and lived to tell the tale. One day, after bemoaning my fate in a telephone call to a childhood friend, I received a "Father of The Bride Care Package." In the interest of worldwide male solidarity, I pass on the list of contents and instructions of this survival kit to future fathers of the bride. It is also quite instructive for the ladies.

My friend wrote that I was no doubt overburdened and excessively bugged. He said, "To assist you during this most difficult fortnight before the Big Event, and having experienced the grievous effects of this sort of tension in the past, I enclose the following aids."

This is a man-cave treasure, because it is a humorous reminder to keep things in perspective. Here is what was in the care package he sent to me:

1.   One pound of $1,000 bills. When the wedding is through,

and all the charges calculated, you will need every last one!
(Unfortunately, these were not real.)

2. Receipt book. There are 32 receipts in the book. I can assure
    you that these will not be enough, but it's a start. Good luck!

3. Aspirin. This may look like a big bottle, but no bottle could be
    big enough.

4. Post-its. Your wife and daughter will come up with so many
    ideas, suggestions, demands, and orders, that you'll use up this
    book of 100 post-its by tomorrow afternoon.

5. Kleenex. No, these aren't for the moment when you hand your
    daughter over to the groom. They are to absorb your tears as
    the money flows out the door.

6. Imodium A-D. It's true; you aren't just losing a daughter. You
    are losing your money, sleep, patience, and golf game, and this
    will help to plug the leak.

7. Olives. Martinis will help get you through.

8. Matches. When the arguments and discussions about the
    reception, flowers, dinner, wine, hard liquor, band, and song
    list become overwhelming, you have my permission to "torch
    the hall."

9. Ear Plugs. To help you retain your sanity.

10. A "Show Me the Money" desk plaque. Yes, it's just a plaque to
    set on your desk, but it sends the right message!

The Vest

After all was said and done, I wanted to add the perfect "priceless" gift for
our daughter on her wedding day. I considered all the options, such as
boxing up the old posters in her bedroom, or giving her two paid holiday

days at work, one before the wedding and one after, or giving her an envelope full of valuable coupons from the newspaper. All those seemed good, but were perhaps excessive. I wanted to send the right message, after all.

Finally, I decided that what she would want most would be for me to invest in my wedding wardrobe. What if I was to wear a vest with more than 75 pictures silk-screened on it? That would get her attention! These pictures would span our daughter's life from birth through a few months before the wedding. Now I finally had something to work on before the wedding.

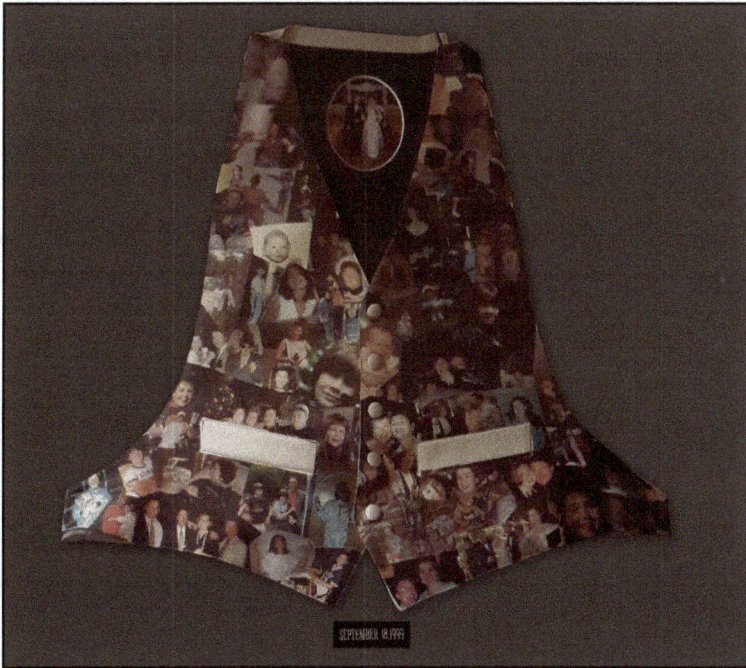

Wedding vest of the father of the bride

It was quite the challenge to find a vest where the silk-screen process would work. I eventually found it, though, and meticulously picked out the pictures to include in the photo montage. When the big day rolled around, I put on the photo vest along with my tuxedo. With my tux buttoned, you couldn't even tell the vest was on, but what an impact it had when my jacket was open!

On the way to the church, I showed my daughter the vest. My heart sang when she saw it. Her complete surprise blossomed into utter joy. How fun and meaningful it was to see the pictures of her life flash before her eyes! I guess I was a flasher that day, but it was OK, because my body was picture perfect!

After the wedding, I had that one-of-a kind vest framed. I proudly display it in my man cave. I added in a photo of me walking my little girl down the wedding aisle, and yes, my wife was right. I had dreamt about doing that ever since we had a daughter. Actually, when she was in sixth grade, I tried three times to give her away. Just joking. It was really in eighth grade. Nonetheless, there is a note on the back of a picture I keep with the vest that reads, "May the best day of your past, be the worst day of your future. Love, Dad." Surprising my daughter with a unique vest was Memorable Moment #50.

Let me be clear, because sometimes my humor obscures the truth. Every penny spent on that wedding was worth it! I love my daughter. I love my son. I love their families.

Webster's Dictionary Pages

My Man Cave has a couple of original 100-year-old Webster's Dictionary pages with stenciled messages handcrafted over the original Webster's page. This creates a piece of "message" artwork with an unusual background, the dictionary definitions.

The first page reads, "When people stare at me I assume it's because they are taking notes on how to be awesome."

The second page reads, "I may be crazy, but all the best people are."

I take these messages to heart. After all, they are in the dictionary! What a great money making idea. Use old dictionary pages as a background to display a funny bit of inspiration. I like innovative ideas such as these, and you know I love jokes! It is the perfect message to display in my man cave.

The Elephant

I have a hand-carved and hand-painted elephant made of kadam. That is a kind of evergreen prevalent in certain parts of the world. This little treasure was made in Rajasthan, India. Kadam wood is well known for its strength and long life and therefore is often used for making decorative sculptures such as Buddhas, elephants, and nature scenes.

The elephant is said to never forget. I try to be a person who remembers important moments in life, people I have met, and promises to keep. The elephant is also known for its longevity, social cooperation, and loyalty. These are all qualities I want in a big way. I am happy to have plenty of room for an elephant in my man cave!

The Money Dome

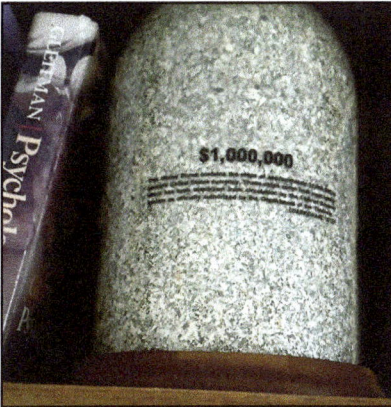

Money dome

My money dome contains $1,000,000 in genuine United States currency. The only sad part is that the money has been shredded into little chips. These chips were once legal tender, which was withdrawn from circulation by the Federal Reserve System as officially authorized by the Department of the Treasury.

In my man cave I am reminded that money comes and money goes! To everything there is a season, my friends. The money dome has become a daily reminder to limit my appetite and follow humorist Eileen Mason's advice, "My favorite dish is mixed greens: Twenties, Fifties, and Hundreds." Memorable

Moment #77 is having $1,000,000 in cash always available at my fingertips.

Perfect Vacation Life— Memorable Moment #78

For years, I joked the perfect vacation would be to spend one year traveling with my wife to every major sporting event in the country. However, it seems my family has other priorities as to how I should spend my money. Jetting from one great sporting event to another doesn't hold the same appeal to them as it does to me. So these sporting events have been spread over many years. It is all part of accommodating other interests into our vacation plans with our kids and grandkids. I have had the pleasure of attending lots of great sporting events and hope for many more to come. I am the kind of guy who keeps ticket stubs and VIP passes, and guess where I store them? That's right, my man cave!

Among the highlights have been two World Series Baseball Games, and one National Football League Super Bowl (XXXII). I saw the Broncos beat the Green Bay Packers in San Diego, CA! There have been hundreds of other sporting events that I have attended, most of them amateur sports. I am a competitor, and I love to see competition in action. My man cave is the place where I keep the various mementos I have collected over the years.

Avalanche Hockey Stick and Jersey

My man cave is a little cooler because of the National Hockey League souvenirs I keep on ice. Sorry, I meant to say, I keep them near my ice bucket. Just before the NHL 1995-1996 season, the Avalanche moved from Quebec to Denver. We were first in line for tickets. I have sports memorabilia from both Avalanche championships in Colorado. One of my treasures is a hockey stick signed by nine key members of the 1996 Stanley Cup Champions!

The other unbelievably cool item is that I was able to get Avalanche Captain Joe Sakic's #19 jersey signed by every member of their 2001 team when they also won the Stanley Cup Championship. Many of the signatures on the stick and the jersey are from players in, or destined for, the Hall of Fame. These items are man cave excellence at its finest.

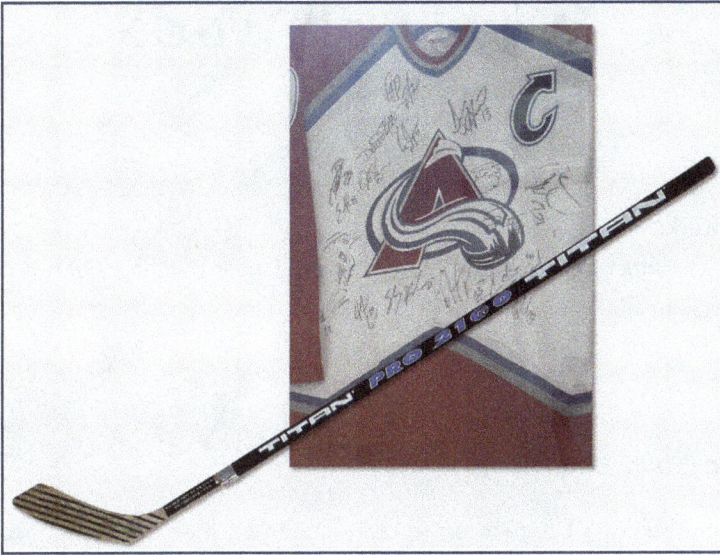

My signed jersey and hockey stick

"Diamond Dream" Baseball

During World War II, women's professional baseball teams drew thousands of fans. It was top-notch wartime entertainment. I have a baseball signed by a number of excellent baseball players, who played in the American Women's Professional Baseball League, including first baseman Dorothy Kamenshek, second baseman Sophie Kurys, and pitcher Jean Faut. While I have many signed baseballs, this is the only one I have signed by these famous women.

That's right, women are allowed in my man cave. Inspiration comes in many forms.

My main point here is that I have selected the things, images, quotes, and symbols I have in my man cave. I surround myself with excellence, humor, faith, and beauty. In your special place, what surrounds you? I'll share more man cave stories in my next book.

CHAPTER TWENTY

Why I Still Work

I AM IN MY MID 70S, SO YOU MIGHT ASK, "WHY DO YOU STILL work?"

The short answer is that my wife is the Chick In Charge of our company, and she won't accept my resignation.

For a more complete answer, read on.

The Steel Foundry

It could be that I don't want to retire, because I have seen some people who have retired, and I don't want that to happen to me. As an example, let me share a story from years ago.

The VP of sales at a steel mill in my old IBM territory became one of my clients. I couldn't get him to spend much more than a dime on our IBM products, but I did get to know him in the process of trying.

To describe this VP of sales, I would use adjectives like strange, weird, bizarre, offbeat, and unconventional. When the IBM Selectric typewriter ruled the universe, he preferred his secretary to pound the keys out with an old-fashioned manual typewriter. Anyway, the steel mill was sold in 1972. Rumor had it that our VP friend got a golden-parachute payout and retired.

From then on, all he did was play golf, play gin rummy cards, and drink lots of cocktails. He had a golfing and drinking buddy that he hung out with almost everyday. That is, until his friend decided that he wanted more than golf, cards, and drinks everyday. He took a consulting job, which led to full-time work, and even overtime. He had no time for his old pal who was still retired.

A few years later, that old golfing buddy died. The former VP of sales shared remarks at his best friend's funeral. He was abusive, insulting, and critical of his friend. He used profanity during the service, blaming his death on going back to work. He thought the most important part of life was golf and drinks.

No thank you. That is not the life I want to live. I guess my VP friend never heard Robert Byrne the writer say, "The purpose of life is a life of purpose."

Why retire when I have a purpose at my work?

77 and Still Working

My wife thinks I'd get bored retired. After all, what could I be doing? Off the top of my head I'd say, exercise, relax in the hot tub, sip coffee, read the paper, golf, play a card game with pals, drink a martini, watch Friar BB game, have sex with wife, and write another chapter in my next book. My wife has not approved this list.

She also believes a retired husband becomes a wife's full-time job. The real truth is my wife can't afford for me to retire. To start with, I work the first 7 ½ months of the year to support my wife's Christmas habit. She is more generous than Santa Claus himself! The next five months go just to pay taxes. Now you do the math. I end up a ½ month in the hole! Retire? Are you kidding me? We can't afford to have me retire.

My new work contract secures four more years of my life, which is just enough time to pay off current taxes. I hope the good Lord is listening about that four-year extension. I don't want to die before I give Uncle Sam every last drop from this old turnip. But hey, there is always a positive if you look for it. Even though I'm working, I'm now allowed to take Wednesdays and Fridays off to play golf with the retired whippersnappers at our Country Club.

I guess the cynics are right—the money is too good to pass up. It also helps me to contribute to causes I believe in, which is Memorable Moment #98.

Attaining the Perfect Swing—
Memorable Moment #22

As I see it, life is not about money. But it is about continuing to work. One of the things I am still working at is to attain the perfect golf swing. After I had found the perfect wife, and the perfect line of work, I started trying to find the perfect golf swing. I'm still at it. I've tried every technique and have taken lessons from lots of pros, always looking to find the perfect theory to actualize the ideal swing.

After many years of frustration, I decided to try hypnosis. I didn't set out to be hypnotized, but I told my sad story of frustration to the wife of one of my managers. She had a degree in psychology and worked as a therapist. Her suggestion was to make an appointment, and she would get me the results I so desired. To make this work, I needed to select a code word. She would take me through a process to put that code word into my subconscious. Then, all I had to do was to say that word before I took a swing.

This therapist also told me to bring my wife. I mean, I love my wife, but can you imagine the risks of taking my wife to such a session where she would have the opportunity to plant her trigger words into my subconscious? For instance, from that day on, she says "jump" and I get up and start vacuuming, or she says, "snap" and I start polishing the silver. No thank you.

So what happened in my wifeless therapy session? Well, the therapist suggested I imagine walking down a flight of stairs and at the bottom I would be asked to give my code word to attain the perfect swing. I don't think I ever was completely under her power of suggestion, but I can honestly say, it didn't work. My voyage into the imaginary led to an overgrown, thorny, prickly path. My perfect swing became even more elusive as I found myself bombarded by annoying thoughts every time I picked up my clubs. It wasn't worth the experience, but hey, I'm glad I was willing to try something new. Just don't say my code word "rutabaga" before I take my next swing.

I took golf lessons from many pros over the last 50 years and only once had the perfect swing. Mike Adams at the PGA school in Florida was late for my lesson. When I finally had him tracked down, we moved to an isolated practice area. After two swings, Mike guided me through a swing adjustment, and suddenly my drives were thirty yards longer and straight as an arrow. Two more Palmer-like swings and Mike vanished. So did my perfect swing. I now must find my perfect swing by reading the gospel according to St. Titleist.

Putting all kidding aside, I think I have found the perfect swing. It is based on a simple image and phrase. To get the perfect swing you simply say to yourself, "Lift club past ear." From there you just do what comes natural. Yeah, that's the ticket. I am willing to teach people this innovative approach. Give me a call, and for a large donation to a charity of my choosing, I'll happily teach you everything I know about the perfect swing. This is why I still work.

Shoot My Age in Golf

I'm taking vitamins, exercising on the treadmill three to four times per week, and having sex on a regular basis (dreams can be beautiful). I am doing all of this in order to live long enough to score my age, or lower, in golf before I pass into the great fairway in the sky. I am really hoping I don't end up in the endless sand trap, or plummet into the never-ending water hazard. I feel if I stay active into my 90s, I'll have the opportunity to realize this Memorable Moment #99. Remember, a guy has to have goals to work toward. I like the unknown author who said, "If you're not sure where you're going, you'll probably end up somewhere else."

Cousin Silly Goose

I have a cousin that I'll call Silly Goose. He was able to retire twenty years ago, at age 48! That's the dream right? Retire early so you can enjoy life! Listen to me carefully when I say, "NO." That is a myth. We need to keep working, even if it is at your golf game.

The Silly Goose spends all his time in front of his TV. No thanks.

That is not listed as one of my 100 Memorable Moments. Life is for living, not for watching.

What? The game is on! OK, I'll watch for a little while.

22 Years Old in 1965

Back in my early years, I already noticed that life keeps marching on, and in a way we are playing it in quarters, just like a football game. When I was 22 years old, I was starting my second quarter of life, which was Memorable Moment #29. Now I am in the fourth quarter of my life. Anyone who has ever watched sports knows that the fourth quarter is the most important. It is when the game is won or lost.

Bernard Baruch, famous financier and advisor to Presidents Wilson and Franklin D. Roosevelt, stated his definition of old age as anyone 15 years older than he was. I love that. When I was in my early 20s, I was positive I'd be retired by the time I was 30, then 40, after that 50.

O.A. Battista, famous Canadian chemist and author, describes age as deceiving. He notes that it as amazing how much faster 60 comes after 50, compared to 50 after 40!

With that in mind, the rest of this quarter of life is going to fly by. My goal is to stay in the game. Heck, in just 15 short years I'll enter the threshold of old age. Perhaps late in the fourth quarter of my life, I will write my third book in a secret code that few people will be able to read (cursive writing).

I Slept with a Grandma— Memorable Moment #53

In 1999, my wife and I arrived in Florida for a two-week vacation in late December. We were trying to escape the Colorado cold and my business workload. However, the most important reason was that our son and daughter-in-law were days away from welcoming our first grandchild into our lives.

Once the baby came, the first night of celebration was followed with a very shocking and upsetting interruption of sleep. In the middle of the night, I suddenly awoke and a jolting thought made me sit up straight and my eyes move toward my ears. I realized, "I am sleeping with a GRANDMA!" My abrupt actions, followed by a gasping for air, caused my wife to awaken and ask, "What's wrong?"

Of course, I felt bad that I had woken her up. She was a grandma; she needed her beauty sleep. Nonetheless, I let her in on my shocking realization. My response started with the catchphrase of the legendary baseball player and broadcaster Phil Rizzuto, "Holy Cow!" I followed that by saying, "I'm sleeping with a GRANDMA!"

Very interestingly, my wife replied, "Holy Haberdashery! I'm sleeping with a GRANDPA."

Now wide-awake, I moved closer and whispered, "No you are not. You're sleeping with a distinctive, impressive, elderly gentleman with a grandson named the IV."

That playful romance isn't just for new grandparents. It is worth working at your whole life, for as long as you have breath in your lungs, and for as long as you want to have a loving relationship with your spouse. Consider yourself lucky if you're still able to work at it a little bit each day.

Sleeper Definition

I don't believe God wanted me to pop out of bed early in the morning to exercise. If he did, he would have had me sleep in a toaster. But, I still have the drive to want to make a difference and to do something useful. So I start most days early in the morning. One day, though, I should probably be able to sleep in. I've already started practicing.

My training for a leisurely retirement includes oversleeping, napping, dozing, passing out, catching z's, and resting. Once I become proficient, I'll have the proper credentials to qualify for full retirement. That will take considerable knowledge and experience derived from long training and practice of the slumbering exercises.

Line of Sight

So much of life is how you view it. It is all about perspective and line of sight. It's my guess that it is time for full retirement when my line of sight shows me all of these things.

- I try to straighten out the wrinkles in my socks and discover I am not wearing any socks.

- I brush my teeth while holding them in my hand.

- "Getting lucky" means I remember where I parked my car.

- I'm still alive–just to piss off Medicare.

A favorite quote I heard is from college basketball coach Abe Lemons, "The trouble with retirement is you never have a day off."

Finding Little Ways to Protect Retirement— Memorable Moment #73

I am learning that there are three ways to affect your future retirement. First, how long you opt to continue to work. Second, how you manage your investments. Third, how much attention you pay to the escalating costs of your quality of life.

The following is an example of the third way to preserve your money. One weekend, I decided to stay at home, trying to relax and watch the game. Not like my cousin the Silly Goose, mind you, just watch one game. However, my frustration with poor satellite reception soon took control of my afternoon. After pulling out a good portion of what little hair I have left, I decided to pull out my recent satellite bill instead.

Just as I thought, I was being charged for shows and channels I don't use and don't want. The key to lessening one's frustration is to call the cancellation number, because the satellite company should want to ease your pain and keep you as a customer, or so I thought. When I finally talked to a real person, I asked her why I must pay for Spanish channels and regional games when I don't watch either one. She explained that I don't pay for it, but it's part of my package. I clarified for her that if it is part of my package, I am paying for it!

She was very appreciative of my lesson, and offered me a $10 rebate on my next bill.

Then, I got to my main point, my overall monthly cost. It had risen from $60 to $115. She knocked it down a few dollars and we ended that day's call. But six months later, my bill came roaring back, higher than ever! Enough is enough. I took decisive action. I moved our account to my wife's name, with the same address, but a different cell phone number, and a different billing account number. I set this new account up for a two-year plan at $60 per month, which was half of my last bill.

Why do the cable, phone, and satellite companies do this to us? Don't they know we aren't going to take it? Anyone who is working to retire, or who has already taken that step, needs to keep careful control of his or her costs. A bill like the one I was getting is too much to swallow.

The companies would do well to remember what songwriter and poet Carroll Bryant said, "Don't bite off more than you can chew, because nobody looks attractive spitting it back out.

As I Have Grown Older

I've learned that pleasing everyone is impossible, but pissing everyone off is a piece of cake. On the downside, pissing people off usually makes my stress level soar. I now have 21 stents and possibly more coming. I'm not kidding. This procedure has become so routine for me, that during my last procedure, I was totally awake. Oddly enough, I kept asking the nurse to hold the bedpan for me. Three times I needed to urinate.

Perhaps it was just the medication, but I swear all the nurses took interest in me at that moment, and I think one even pulled out a cell phone to get video of this old Italian stallion.

For one of my past procedures, I was asked if I wanted to watch the operation on the monitor aside my surgery bed. "Will it be in color?" I asked.

"No," the nurse replied. Therefore, I declined.

Then there was the time I was asked what type of music I preferred during the procedure. I responded that I was Italian and could make my own music. I began to sing, "O sole mio." They immediately stopped me and said I was out of tune. The nurses suggested I pick a recorded song. So I said I wanted the music that would make the surgery team most proficient. They put on the theme from "Jaws."

During one of my follow-up visits to my cardiologist, my wife asked if there would be any sexual limitations imposed on me. He explained that strenuous sex was like walking up two flights of stairs. He asked me, "Do you think you could walk up a couple of flights of stairs?"

"Well, if my wife was beckoning for me at the top of the stairs, yes I do believe I could make it."

The doctor asked, "And what if she wasn't at the top of the stairs, but you had to walk up to get your medication anyway, then would you have any trouble getting up the steps?"

"It all depends," I said.

"On what?" asked the doctor.

"Whether the steps were on an escalator, or if they were the old-fashioned type that you have to lift your feet up for every step."

The Doc's order, "Take it slow, and limit the number of steps."

A Beautiful Poem About Growing Old

One day I was sitting in my rocking chair when I realized I was getting the same sensation from my chair I used to get from riding a roller coaster. That's when I decided to write this poem and share it with the world. It reads as follows:

"Rock with me while I age."

Unfortunately, I have forgotten the rest of the poem, but it's good so far, isn't it?

Victoria's Secret Fashion Show

Being a red-blooded American male, it is not hard for me to admit that Victoria's Secret, the women's lingerie shop, seems appealing to me. Earlier in my book, I mentioned that I would like to attend one of the famed Victoria's Secret fashion shows—with my wife at my side, of course.

As it turned out, 2019 was the last version of the show. They cancelled it to "evolve their brand." Ratings had dropped, and there had been numerous complaints about the scantily clad nature of the program. I thought my future memorable moment had disappeared, but as is so often the case, when God shuts the door, a window opens.

On a recent trip to Florida, my wife came up short in the unmentionables category. She forgot to pack enough underwear. OK, I know, I just mentioned the unmentionable, but I kind of had to for this story to make sense. So anyway, we drove to the local mall, and right there by the entrance was the Victoria's Secret shop. My wife had actually never purchased anything in there before, but we had to do something about the, ahh, situation. So, I led her into the store to save the day.

I have good taste in these matters, and let me tell you, she picked out a pair of underwear that was really sexy. She said, "What do you think of these? Shall I get 'em?"

I smiled, "Yes indeed, but don't stop with just one pair. That wouldn't be prudent. It would be best to get several, just to be safe." And so, she got about a half dozen assorted pairs. We paid the bill, and home sweet home we went. I have to say, it doesn't get much better than that! My wife was the one and only model for my Memorable Moment #101— Watched Victoria's Secret Fashion Show in Person with my Wife.

Never mind the fact she didn't strut her stuff down the runway and show me all the best angles. I'm a salesman. I can imagine how it all looks!

Burial Plot

Earlier in the book, I wrote about my ideal cemetery plot. Since I'm almost done with my book, it's probably fitting to add one more tombstone story. A friend with only nine stents ignores all diet recommendations, regardless of who gives them to him and why. Every Friday night at the club, he devours a slab of roast beef big enough to choke the proverbial horse. We all know where that leads. So I asked him what he wanted on his tombstone. One day he answered my question, "Medium rare with extra onion rings."

Veritas Torch— Memorable Moment #87

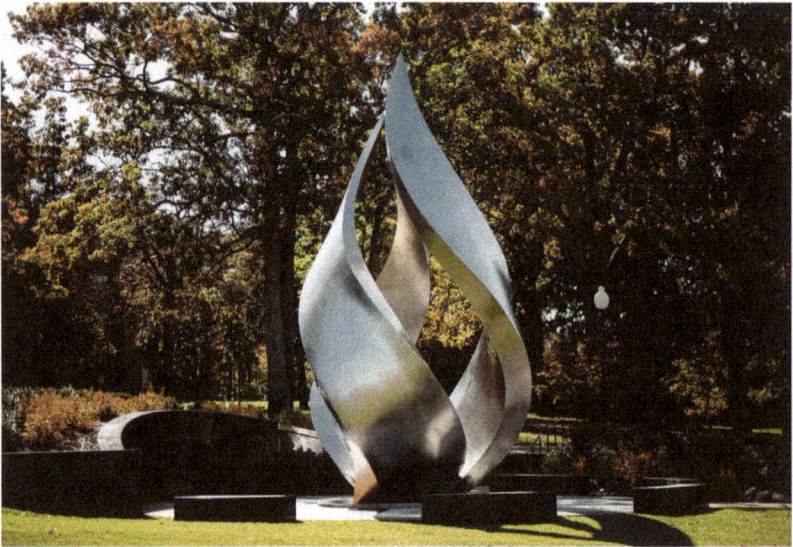

A few years ago, Sugar and I attended a celebration at Providence College. This event brought together key donors and featured food, fellowship, music, and entertainment. At one point in the evening, an all-American runner from the college ran between the tables carrying a torch. It was a striking image.

Later that evening, Sugar and I went for a stroll on the campus grounds. That image of the torch runner was in our minds. In fact, the symbol of Providence College is the torch of truth, known in Latin as Veritas. The college is dedicated to that pursuit of truth. As we continued hand in hand on our romantic walk that evening, it occurred to us that there was no actual torch at the campus. Perhaps we were being called to provide the funds so that one could be built.

A few moments after we had this idea, we came to a crossroad—another path going across the campus. Walking on that other path was the president of the college, Fr. Brian Shanley. Sugar told him our idea and said, "With your approval, we would like to build a torch on campus." He immediately liked that idea, and soon we shared it with our friends and staff at the college. Gradually, the plan took shape. This would be more than a torch. This would be a plaza for students and visitors to enjoy. It would be a tangible symbol of the college, a destination site. It would be called "Calabria Plaza."

In this case, Calabria Plaza has more than one meaning. Read on.

The decision was made that there would be no actual flame but that a striking stainless-steel sculpture, along with special colorful lighting, would symbolize the fire of truth. Drawings were made. The plans were analyzed. There would be many symbolic elements to the plaza. The sculpture of the torch would rise up 33' into the air, which was inspired by Christ's 33 years of life. There would be a round base at the sculpture representing the halo of St. Dominic. The black granite wall would be 7' high symbolizing the seven days of creation.

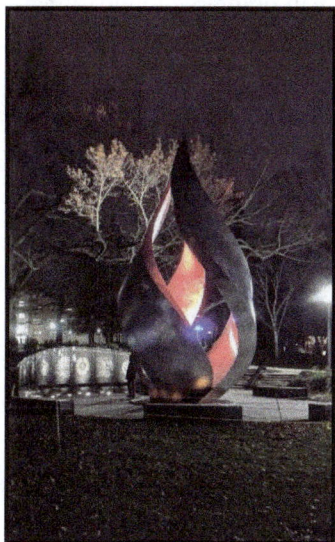

The ground was broken, and the work began. There were numerous difficulties. This was hard for me to take since I thought Sugar and I were offering such an important gift to the campus. Shouldn't God bless and make such an effort smooth? One difficulty was that both the black granite for the walls and the stainless-steel sculpture itself, for various reasons, needed to come from China. The sculptor worked with his team in China to create the architectural drawings for the plaza. When we at the college got them, we found they were done using the metric system, and notes for the project were recorded in Chinese. This, of course, ensured that they would be clear as the order was fulfilled in China, but for us to understand and approve it, we had to get everything translated. Sounds easy enough, but it was quite a challenge.

The sculpture arrived from China by boat at an international shipping yard in California. Because it was massive, weighing 19,000 pounds and being more than 30 feet long, the sculpture was an oversized load and had a very complicated shipping route across the country. Only certain highways can accept an oversized load this big. At one point, the truck driver missed an exit. He then was forced to go under a bridge that was too short for his load. He got the truck stuck under that bridge. Fortunately, by deflating the tires of the truck, they were able to extract it from under the bridge. Finally, the shipment made it to the college.

During this time, I attended a trustees meeting. I walked to the plaza site before that meeting to see how it looked. After the meeting, I went back to see what was accomplished that day. I was a little irritated at the slow progress of the construction. So I talked with the skilled craftsman doing the foundational stone work for the sculpture and the entire plaza. Standing at the construction site, he told me that he wouldn't be rushed. In fact, he had been trained by his father, and his father was from Calabria, Italy. Furthermore, I learned his father had passed away only a couple of months earlier. In an emotional moment, he said that his father was guiding him with every block of granite he laid. Wow. There was no way I could tell him to hurry up. The truth of the matter was that the project was proceeding at God's speed. The truth was that more than one Calabria family was contributing to the success of the project. God's truth has a way of making these connections known. God's truth is not always easy, even when we have the best of intentions.

In the end, it all got done. The stone work by that artisan granite setter was perfectly laid. When the sculpture was erected, not a single stone shifted. It was done to perfection. Calabria Plaza has truly become one of the centerpieces of the college, a destination point for all those who are seeking truth. As one descends down the steps of the plaza, they can read the words: "Where the search for Veritas begins."

Sugar and I have contributed to the college in many ways, but John Killian, the president of the board of trustees at the college, told us: "This contribution will be the most important thing you have done. This is how you will be remembered."

It is truly Memorable Moment #87—Built a Veritas Tribute Plaza on Providence College Campus.

Near Death

I joke a lot. You know that by now. This story is serious, but it has a funny ending. On one of my stent operations, there was a complication. I developed a clot. This was a medical emergency, and I nearly died.

I can't really report on what happened for the surgical team, but I do remember what happened for me. I was in a state somewhere between asleep and awake. Suddenly I knew I was dying. I had this feeling that my life was slipping away. In that moment, I felt I had a choice.

My decision was to fight to stay alive. I wanted everyone to know that I wanted to live. I was praying, begging, fighting for my life. Suddenly there was relief, and I got this distinct feeling everything was going to be OK.

When I awoke, I was being wheeled out of the surgical theater and transported down the hall. I saw my daughter, who was obviously relieved to see me awake, but then she started to laugh.

"What?" I asked.

"You'll never believe what just saved your life," she said.

"What was it?" I mumbled.

"Rattlesnake venom. They used it to break up a blood clot that was about to kill you."

Snakes. I hate snakes, and I am afraid of them. My daughter knew that. How funny is life? The thing that I am most afraid of saved my life.

The Decision Is Made

So, my wife tells me she has something special for my 76th birthday, and if I get in her car, I will get my surprise present. What an offer! As my Uncle Frank used to say, "This is one I can't refuse."

When she put her Buick SUV in gear as I sat back in her heated leather seats, I thought, as I have many times, this is the sweetest woman alive; it is no wonder her nickname is "Sugar!" As we drove, I wondered if she would pull the vehicle over on some tree-covered, private lane. Perhaps we were headed to the backseat. I imagined her turning up the music, opening her coat, and saying, "Happy birthday, Mr. President."

Well, she must have sensed what I was dreaming because before I knew it, we turned into the church parking lot of Sacred Heart of Mary Catholic Parish. "How sweet," I thought. "She wants to renew our vows."

That was not the case. In fact, what she had decided was that it was time to pick my final resting place. As she explained this to me, I wondered if this might be my last birthday present. For just a moment, I envisioned that she might be dropping me off! I followed Sugar into the parish office. This was the only local church in Boulder with a Catholic cemetery. It wasn't our parish, but it was one we occasionally attended. This time, evidently, we had an appointment with a lady named Peaches. She is the one who sells the plots at the church cemetery.

"I am not dressed for such an occasion," I said to the two ladies as they briskly walked into the cemetery. They clearly were on a mission. We stopped to look at some burial sites set aside for cremation. They were nestled in a patch of grass that hadn't been cut in a while. I said, "I think I'd rather be in Aruba for the long haul. Things can get pretty cold here."

"Where you're headed," said Sugar, "the cold is not the thing to worry about."

Peaches smiled, "Let's keep looking. Shall we?" She gestured for us to follow her along the cemetery path. Peaches had attractive blonde hair and a cheerful disposition. Sugar, the woman of my dreams, walked next to her.

As I took in the view, I said to myself, "This isn't all bad."

The wind kicked up, and I felt a chill from the overcast skies. Peaches led us to a newly built mausoleum. It was surrounded by mud, and there were no benches to sit upon. "This looks perfect," said Sugar. "This could be your final resting place." She pointed to an open space in the wall near the bottom of the burial niches. "Our grandkids could come and touch your marker and sit by your side."

I looked deep into Sugar's eyes, and I could see she really wanted this. And by this, I mean when the time comes for me to die, she didn't want to have to travel to Aruba to visit me, nor did she want our kids and grandkids to have to travel. She wanted me here, by her side, near the home we built together.

"Oh, no you don't," I said. "I'm not going down there. I don't want people laying on top of me for all eternity. If you want me here, you are going to have to buy me the penthouse suite!"

Peaches asked, "And, by that, you mean top row center?"

"That's right," I said.

"As you can see," said Peaches, "that spot is taken...on this side." She walked us around to the other side. "But look at that." She raised her hand and pointed to the empty top row center. "This faces the mountains and has a beautiful sunset every night."

"We'll take two," I said.

"Why two?" asked Peaches.

"Well, one for me and one for Sugar."

"Joe," said Peaches, "the niches can hold two urns. It will be a little tight, but you and Sugar can be together for all eternity in your private penthouse."

"Now wait just one minute," I said. "It may not be immediately apparent, but there is more to me than meets the eye. I think it could be difficult to, ahh, stuff it all in to such a tight space."

Sugar let out a little laugh. "Dear, I have no doubt that we will be able to get you all in that little container. You know, you're not quite as big as you think."

"OK, my beautiful wife, very funny, but think about this—there will be no room for a TV to watch, no room for a radio. What am I supposed to do for all eternity? Will I be forever immersed in silence?"

"I'll keep you company," says Sugar. "Silence will not be an issue."

"So, I'm supposed to listen to you for all of eternity? That's my birthday present?"

Sugar gives me one of those looks. I can see this is a losing battle, I mean, a time to be filled with gratitude. But I say, "My buddies are going to want to come by and smoke a cigar and talk to me about guy stuff. Will there be a place for cigars?"

"I'll give them a cigar when they come by," says Sugar.

"What about me?" I ask.

Sugar smiles, "You're going up in a puff of smoke. Remember that when your boys come around."

Peaches chimes in, "You have some choices on the engraving that goes on the vault cover. Would you like to upgrade for the color versions on your marker?"

"Absolutely," I say. "And can we add in heating and air-conditioning?"

Sugar says, "You don't need to worry about being cold when you are filled with hot air."

"You know," I retort, "I have done a lot of good in my life. I'm not all hot air. If it wasn't for us, there wouldn't be the Veritas Torch shining light and truth at Providence College. I think on our marker, we should have a color picture of the torch along with our names—Joseph M. Calabria, Jr. and Sugar Calabria."

"Slow down, mister. I am not going to be listed as Sugar Calabria. My full name will go on our marker—Marlene R. Calabria."

"We can't do that!" I say. "Nobody knows you as Marlene. People will think I am sleeping with another woman."

Sugar shakes her head at me and says, "I should be so lucky. Happy birthday, honey."

Without saying anything, I start to ponder the situation. Dollar signs flash by my eyes. I realize that this final resting place costs a significant amount of money. I note that it is locked from the outside, which means, once I go in, I won't be able to get out. Yet, it is likely that it will be vacant for some time to come. I wonder if I might put it on Airbnb for the near term. I start thinking of the selling points...It has a beautiful view of the Rockies and the highest elevation of any place in the cemetery. It is as close as you can get to God.

Sugar takes my hand. Our eyes lock. She raises her eyebrows. And just like that, my fate is sealed. My birthday present received. Memorable Moment #75 is fulfilled. We have planned the perfect burial plot.

I turn toward Peaches, "Who do I write the check to?"

Non-profit Corporation for Scholarships

I am a for-profit kind of guy, but as I am about to get to the final section of this book, I want to say that one of the things I am most proud to have achieved is starting a non-profit corporation. Of course, it is not just me. Sugar has as much to do with it as I do, and it never could have been possible to do without the success of my business, all our employees, and all of the customers that have purchased products from us.

We meet the guidelines for the IRS code of a 501(c)(3) corporation. And what is this non-profit organization? It is a charitable foundation set up to give scholarships to those who need help financially so that they can get the education they desire and deserve. I want people to have the opportunities that I have had.

"What we do in life echoes in eternity," Marcus Aurelius the Roman Emperor said. This quote resonates for me. I realize things Sugar and I do now can have rippling effects for decades to come and hopefully much longer.

This book is a kind of education that I am sharing with others. It is much less expensive than a college class, but I offer it in the same spirit as our new non-profit—to give people opportunities to learn so that they may live life to the fullest. It is my Memorable Moment #102—Started a Foundation for Scholarships.

Why I Still Work

In this last quarter of my life, I have a chance to do good things for the world. I fought to stay alive. I intend to make a difference in this world.

Why do I want to keep working? It is because I have more people to help, more causes to support, and more projects to complete. My wife and I are committed to doing good to help people of the next generation succeed. We want to invest in education. Yes, Providence College will benefit from our generosity and hard-earned wealth, but there are other places and people we care about.

I can't earn enough money. People sometimes ask, "How much is enough?" There is this sense that wealthy people only want wealth for wealth's sake. That is certainly not the case for me. I can't earn enough, because there are so many ways that I would like to give my money away.

This is why I still play the lottery. I get excited thinking about all the good I could do if I was to win big. Sure the odds are 324,000,000 to one, but the cost of the ticket is insignificant compared to the pleasure of dreaming about all the good I could do with the winnings. My mind starts thinking that I would be able to donate an entire building to Providence College! I am going to keep playing the lottery. I am going to keep dreaming about all the ways I could feed the hungry. And, I am going to keep working. Remember, the more you have, the more you can contribute, so you can never have enough money.

This book has been work, hard work, long hours, and little monetary pay. I like to translate my first royalty check into pennies to make it sound huge—594! On the other hand, writing the book has made me take stock of my life. It has forced me to look at my life in a deep and meaningful way. That has been wonderful. It feels like I have lived five lifetimes.

Many people are not happy with their lives. I am absolutely thrilled with mine. My memories make me happy, elated, joyful, smiling, and whistling a happy tune. I am so lucky to have the wife that I have, the kids, grandkids, family, friends, and loyal employees that are part of my life.

If I had to sum up my life in one sentence what would I say? I am still deciding, but I like one of these:
- "I Savored Every Second of My Life."
- "Proud to be a Friar who Overachieved."
- "Buried with a 100+ Bucketload of Memorable Moments."

I hope you will live your life to the fullest my faithful reader. Thanks for making it with me to the end. May your Memorable Moments continue to bless your life. Please know that Divine Providence is with you.

Always remember, as AUTHOR Joe Calabria said in his book, "Make sure you know what keeps your ticker ticking!"

CHAPTER TWENTY ONE

The 100+ Bucketload of Memorable Moments

Note: Some are in process (IP)

1. Married the Woman of my Dreams

2. Blessed with a Son and a Daughter

3. Earned Thirty Thousand Dollars by Thirty Years Old

4. Springboarded a BS in Physics into a Successful Career

5. Scored my First Triple-Double

6. Won at the Racetrack

7. Honored the American Flag

8. Served on 1965 Bachelor Ball's Planning Committee

9. Developed and Incorporated Calabria's Laws

10. Gave my Wife an Unlimited Budget

11. Developed the CPI Financial Model

12. Perfected Theory for Compensation

13. Accepted to my First Country Club Membership

14. Recognized in Who's Who Among Students in America

15. Left College with a Diploma

16. Pledged to Help Someone Everyday

17. Each Day Celebrate the Million Reasons to Live this Life

18. Live Off Interest or Dividends

19. Built my Man Cave Office

20. Own a Home on a Golf Course Fairway

21. Shot a Hole-in-One

22. Master the Perfect Golf Swing (IP)

23. Completed my Military Obligation ASAP

24. Have Grown Garden Miracles

25. Got B+ in at least one Physics Class

26. Threw a Coin with a Wish into the Trevi Fountain in Italy

27. Climbed onto the Train of Life

28. Came to Understand Fairness Through the Equal Sign

29. Started Second Quarter of Life in 1965

30. Entered the Corporate Workplace

31. Bought a Home at the Ocean

32. Learn to Speak Italian (IP)

33. Reached my Quota in First Sales Territory

34. Win the Lottery (IP)

35. Edged my Way to Respect from Bank Teller

36. Learned to Control Business Costs

37. Earned Order of Arrow Boy Scout Honor

38. Took Revenge with the Nerds

39. Learned from the Board Meeting Debacle

40. Got to Albuquerque Balloon Fiesta

41. Witnessed Rose Parade

42. Created Corporate Jargon Game

43. Impressed Grandkids with my Treasure Chest

44. Coined a Phrase

45. Won Election to Student Congress

46. Voted in as Student Congress Treasurer

47. Earned Faithful Friar Award

48. Received Friar Hockey and Basketball Jerseys

49. Parasailed at Turk and Caicos Islands

50. Wore a Unique Vest for Daughter's Wedding

51. Elected my Granddaughter President (IP)

52. Stomp on Grapes to Make Wine (IP)

53. Slept with a Grandma

54. Got Off Unemployment Line

55. Displayed My Golf-Bag-Tag Collection

56. Started my Own Company

57. Rode a Horse Through the Garden of the Gods

58. Dreamed to Reduce Corporate Taxes Due

59. Instructed Tax Auditor to Conclude "No Tax Due"

60. Managed Escalation Costs

61. Met Terry Bradshaw

62. Received Note from Arnold Palmer

63. Promoted to IBM Branch Manager

64. Became Skilled in the Business Planning Processes

65. Got Photos and Baseball Cards Signed by the Babe and Yogi

66. Watched a Sunset in Aruba

67. Got Joe DiMaggio to Sign my Menu

68. Let My Wife Sleep with a Champion

69. Took Romantic Carriage Ride in Bermuda

70. Used SWOT Matrix—Strength, Weakness, Opportunity, Threats

71. Visit Fatima (IP)

72. Experienced the Ketchup Bottle Effect

73. Found Little Ways to Protect Retirement

74. Watched Wife Ride an Elephant

75. Planned the Perfect Burial Plot

76. Gave the Priceless Gift

77. Bought the Memorable Money Dome

78. Preparing for the Perfect Vacation (IP)

79. Selected to the Providence College Board of Trustees

80. Attended Baseball World Series

81. Attended Football Super Bowl

82. Attended PGA Golf Tournament

83. Attended College Basketball Final Four Tournament

84. Attended Stanley Cup Hockey Tournament Final

85. Received Friar National Championship Hockey Ring and Big East Basketball Championship Ring

86. Attend Kentucky Derby (IP)

87. Built a Veritas Tribute Plaza on Providence College Campus

88. Studied Quantitative Analysis

89. Watch our Grandchildren Graduate from College (IP)

90. Publicly Recognized as Business Innovator

91. Wrote a Book

92. Offered Book Readers a Movie Contract

93. Took Gondola Ride in Venice, Italy

94. Attended an Ice Hockey Friar Championship Game in the Frozen Four

95. Attend a Basketball Friar Championship Game in Final Four (IP)

96. Write Second Book Called *Illegitimi Non Carborundum* (IP)

97. Own Stock in my Start-Up Company

98. Work After Retirement Age to Contribute to Causes I Believe In

99. Shoot My Age in Golf Before I Die (IP)

100. Became a Millionaire

101. Watched Victoria's Secret Fashion Show in Person—with Wife

102. Started a 501(c)(3) Foundation for Scholarships

Note: "Between saying and doing, many a pair of shoes is worn out." Italian proverb.

CHAPTER TWENTY TWO

Soon to Be a Major Motion Picture

A COLORFUL BOOK LIKE THIS, DESPITE WHAT MY WIFE THINKS, IS destined to become a major motion picture. I can see the scenes of the book coming alive on the big screen at the last surviving theater, and guess what? Your local theater might be the last survivor.

Get your popcorn ready, and watch your theater for the listing of showtimes.

But for now, let me share a few scenes from the movie with you, my faithful reader who has made it to the end of my book, and then, I have a simple contract for you to sign. After all, you're part of the story.

Hello, How Are You? —THE MOVIE

Opening Scene

At sunrise on the first tee of a mountainous golf course, our narrator begins to speak: "You want this life? Who doesn't? It's possible. You can go from rags to riches." He takes a long drag of his humongous cigar and lets out a tremendous cloud of smoke. "Here is how it happens. Watch carefully, and enjoy the ride." He takes a swing from his driver, and his ball goes straight and long. The story begins as a little, good-looking Italian boy is born. The doctor slaps the baby's rear end, and the boy lets out his first scream. His father beams with delight and says to his mother who is now holding the boy, "One day, this boy will go to college!"

Scene 2

The baby has grown into an intelligent boy with perfect hair. His mother says to him, "It is time to start saving your pennies for college. Go and cut the lawn and the neighbor's lawn as well." Time passes and she says, "Now you must also get a paper route delivering newspapers in good weather and in bad." We see him riding his bike delivering the paper with the sun shining brightly, then thunder blasts and rain pelts the young newspaper boy.

Scene 3

Our narrator is about to take a putt on an undulating green. He says, "If you want to get onto the golf course of life, you have to get yourself educated. Picking the right school is key." He sinks the putt and the story flashes ahead to our hero, age 17, watching Providence College basketball on TV.

The young man lying on the couch eating potato chips decides that Providence is the school for champions, the school for him.

Scene 4

All those pennies saved from cutting lawns and delivering papers are enough for the first year of college, but what will happen if the boy makes it through to the second year? His grades are marginal, but it looks like he's going to pass. Our hero takes a summer job selling cookware. It is the best way to get dates and earn money at the same time! We see him close deal after deal of cookware and kisses. And our hard-working college student becomes the number one salesman in the nation that summer.

Scene 5

As he cranks his golf ball through the ball cleaner, our narrator says, "Cleaning is a business that will never go out of style. Smart people take advantage of this fact of life." We now see our college student looking at his tuition bill. He has got to find another way to earn money to pay his bills. He starts a laundry pickup and delivery business in his dorm parlor. He wonders how to get customers to notice him? Since he is in an all-male college, he decides to try hanging a tampon in his doorway! Yes, that gets the people talking. The money follows as his customers line up to get their shirts cleaned.

Scene 6
Senior year is here, and Providence College once again insists on being paid. After studying his physics and math books, the young entrepreneur heads to the horse track. Wearing a striking Fedora hat, he creates an algorithm to sort through the horseracing scenarios, and it works. As the horses cross the finish line, he wins big time after time. He goes to the bursar's office and pays off his remaining college tuition. Our hero graduates debt free. His parents rejoice.

Scene 7
Relighting his cigar, our narrator says, "Remember this: Everybody has a mother, and you better believe she will influence your entire life, even if you think you are making your own decisions." He puffs the cigar, and we see our hero holding his diploma in his hand. With college behind him, he decides to become a professional gambler, but his mother has other plans. She says, "Apple pie, mamma, and IBM." She signs him up for an interview, and he gets the offer to join "Big Blue."

Scene 8
In the first year, competition to employ our hero's services comes from a manager in another division of IBM. He offers our Italian hero a sales position in his division. Our young star breaks the news to his girlfriend about the offer. She doesn't want him to make the move since he would be going from the prestigious data processing division to the less glamorous office products division. He says to her, "Perhaps a ring might help you to decide?" She agrees, but our dashing hero doesn't have a ring to give. He pledges that she won't have to wait long. He tries his luck at the track and comes up short one week but wins big the next.

Scene 9

The star of the show has surpassed his quota for the first year and gets invited to the annual sales recognition conference, and there he hears the words from the VP of sales, "Hello, how are you?" It's thrilling but quickly seems insincere as the VP says it over and over again, never paying attention to how people respond. Our hero vows to make better use of that powerful phrase—perhaps even to one day make it into a book and then a movie!

Scene 10

The narrator is back on the green. He is hitting one ball after another toward the cup and missing. Finally, he sinks the putt. The story continues as our dashing salesman hands a small box to his true love. She opens it to find the diamond ring she has been waiting for. Wedding bells chime, and the couple exchanges vows. Our hero is thrilled and tells his new wife that she is the best thing that ever happened to him—better than a stiff drink and every bit as good as a Cuban cigar.

Scene 11

Driving in his white golf cart down the fairway, our narrator says, "You might not think you will ever get admitted into the golf club of your dreams. But then one day, the wind shifts, and your chance arrives." Our star drives down the long tree-covered lane to an exclusive golf club. In the clubhouse, he can't remember the longtime members' names so he calls them "Sir" and "Madam." They love that and make him one of their members, as long as his check for the membership fee will clear.

Scene 12

Our rising IBM star proves there is a method to his madness that has allowed him to become a success. He chews on a pencil as he creates his own set of laws. He scribbles on a napkin and smiles broadly. Summer turns to fall. He types up his laws, frames them, and puts them up on his wall. He calls his employees over and explains they must memorize each of these truths of life and business. The next day, he tests the staff to see

if they know the laws. Three people are sent packing. They are fired for
not learning their lesson!

Scene 13

Our narrator slices a tee shot into a deep, dark woods. "Welcome to scene
13. That ball will never be found. It's as if it never existed. My advice is
to forget about that gold Titleist and move to the next scene of your life."

Scene 14

"There is always another shot to take and another hole to play." The narrator chips a shot onto the green. Our hero signs the paperwork to accept
a new job. We see the couple loading their possessions into a moving van.
There are now kids getting packed into the van as well! He closes a giant
deal for the startup, but the company fails.

Scene 15

Always creative and hardworking, our Italian superstar, between jobs,
pieces together a series of escalating barter trades that makes him thousands. The adding machine spews out tape as the sales add up. This is just
what his young family needed for a happy Christmas. Presents abound
under the tree.

Scene 16

Our narrator holds a seven iron in his hand. He prepares to tee off for
this par-three hole. "When everything comes together in your life, is it
luck or is it skill? Nobody really knows, but I'll tell you this. If you don't
keep playing the game, you'll never know how it turns out." The narrator
swings, and his ball lifts high into the air, lands on the green, and rolls
into the cup. The calendar turns to a new year. Our hero and his wife sign
papers and shake hands as they start a new business. Flying through the
air and going straight into his pocket and her purse are one-dollar bills,
then fives, tens, twenties, fifties, and hundreds. They fill in a graph that
quickly shows their company hits a million dollars in sales. The graph
keeps growing upwards.

Scene 17

Our narrator takes a swing while in the sand trap. The ball goes six inches as the sand goes twenty feet. Our hero pays taxes, taxes, and more taxes.

Scene 18

We hear the crack of a club hitting a golf ball. We see the ball does a slight hook and plops into a pond. Our narrator drives up in his cart, pulls out his ball retriever, and scoops the ball back onto the fairway. He takes another swing and shanks the ball back into the pond. Our story continues as our millionaire business owner goes to one lawyer, another lawyer, and another lawyer.

Scene 19

Life is stressful for the successful couple. To relieve the tension, we see our hero out with his buddies playing golf! One of them jumps out of a tree to surprise the others. The group falls down laughing.

Scene 20

We see our hero back at work in his office. He shares cups of delicious coffee with his staff. The sales graph keeps going up. It hits $100 million. It doesn't stop. It passes $200 million. It doesn't stop. The last number we see is $260 million.

Scene 21

The impeccably dressed Italian man and his loving wife are signing a giant check and handing it to Providence College. Money is going out of his pocket and her purse and into the hands of the needy, the hungry, and the vulnerable.

Scene 22

The narrator adds up his score while sitting in his cart. "Some holes were better than others, but I loved every minute of it—well, as much as I could love my time in the sand." Our hero scratches his head and his life flashes before his eyes—cutting grass, winning at the horse track, graduating college, winning deals, wedding vows, moving, children, money in his pocket, joining a golf club, giving back to others. He types it all into his long-awaited book. The book gets published. Readers tear up, laugh out loud, and sigh in recognition of sage advice.

Closing Scene

Our narrator is putting his clubs into the trunk of his Cadillac. "Is it possible to live this life? Of course it is. I am living proof because this is my life. But the real question is what is possible in your life? Golf may not be for you, but I bet you a million bucks that there is something for you. Every one of us is meant for greatness; I just happen to be the hero of this story." He shrugs his shoulders, closes the trunk, and drives off. He has left his golf shoes at his parking space.

Hey, so that's the movie. You can see that you, the reader, are in it. So, here's the thing. My lawyer needs you to sign the movie contract. But he constantly overcharges me, so I have written the agreement up myself. Personally, if I were you, I would just treat it like any other agreement. Scroll to the bottom, and hit agree. If, however, you choose to read the whole thing, please know that it is standard business practice, nothing to be alarmed about. You never have any rights, nor should you expect monetary gain.

Your Motion Picture Contract

The Contract – Memorable Moment #92

Without any formal legal training, I felt qualified to write and publish my movie contract. This is YOUR chance to be in the movies!

Official Movie Contract for My Readers

Preamble:

The party of the first part (herein referred to as the OWNER of the manuscript "Hello, How Are You?") being of sound mind and fairly good body agrees to the following with the party of the second part, that's YOU! (herein referred to as the obviously intelligent, HONORED READER).

THIS AGREEMENT, WHEN ACCEPTED BY HONORED READER, WILL CREATE A BINDING AND COMICALLY ENFORCEABLE CONTRACT BETWEEN YOU AND OWNER OF MANUSCRIPT.

THE OWNER reserves the right to add, delete, and/or modify any of the terms and conditions contained in this contract whenever the Owner wants, especially on Wednesdays, which is my day to play golf and, thus, most productive. Don't worry, Honored Reader. All this legally binding nonsense is standard legal practice. You can spot it if you use a magnifying glass to see the complete terms in any on-line agreement.

1. Terms of Service:

Honored Reader gets no guarantees, but the Owner will attempt to film your likeness from your best side.

2. Authorization:

Honored Reader's consent is non-exclusive (meaning you have no rights); all rights granted by Honored Reader to Owner under this Contract are exclusively created for his benefit—for Eternity. All this means to you, Honored Reader, is that you are forever famous!

3. Payments to Honored Reader:

A bag of peanuts provided during the filming of your scene. If you are allergic to peanuts, you'll receive one marshmallow.

All the popcorn you can eat and half-priced sodas during the movie premiere.

4. Payments to Owner by Honored Reader:

Your smile will be sufficient, but a genuine laugh would be appreciated.

5. Wardrobe for Honored Reader:

Honored Reader is entitled—and, in many instances, required—to be fully clothed during filming. Note: no exceptions, even for bathtub reading scenes.

6. General Provisions:

Any notice, approval, request, authorization, direction, or other communication under this agreement shall be deemed to have been delivered as long as the Owner thinks about it!

Any Honored Reader who appears in the movie but does not actually finish the book is required to return all payments, i.e., peanuts.

No resume necessary.

7. Scope of Enforcement:

The terms listed shall apply equally in all countries, municipalities, planets, and star systems within the Milky Way Galaxy.

Those residing within the Snickers Galaxy must individually negotiate their contract.

If any Honored Readers are from the Almond Joy Galaxy, please note that your home is about to be eaten!

8. Instructions:

By checking the box below, signing, and dating this agreement, Honored Reader authorizes all provisions, terms, and intentions of this contract to be in full force and humor. This is a strictly laughing matter, and the Owner knows who you are and where to find you!

Note: Those of you who are married, please have your spouse sign your life away. Those of you with significant others, please get your better half to give your likeness away. Those of you who are underage and with parents, please have your parents sign below to give you a chance to appear on the silver screen. Everyone else, sign for yourself.

I hereby accept the terms of this contract for myself, my spouse, my significant other, my child, any rebirth or transmigration, and anyone else the hidden camera captures.

_____

My Signature   Date

[ ] Click the box to activate the hidden camera and have one moment of your life forever preserved in the movie. You will not be able to tell that you are being digitally recorded, but you will be, so smile and talk to the pages. Also note that, by clicking the box, there will be an automatic withdrawal from your nearest credit card as you donate to the Calabria Charitable Foundation for Scholarships.

Joseph Calabria, Jr., is a great example of a self-made man, but he is the first to point out that he has had help along the way. He acknowledges the huge impact Providence College and the whole Friar family has had on his life and career. One of his continuing goals is to give back to that institution.

Calabria has more than 50 years of business experience. Throughout his career, hard work has been his signature. And strategic thinking has been his focus. Humor has been his connector.

His business, CPI, provides information technology equipment and services to industry and government. This grandson of an Italian immigrant has risen from the meager surroundings of a working class family to the owner and president of his own multi-million dollar company.

An anonymous writer from *Golf News* posted this poem about Calabria:

While Basking in the Florida Sun, Joe Calabria Sinks a Hole-in-One!

December 30th was the day,
That Joe Calabria made his way,
To Boca Raton's Municipal Course,
To see if his stroke still had the force,
To accomplish a golfer's oft-dreamed-of feat,
A hole-in-one...despite the heat.

On the beautiful 7th, Par 3 was the goal,
132 yards away was the hole.
The ball, with magnetic force it would seem
Accomplished that often-sought-after dream.
A hole-in-one, oh what joy, what delight!
The third of its type for Joe! What a sight!

The foursome players led the applause.
Joe's fame, now renown, has given the cause
To digress into verse, and acclaim his prowess,
Joe Calabria, man, you sure are the best!